STRUCTURAL CONCRETE COST ESTIMATING

John E. Clark, P.E.

STRUCTURAL CONCRETE COST ESTIMATING

McGraw-Hill Book Company

New York   St. Louis   San Francisco   Auckland
Bogotá   Hamburg   Johannesburg   London   Madrid
Mexico   Montreal   New Delhi   Panama   Paris
São Paulo   Singapore   Sydney   Tokyo   Toronto

To Al Mestiula
with regards

John E Clark
10/28/86
Lorton Va.

Library of Congress Cataloging in Publication Data

Clark, John E. (John Eric)
  Structural concrete cost estimating.

  Includes bibliographies.
  1. Concrete construction—Estimates.   I. Title.
  TA682.26.C55 1983   624.1'834   82-12693
  ISBN 0-07-011163-4

1 2 3 4 5 6 7 8 9 0   DOC/DOC   8 9 8 7 6 5 4 3 2

ISBN 0-07-011163-4

The editors for this book were Joan Zseleczky
and Celia Knight, the designer was Elliot Epstein, and the
production supervisor was Paul Malchow. It was set in
Caledonia by Progressive Typographers.

Printed and bound by R. R. Donnelley & Sons, Inc.

CONTENTS

v

PREFACE

At best, an estimate of cost is a rational approximation. An estimator's chore is to make the best approximation possible. Experience is an important factor in determining the best cost estimate.

Estimating cost for construction work in the 1980s is a considerable challenge. Spiraling inflation combined with greater design sophistication and broadening world markets demands more and more technical and economic understanding in the field of cost estimating. With such development, there is a need for improved instruction and technical support. This book helps the construction industry with that need as it relates to structural concrete cost estimating.

It is surprising to find that so few of the many professionals who earn their living estimating construction cost really know how to estimate the cost for structural concrete. Possibly some of those professionals are basing their estimates on misunderstood concepts or on patented, cookbook approaches—thereby appropriating large funds or submitting substantial construction bid proposals. If this is a reality, then the estimating profession needs a book that deals specifically and in detail with the single subject of structural concrete cost estimating.

There are many publications written on the subject of estimating. This book, however, is not a *how-to-estimate* handbook; rather, it is a sharing of experience and an illustration of the many facets which influence the direct cost of structural concrete. To best cover the subject, the procedures for the take-off and cost estimating of structural concrete are first thoroughly discussed and then supported with a complete, realistic example involving a hypothetical highway construction project. The highway construction project is chosen because it offers a great variety of estimating challenges in concrete construction and represents the broadest and most often repeated type of construction in the nation. Competence here will be useful in any construction cost estimating.

Estimating the cost for structural concrete is a matter of applying knowledge to the many aspects involved in the work. Experienced estimators may vary their approach to this subject, but the objective always remains the same: to obtain a good and reasonable estimate of cost.

Many of the principles applied in structural concrete cost estimating are basic to all cost estimates. For instance, the total cost involves the summation of all labor, equipment, material, and subcontract cost. The format for assembly of those costs is a matter of choice. This book explains. the many influencing facets of structural concrete cost through the development of a procedure that will lend itself well to other types of cost estimates. Its purpose, however, is to be a vehicle for the clear and thorough explanation of structural concrete cost estimating.

Structural concrete construction projects vary so widely in scope that it would be difficult to cover all the possibilities with necessary instruction and illustration in a single text without destroying the prime purpose: to develop a basic view of direct cost for structural concrete. The manufacture of concrete mix on the job, for instance, is not addressed in great detail, nor is the use of commercial forming systems. Instead, the subject is confined to what is most often found to be the typical highway project in which the use of commercial concrete plants and wood form systems applies. It is certain that, once the basic concept is understood, the estimator's capability to practice what remains a mystery to many otherwise experienced and competent professionals will have expanded.

It is suggested that the entire book be read and a careful study be made of the illustrated examples of the take-off and cost estimates. Thereafter, it is up to the estimators to develop their own approach for their objectives—with the text serving as a convenient reference tool.

The information contained here is provided for demonstration only and is not intended for any purpose other than to assist the estimator in understanding the particular issue. The estimator alone has the entire responsibility to develop and establish real cost estimate criteria.

John E. Clark

ABBREVIATIONS AND SYMBOLS

A	Area
AASHTO	American Association of State Highway and Transportation Officials
ACI	American Concrete Institute
AISC	American Institute of Steel Construction, Inc.
APA	American Plywood Association
ASTM	American Society for Testing and Materials
B	Bid wage rate
b	Width of beam (inches)
bbl	Barrels
BF	Board finish
bf	Board feet
bf/lf	Board feet per lineal foot
bf/sf	Board feet per square foot
C	Equipment ownership cost
CCC	Common concrete cost
cf or cu ft	Cubic feet
cfm	Cubic feet per minute
cy or cu yd	Cubic yards
DB	Drainage backfill
DP	Dampproof
E	Escalation
ED	Expansion dam
EOE	Equipment operating expense
F	Fuel and lubricating expense—equipment
F	Fringe benefits
°F	Degrees Fahrenheit
ft or	Foot or feet

ft/hr	Feet per hour
gal	Gallon(s)
gal/sy	Gallons per square yard
H	Hours worked
H_l	Lost time hours
H_p	Premium time hours
h	Height of a beam (inches)
I	Insurance and taxes
I	Interest, taxes, and storage expense—equipment
in or "	Inches
JS	Joint seal
K	Kip (1000 pounds)
L	Lost time factor
L	Economic life in years—equipment
LO	Linseed oil
lb or #	Pound
lf	Lineal feet
lb/gal	Pounds per gallon
lb/cf or pcf	Pounds per cubic foot
lb/ft	Pounds per foot
lb/sf	Pounds per square foot
lb/sq in or psi	Pounds per square inch
P	Premium time factor
P	Total investment—equipment
PVC	Polyvinyl chloride
pcf or lb/cf	Pounds per cubic foot
psf	Pounds per square foot
psi or lb/sq in	Pounds per square inch
R	Repair expense—equipment
R	Rate of concrete rise in forms (ft/hr)
S	Salvage value—equipment
S4S	Surfaced on all four sides
sy or sq yd	Square yard(s)
sf or sq ft	Square feet
T	Time factor
T	Tire expense
tn	Ton
T/sf	Ties per square foot
W	Basic wage rate
WP	Waterproof
WS	Waterstop

1

TAKE-OFF

1.1 DEFINITION AND SCOPE

Take-off, as it applies to construction cost estimating, is an often misunderstood and misused term. Too often, even professionals think of take-off as the determination of quantities. The following example demonstrates this point.

An estimator who is assigned the take-off responsibility for a project described as a foundation excavation first thinks that the quantity to be excavated must be computed. Although the quantity is certainly important, the answers to other questions are equally important: (1) What is the nature of the material to be excavated? Is it earth or rock? Is it wet or dry? (2) What are specified requirements for disposal and/or use of the excavated material? Is it suitable for its intended use? Is it marketable? Will handling be difficult? (3) Are there any dewatering requirements, and if so, what are the scope and duration for such dewatering? (4) Does payment for excavation include placing of backfill at a later date? (5) Are all measurement and payment terms clearly stated? (6) Do local ordinances affect the work?

Answers to any of these questions could materially affect the cost of the foundation excavation. The point made is that, regardless of the nature of construction, the take-off is so critical to the cost that, if not properly understood and executed, any resulting cost estimate will be worthless.

To state this another way, the principal purpose of a take-off is to isolate and explain each of the individual influencing factors of importance to the cost. To accomplish this requires clear understanding of what is needed and how it should be presented. Take-off, therefore, includes (1) the *investigation* to get complete understanding of the project through a study of the plans and specifications, a project site visit, and testing or other field investigation; (2) the *quantity take-off* to determine the physical extent of the work and the basis for productive time; (3) the *preliminary progress schedule* to show the interdependence of major activities and resources in time; and (4) the solicitation of prices from *suppliers* and *subcontractors*. Each element is discussed under its own heading later in this chapter.

The presentation of a take-off will vary with the nature of the work being estimated. So long as all factors are clearly and briefly defined, any format is acceptable.

The rest of this chapter along with Chapter 2, "Illustration of a

Take-Off," will help the estimator understand how to apply this approach.

1.2 INVESTIGATION

The isolation and explanation of each factor influencing the cost of the structural concrete is a qualitative as well as a quantitative requirement. For instance, the consistency of a concrete mix can be as important as the determination of the correct volume, or a complete description of the application requirements for a special surface finish is as necessary as the computation of the overall area affected. Recognizing a limiting work-site access problem which will affect the cost of placing concrete is also important. Within the time frame allowed, a good estimator finds it imperative to understand the plans and specifications and to be so familiar with the project site that, when the take-off is completed, each item has been clearly and fully exposed. This investigative approach will aid and ease the entire take-off process and yield a quality estimate. It is also worth stating that an orderly and systematic recording of all investigative information is necessary to the quality of the cost estimate.

Plans and Specifications

Every estimator is familiar with the use of plans and specifications. Very few cost estimates are made without some depiction of the designer's intent. Those not familiar with structural concrete cost estimating will find, even by casual observation, that the plans and specifications for concrete work are often extremely complex. Plans are immersed in notes, dimensions, and detailed drawings to cover needed information for reinforcing, joints, hardware, piping, concrete, and many other features found in a complex structure. This design practice tends to clutter the plans, and at best, render them difficult to read and understand.

Specifications are normally assembled in an orderly fashion, whereby an estimator can usually find all the subject matter with relative ease. One pitfall to watch for is that, while reading and attempting to understand a specification, the estimator can still completely miss a small, unobtrusive note or detail on the plans that entirely changes the character of the work. With heavily detailed plans, this is an easy trap to fall victim to. To miss such information can be very expensive to the estimator's employer—and perhaps to the estimator.

Study of the plans and specifications for a proposed project is an early order of business. For structural concrete, in particular, it is vital to gain knowledge of all factors that affect the cost.

Project Scope

Any estimator, regardless of assigned estimating task, should become familiar enough with the entire set of plans and specifications to develop an overview of the project. This will evoke greater interest in the project and deeper insight into how the assigned portions relate to the whole. Particularly, the estimator may learn of some serious external influence that could impact the cost of the concrete work to be figured.

Concrete Work Scope

Nearly all work item specifications are written in this manner: the item is described by the first paragraph and the measurement and payment for the completed work is explained in the last. Those paragraphs define intent—what the owner or designer expects to get and how the owner or designer expects to determine payment for it. With structural concrete, there is no exception to the rule that these paragraphs must be thoroughly read and understood. It is here that the estimator may discover that payment for the concrete also includes the reinforcing steel or wrought iron rails, or that payment does not include the cement or the rubber waterstop. Such additions or omissions can make a significant difference in the cost estimate.

Specification Details

Within the body of all structural concrete specifications are detailed requirements for materials (incorporated or unincorporated); equipment and its applications; the mixing, batching, delivery, placing, consistency, finishing, curing, and testing of the concrete; forming and shoring; and many other requirements to cover the great variety of possibilities. Each written detail is at some point applicable and important to the construction process. In the interest of time and efficiency, however, an estimator must develop a capability to view specifications with an eye for those details in the maze that are crucial to the cost of the concrete to be priced. This is a subtle practice which should develop and improve with experience.

Specification details for structural concrete that the estimator should faithfully extract for each new project are as follows:

- Mix design
- Additive requirements
- Temperature limitations
- Joint types
- Form-type requirements
- Placing requirements

- Curing requirements
- Finishing requirements
- Protective coating requirements
- Incidental items required
- Unusual requirements
- Quality control requirements

If consideration is to be given to an on-site concrete batch plant, then the list would be expanded to include details for materials supply, batching, and equipment.

Something should be noted here about *Contract Special Provisions*. The estimator is familiar with special provisions as they relate to the specifications in that they amend, add to, or delete from portions of the standard specifications as written. Regardless of time limitations, the estimator should read *all* applicable special provisions because this is one place to find the unusual requirement that may influence cost.

Plans

For structural concrete take-off, the plans will be the source from which the estimator will identify the various structural components and take off much of the detailed information necessary for a cost estimate. Therefore, the estimator must understand the plans completely.

Construction plans are a pictorial presentation of what a designer wants built; they contain many details that could not be otherwise described. Plans are also used by designers to supplement their specifications with notes and/or descriptive details. A careful reading of the plans is mandatory. This includes general notes and standard sheets that contain supplemental information.

With the knowledge gained by a thorough review of the plans and specifications, the estimator is intelligently prepared to complete a take-off computation format.

Project Site Visit

Sometime during the take-off process, the estimator should make it a point to visit the proposed project site. Such a visit can completely alter the character and nature of the project from the impression gained by studying the plans and specifications. A visit to the site—as it relates to structural concrete—can yield information typical of the following:

· Existence of extreme traffic conditions
· Availability and adequacy of local labor forces
· Availability and adequacy of a plant setup site
· Location of aggregate sources
· Location of new sources of supply
· Location of overhead utility hazards
· Location of underground utility hazards
· Existence of access difficulty
· Existence of extremely high water

It is even a good idea to bring along a camera to photograph features of the project site. Photographs can serve as documentation of original conditions on which the estimate was initially founded.

Testing
Most materials used in structural concrete require quality assurance testing and certification to ascertain that the requirements of the specifications are met. In bid preparation, for instance, where it is the intent of the contractor to quarry, manufacture, and supply the concrete aggregates, the estimator has the responsibility—in some manner—to ensure that the proposed bedrock meets the requirements. This requires sampling and testing and can be an important segment of bid preparation.

1.3 THE QUANTITY TAKE-OFF
The purpose of quantity take-off is to determine and summarize quantitative data that must be used in computing cost. To a great extent, the choice of quantitative data to take off is dependent on the estimator's approach to computing cost. For example, if the estimator prefers to price chamfer strip separately, a take-off of the total length of chamfer strip is necessary; however if it is to be in some way included in the cost for forms, then the take-off is unnecessary.

The following subsections will develop a quantity take-off procedure and explain in detail what each computation covers and what mathematical accuracy to use. Quantity take-off for structural concrete involves so many variables in addition to the requirements for accuracy and speed that a somewhat regimented system for performing computations is necessary. *Remember:* Simplicity and thoroughness are the key factors.

Identification of Components

Structural concrete take-off in heavy highway construction requires the gathering and tabulation of more information than most types of construction require. If an estimator learns how to identify the significant component parts of a structure and how to analyze each of those parts, the task is fairly easy. The significant component parts of concrete structures are identified as follows.

Footing A footing is the foundation or base component of a structure. It is often rectangular in shape and larger in area than the structure it supports. Its purpose is to evenly distribute the weight of the structure and its burden loads over the excavated subgrade on which it rests. The depth of a footing is a function of the load and the area over which it must spread that load. Usually, a footing will have a depth equal to, or greater than, the distance from its edge to the edge of the nearest loading component.

Slab on Grade A slab on grade is similar to a footing in that it is located on the ground at or below grade. The difference is that the slab on grade almost always requires greater precision in construction, and it is often greater in area relative to depth than is a footing. Concrete highway pavement slabs, bridge approach slabs, on-grade floor slabs, box culvert outflow aprons, and box culvert floor slabs are examples of a slab on grade.

Abutment The principal function of an abutment is to act as both an end bearing structure capable of absorbing loads and a transition structure capable of withstanding associated impact and retaining loads. Abutments for bridges can be described as a series of interconnected walls of varying length, width, and height. They are often very complex structures involving special shapes, skewed corners, and multiple concrete pours. Although the various parts of a bridge abutment, such as the seat, backwalls, wingwalls, and parapets can be identified separately, they are almost always constructed in a continuous manner—thereby explaining why an abutment is often considered a single structural component. Abutment concrete take-off is separated into two categories: 0 to 8 feet in height, and over 8 feet in height.

Walls Concrete walls serve as guides, dividers, barriers, earth retainers, and load bearing structures. A wall is distinguished from other components by its shape, with its length and height usually much greater than its thickness. Walls that are of great length offer the advantage of repeated construction operations, which can become very efficient. Walls are evaluated as either 0 to 8 feet in height, or over 8 feet in height.

Columns Columns are generally known for their high, slender outline. Usually their horizontal cross section is round, square, or rectangular. However, any geometric section may be used as long as it meets the design requirements for strength and aesthetics. Columns almost always serve as a support structure for beams, floor systems, and other columns.

Beams Structurally, a beam serves as a supporting member to carry other beams, floor slabs, or other loads as they exist over an open space. Functionally, beams provide for free passage beneath; economically, they require a minimum use of concrete. Beams are generally square or rectangular in vertical cross section and must be constructed on top of shoring.

Decks A deck is a relatively thin floor slab that supports itself and the loads it is intended to carry over a short span between walls, beams, or columns. In the case of bridge work, the construction of the sidewalks is usually included with this component.

Slab above Grade A slab above grade describes a heavy roof slab or arch that will ultimately carry heavy loads over relatively great spans. The use of shoring is necessary for a slab above grade construction.

Figure 1.1*a* and *b* contains several simplified sketches of concrete structures with their component parts identified.

The reason that these structural components are separated is that there are specific differences in their makeup. That is, they are formed differently, or there is a difference in the way the concrete must be poured, or they are finished differently, or the design strength of the concrete used in each varies, or a special support of the forms is required. Whatever the reason, the estimator will discover the absolute need to keep these components separated throughout the estimating process until their evaluation is complete. After that, they may be combined to produce the total cost in whatever particular manner is required.

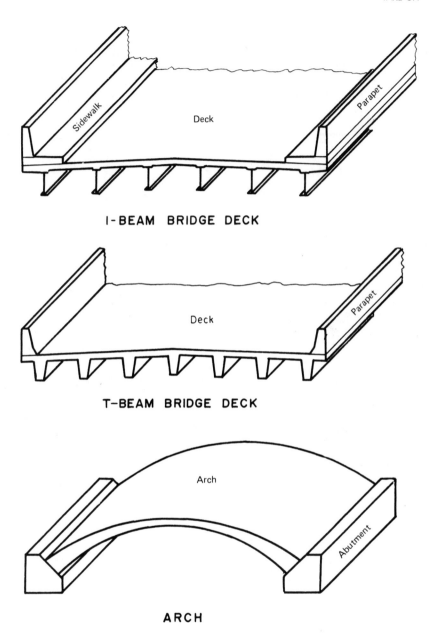

Figure 1.1(a) Structural Concrete Components.

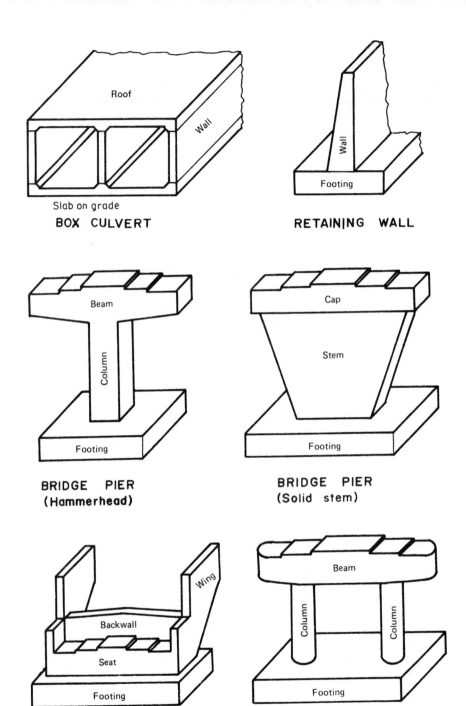

Roof

Wall

Slab on grade

BOX CULVERT

Wall

Footing

RETAINING WALL

Beam

Column

Footing

**BRIDGE PIER
(Hammerhead)**

Cap

Stem

Footing

**BRIDGE PIER
(Solid stem)**

Wing

Backwall

Seat

Footing

BRIDGE ABUTMENT

Beam

Column

Column

Footing

BRIDGE PIER (Round columns)

Figure 1.1(b) Structural Concrete Components.

10

Evaluation of Components

After identifying the component breakdown need for the structure to be estimated, the estimator must next understand what information is necessary for the evaluation of each of the components. For any structural concrete component, the detailed information listed is required as applicable.

Concrete Volume	The volume of concrete required to build each part of the structure (in cubic yards)
Contact Area	The surface area of the concrete to be formed (in square feet)
Joints	The length of special keyway, elastomeric joint, waterstop, etc., to be used (in lineal feet)
Shored Area	The area of formed concrete surface requiring external support to supplement the normal structural capacity of the forms (in square feet)
Finish Area	The surface area of the concrete to receive a specified finishing treatment (in square feet)
Waterproof or Dampproof	The surface area of the concrete to be treated with bitumen, asphalt, or other material, applied for the purpose of protecting the concrete and its housed facilities (in square feet)
Embedded Items	A detailed listing of pipe, hardware, steel, grating, curb, duct, etc., which are specified and included in the price for the concrete (by item and dimension)
Miscellaneous Items	Details of the unusual, or normally non-associated work, such as reinforcing steel, excavation, and backfill

As the take-off is developed, the significance of all of the preceding factors will become apparent. One thing that cannot be emphasized too strongly in performing the take-off for structural concrete work is the need for an orderly and systematic approach for exposing all important cost influencing factors.

Concrete Volume

The volume of concrete for each of the structural components is generally computed with two purposes in mind: First, to gain a separation of the overall volume of concrete by structure components and, second, to get a check on the pay quantities as provided by the plans and specifications.

Calculation of concrete volume for estimating purposes does not warrant an extremely high degree of accuracy. Generally, the necessary accuracy will be established if the estimator uses dimensions to the nearest one-tenth of a foot and records the concrete quantities to the nearest one-tenth of a cubic yard. This approach usually yields a 1 to 2 percent accuracy. The quantity can be rounded to the nearest even cubic yard in summarizing the concrete volume for each structural component.

For example, assume that a particular structural component consists of three masses (A, B, and C), of similar shape and construction—each with the dimensions listed:

	$\dfrac{\text{Length}}{\text{(feet-inches)}}$ ×	$\dfrac{\text{Width}}{\text{(feet-inches)}}$ ×	$\dfrac{\text{Height}}{\text{(feet-inches)}}$
A	20 - 0 ×	12 - 8 ×	3 - 7
B	16 - 4 ×	10 - 6 ×	2 - 10
C	18 - 10 ×	12 - 2 ×	3 - 6

The computations for volume of each would be as follows:

	Length (feet) ×	Width (feet) ×	Height (feet) ×	$\left(\dfrac{1}{\text{cf per cy}}\right)$ =	Volume (cubic yards)
A	20.0 ×	12.7 ×	3.6 ×	$1/27$ =	33.9
B	16.3 ×	10.5 ×	2.8 ×	$1/27$ =	17.8
C	18.8 ×	12.2 ×	3.5 ×	$1/27$ =	29.7
				Total volume	81.4

The total would be listed as 82 cubic yards. The choice of rounding is up to the estimator, but the system should be consistent.

There are exceptions to the one-tenth-of-a-foot rule in the case of floor slabs, walls, or other large areas with thin sections. For example, the volume of concrete for a bridge deck that is 8 inches (0.67 feet) thick should be computed as $500' \times 40' \times 0.67' \times 1/27 = 496.3$ cy, rather than 500′ × 40′ × 0.7′ × ¹/₂₇ = 518.5 cy. Note that the 0.03 feet made a 22-cubic yard difference in quantity for the deck. This difference is too great to ignore.

Contact Area

Formed area, or *contact area*, for the various components of a structure (as classified under "Evaluation of Components" in this section), is of utmost importance to concrete cost, since formwork is the most expensive single part of the concrete. Contact area is a representation of all forms to be erected. Formwork cost consists of the cost for all forming lumber, plywood, wales, stiffbacks, nails, hardware, chamfer strips, keyways, and added support.

Remember: A wrong contact area will yield a wrong concrete cost. Every surface to be formed must be calculated. It is not necessary that the contact area be calculated with an extremely high degree of accuracy. The principal idea is that the estimator should consider the mathematical ramifications of the contact area take-off and then consistently govern the accuracy of computations accordingly. Generally speaking, if the estimator uses dimensions rounded up to the nearest even foot in calculating each area and then rounds the total of the computed areas up to the nearest even 10 square feet, the accuracy will be sufficient to represent a neat contact area.

If, for example, a footing form is dimensioned as shown in Figure 1.2a, the contact area (perimeter × height) can be calculated exactly as 65.00′ × 3.67′ = 239 sf. In all probability, however, the footing form will be built 4 feet high, and 65′ × 4′ = 260 sf is a more realistic and practical computation from an estimating viewpoint.

Again, reminding the estimator of the mathematical ramifications involved, it should be noted that rounding of dimensions is not always the thing to do. In the case of a square column having dimensions as shown in Figure 1.2b, the estimator might feel more comfortable using a computation such as 14′ × 18′ = 252 sf, rather than 16′ × 18′ = 288 sf.

Another example of the use of judgment along with need for speed is demonstrated in computing a bridge deck contact area. Assume the deck is as indicated in Figure 1.2c. Figuring the contact through all steel beam flanges, the width of the bridge deck form would then be 42 feet for estimating purposes. This approach is much easier than trying to determine the exact distance between beam flanges—and there is much less likelihood of a mistake. Actually, this method would be quite accurate if there are beam haunches required, as shown.

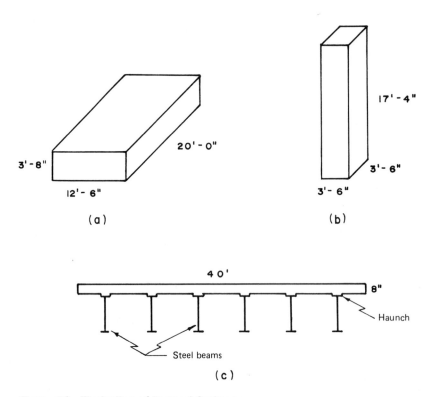

Figure 1.2 Illustration of Formed Surfaces.

The whole idea is to remember that the estimator is looking for a single, fast method to reach a reasonably accurate conclusion that is consistent with the pricing procedures and cost system in use. Good judgment, consistency, and care will accomplish this.

Joints

Examination of most large concrete structures will show there are always construction joints located to provide the contractor with a place to break up concrete work into manageable and practical units. There are also contraction and expansion joints provided for the purpose of handling variable shrinkage or expansion with changing temperatures or some established movement within the structure. Figure 1.3 shows some types of joints in use.

In preparing for a structural concrete quantity take-off, the estimator examines the plans and specifications and notes the types of joint treatment required, deciding whether or not the cost of that treatment is significant enough to be considered separately in the concrete cost estimate. Here again, judgment comes into play. For example, if a joint calls for a small 2- × 4-inch keyway, the estimator may consider the installation cost to be a part of the regular formwork. However if

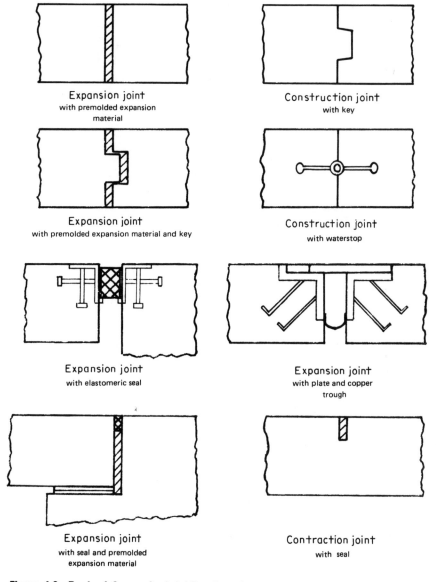

Expansion joint
with premolded expansion
material

Construction joint
with key

Expansion joint
with premolded expansion material and key

Construction joint
with waterstop

Expansion joint
with elastomeric seal

Expansion joint
with plate and copper
trough

Expansion joint
with seal and premolded
expansion material

Contraction joint
with seal

Figure 1.3 Typical Concrete Joint Treatment.

the keyway is to be a larger 6- × 20-inch dimension, the added cost might warrant separate consideration. Joints designed for use of an elastomeric compression seal or rubber waterstop, or for some config-uration of embedded steel plates and angles, are always to be listed separately. Another joint treatment requirement that has become more prevalent in recent years is that of sandblasting or waterblasting construction joints for the purpose of improving the bond. This is ac-complished by cleaning off grout and loose particles and exposing the aggregates. Yet another consideration is that made for added joints that may be necessary for construction practicality. The estimator may list this requirement in the take-off by the square foot, or by the lineal foot, as required.

Shored Area

Forms for floor slabs, beams, roof slabs, arches, or other overhanging spans of concrete often require additional support to prevent exces-sive deflection or failure under the loading of concrete when placed—and until the concrete is cured. Such support is called *shoring*, or *falsework*, and this represents additional cost. The esti-mator should compute the area being supported so that a cost can be estimated and included in the overall cost of the concrete. Computa-tions of the area should be consistent with the accuracy used for con-tact areas.

The estimator must decide which formed areas will require shoring. This may possibly require some preliminary design computations. Experience has established that under ordinary circumstances, signif-icant added support is usually necessary for bridge pier beams or floor beams, overhanging bridge abutment wingwalls, box culvert roof slabs of spans over 7 feet, arch spans of over 7 feet, floor and roof slabs with spans over 7 feet, T beams for floor and roof support, and rigid frame structures.

Finish Area

To many, all concrete looks the same. This is far from true— especially for structural concrete. There is a concerted effort on the part of designers to make exposed concrete surfaces look different and aesthetically pleasing by providing for a variety of surface treatments. With this in mind, the estimator should always determine in advance how each concrete surface is to be finished. As take-off calculations are performed, it is easy to tabulate the various finishes required. The degree of accuracy necessary in the calculations need be no greater than that required for contact areas. Some of the many surface finishing possibilities are described as follows.

Architectural Finish   This is the forming of designs or patterns in the surface of concrete. It is accomplished by adding textured or relief patterns to the surface of the form or by applying specially made form surface material with the required texture or pattern molded into the material. There is an add-on cost for these finishes, and it is always noted separately in a take-off. (See Figure 1.4.)

Machine Finish   Many bridge decks and floor slabs require machine finishing. The finishing machine strikes and rough-finishes the surface to a close, uniform tolerance. Most often, further hand-finishing is required to complete the job. If the finishing machine is not included in the cost of placing the concrete, it must be given consideration as a separate finishing cost.

Figure 1.4(a)   Architectural Finishes. (Symons Corporation.)

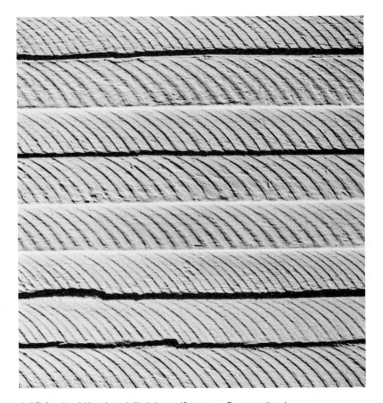

Figure 1.4(b) Architectural Finishes. (Symons, Corporation.)

Float Finish Float finish is a designation for the additional finishing of uniform horizontal surfaces after the concrete has set. The cost is not included as a placing cost and must be added. Float finishing usually involves the grinding of bridge seats to close tolerances or the removal of high spots in a floor slab with a scabbler or grinder.

Rub Finish This finish usually applies to the treatment of an exposed vertical surface and should be done just after the forms are removed. The concrete surface is wetted and rubbed with a carborundum stone until it is uniform in texture and color. The process eliminates form marks and small surface holes. Sometimes mortar is added and rubbed over the surface to accomplish the desired results. The cost is significant and must be accounted for in the take-off.

Ordinary Finish An ordinary finish generally requires that form fins be trimmed and tieholes be plugged and filled. This work is relatively inexpensive and is often considered to be included in the cost of stripping forms. In all probability, the estimator would not list this area separately in the take-off.

Sandblast Finish   Sandblasting is sometimes called for when a particular surface texture is desired or if tile is to be applied. The cost can be considerable and should be noted. Bonded joints may require wet sandblasting or water jetting, although this requirement is not related to finishing.

Tooled Finish   At times, a requirement for roughening of the surface with a hammer is called for in order to accomplish a certain architectural effect. Or, the requirement might be to bush hammer the surface to expose aggregates. Whatever the case, the cost is extra and should be noted.

Burlap Finish   A burlap finish involves the rubbing of a mortar mix over the surface with a burlap pad. Again, this usually is done just after forms are removed. The effort involved is enough to warrant separate cost.

Waterproof or Dampproof

Many protective surface treatments are in popular use. As sturdy as concrete may appear, it is very susceptible to the elements and to the many destructive chemicals people use on it. Salting of highways, for instance, has been one of the greatest, single destructive practices to affect highway bridges. Water will often find its way through concrete, regardless of thickness. When it does, reinforcing bars rust, chemicals from the concrete go into solution, and a deterioration process is established. If corrosive chemicals such as salt are present, the deterioration process is accelerated.

The result created by this concrete deterioration is that the estimator can expect to find protective coating of some type called for in the plans and specifications for most concrete structures. Retaining walls, abutment walls, box culverts, subway tunnels, underground tanks—and almost any other underground structure—receive a dampproof or waterproof treatment of some type. Bridge decks, parapets, railings, walls, and other exposed concrete surfaces are frequently treated with oil, wax, or epoxy coating to resist or seal out corrosive elements. Whatever the protective treatment, the estimator must take off the area of coverage and include those areas in the quantitative summary.

The specified treatment should be described in enough detail that materials or subcontract prices can be obtained intelligently and that the estimator can easily assemble a cost. A 3-ply membrane waterproofing on a retaining wall, for example, may require the following:

Materials
- Woven glass fiber, ASTM D 1668[1]
- Waterproofing asphalt, type A, AASHTO-M115[2]
- Primer, AASHTO-M116[2]

Application
- Clean the surface
- 1 Primer coat
- 3 Layers of fabric, 24″ wide, overlapped
- 4 Layers of asphalt, 15 gal/100 sf

Quantity
- 530′ × 20′ = 10,600 sf

Embedded Items

When plans and specifications for structural concrete require that embedded items, such as anchor bolts, sleeves, conduits, drains, expansion dams, curbing, and flashing, be placed within the structure and that the cost for such items be incidental to the concrete, the estimator must include a summary of the quantities involved in the take-off. Some of the incidental items may require explanation or definition to enable material prices to be properly solicited and to allow an intelligent cost to be computed.

Miscellaneous Items

It remains a very important point to remember that it is the estimator's responsibility to find and point out all the factors affecting the price of structural concrete. Anything missed is lost. The easiest thing to do is to overlook the unusual (and, therefore, unexpected) requirement. When studying the plans and specifications, watch for hidden contractural conditions that require:

- A lump sum payment for some part of the work
- Extremely expensive bearing pads
- Special treatment or payment for concrete placed on blasted bedrock

· Use of lean concrete as a leveling course subsidiary to the foundation concrete
· Reinforcing steel to be a subsidiary to the concrete
· Excavation to be subsidiary to the structure

These and several other unusual requirements appear frequently enough to justify a special alertness by the estimator.

1.4 THE PRELIMINARY PROGRESS SCHEDULE

A preliminary progress schedule is a very simple and useful tool because it assists an estimator in establishing a time frame for principal project activities. The estimator's ability to quickly identify milestone needs for critical supervisory and labor personnel, equipment, and materials and to correctly apply escalation factors to the cost will add to the quality and accuracy of the cost estimate. In other words, the preliminary progress schedule becomes one more important way to use information gained from a take-off to best advantage.

Scheduling of a project again requires judgment and experience just as do many other steps in the estimating process. Background knowledge is necessary in order to judge how long it should take to construct a concrete structure, whether it be a small wall or a complex bridge abutment. Even with this background knowledge, the schedule can only be considered preliminary at this stage, since it does not include all the time factors that will become apparent when pricing is completed.

1.5 SUPPLIER AND SUBCONTRACTOR

Soliciting prices for materials and quotations from subcontractors is part of the take-off process for all types of construction. Structural concrete estimating requires quotations on certain basic materials:

· Concrete mix (ready-mix)   · Form plywood
· Aggregates (on-site plant)   · Joint materials
· Cement (on-site plant)   · Stay-in-place (SIP) metal forms
· Concrete additives   · Embedded items
· Lumber

Each project bid should be prepared with backup quotations for all significant materials and subcontract work. Very little should be left to conjecture. This is where studying the plans and specifications pays off. A situation such as the estimator's neglecting to tell the ready-mix supplier that all floor concrete must contain an expensive retarder is avoided. All needs are recognized in time to do something about them—and nothing is missed. It bears restating that anything missed is lost.

Occasionally, a supplier or subcontractor will require considerably detailed information in order to quote a price for an item. It may be necessary for the estimator to prepare a *Bill of Materials* for the supplier. A Bill of Materials is simply a complete description and summary of needs for a work item. The supplier can use this information to identify and price all the needs. For instance, if a concrete item requires considerable embedded pipe and inserts, a Bill of Materials would provide the supplier with information about quality, quantity, size, length, fittings, etc., so that a suitable quotation could be prepared. In quoting prices, most suppliers do their own take-off and establish their own Bill of Materials. However, the estimator should keep in mind that it is always possible for suppliers to view the requirements differently—and somewhat to their own advantage.

REFERENCES

[1] American Society for Testing and Materials (ASTM), Standard D 1668, Washington, D.C. (latest edition).

[2] American Association of State Highway and Transportation Officials (AASHTO), Standards M115, M116, Washington, D.C. (latest edition).

2 ILLUSTRATION OF A TAKE-OFF

2.1 GENERAL REQUIREMENTS

An excellent way to understand a structural concrete take-off is through the use of an example that applies the principles discussed in Chapter 1. A hypothetical Highway 1 Project is created for this purpose. Plans and appropriate specifications for the Highway 1 Project can be found in Appendixes A and B. Highway 1 requires construction of the following:

Structure 1   Reinforced concrete box culvert
Structure 2   Retaining walls
Structure 3   3-Span simple I-beam bridge
Structure 4   3-Span girder bridge

The estimator's task is to provide a complete take-off for the three structural concrete pay items that cover all concrete work in these structures. They are described as:

Class A Concrete   Decks, sidewalks, parapets
Class B Concrete   Substructures, wall stems, box culvert
Class C Concrete   Footings

It is suggested that the reader now study the plans and specifications in Appendixes A and B, remembering that the illustration will be somewhat overdone for the sake of definition.

2.2 ASSEMBLING INFORMATION

Time is limited, with a deadline to meet and much to do! Recognizing urgency as well as the importance of quality take-off, the estimator must plan for a concentrated, well-organized effort directed toward learning all there is to know about the structural concrete in a short period of time. This is accomplished through two extrapolations.

The first involves obtaining a clear understanding of the project through study of the plans and specifications and by means of a visit to the project site. This will provide the estimator with knowledge of the scope of the project and how external factors affect the structural concrete. The second is directed toward the internal (or direct) details that affect the concrete cost. Factors such as concrete mix, consistency, and special finishes are noted. This assembling of information will become a valued tool throughout the estimating process.

The Project Scope

A project scope is a description of the work that brings out the broad external factors of importance that influence the cost. After a study of the plans and specifications and a visit to the project site, the estimator is ready to produce a project scope as it pertains to the structural concrete work.

PROJECT SCOPE—HIGHWAY 1

Highway 1 is a project one-third mile long with an 18-month contract duration. (See "Plan and Profile," Appendix A.) It has good access via the existing side road, which will eventually be carried by Structure 3. Supplies and the availability of labor and subcontractors are not a problem. Certain parameters affect construction of the structures. A visit to the site and a study of the plans and specifications have produced the following understanding:

Structure 1 This twin 8' × 6' reinforced concrete box culvert should be constructed early since it is at the bottom of a main-line embankment that must be made available for earth materials excavated from the project's earth cuts. Access to this structure site is fair, but must be via a road built along the right-of-way. Stream diversion is not a problem since the flow is very light.

Structure 2 The largest earth cut on the project will have its banks retained by two identical retaining walls 420 feet long. The owner's interest is to minimize taking of land for the highway right-of-way in this area. Before excavation proceeds, an earth support system must be installed outside the limits of wall construction. Then, after the earth cut is removed, the walls can be started. When the site is ready for wall construction, it is anticipated that access will be satisfactory along the highway right-of-way.

Structure 3 This bridge will carry the side road over the main line. The side road can be closed to traffic during construction of the bridge. Excavation for the abutments can start early. The piers cannot be constructed until the main-line excavation is completed at the bridge site. This excavation will be done early since the earth material is needed for the embankments at Structure 4. Bedrock will be encountered in the pier footing excavation.

Structure 4 This bridge will carry the main line over a stream. Although the bridge is simple in design, construction presents several problems of significance. It is quite high (35 feet from roadway to streambed), and has long spans (75 and 100 feet). The stream is 100 feet wide, and access is difficult for construction of the center span and for the movement of personnel and equipment from one side to the other.

Study of the plans and the site point out a need for a stream crossing to haul earth material to the otherwise isolated embankment area. A crossing could be constructed at a location that could accommodate this principal use and also serve the needs of the bridge construction. The cost will be assigned to an excavation item.

The plans require construction of the piers in the dry. To keep the pier excavation dry, it will be necessary to build dikes or cofferdams around each pier and to install a pump (or pumps) at each location. This is an excavation cost; however, the installation affects the scheduling of pier construction. Access to the piers for early construction is poor since a road must be built over rough terrain.

Abutment construction must wait for the construction of the embankment and installation of the bearing piles specified.

Details

The project scope provided a view of the external factors that influence the cost of the structural concrete for Highway I. Equally important is a view of the internal factors or details that affect the concrete cost. As a matter of form, an estimator should list all details of significance and include with the list enough data to aid pricing and soliciting for prices. A well-done take-off for Highway I structural concrete would include the following details.

TAKE-OFF DETAILS, HIGHWAY I

1. Concrete

    Class A

    · Deck, sidewalks, and parapets

    · Include parapets on Structure 4 wingwalls

    · 6½ bag, 3500 psi, 610 cy

    · Must use retarder for deck

    Class B

    · Bridge substructure, wall stem, and box culvert

    · 6 bag, 3000 psi, 2125 cy

    Class C

    · Bridge and wall footings

    · 5½ bag, 2500 psi, 2020 cy

    Class D

    · 6″ subfoundation mat—Structure 4 piers

· 4$^1/_2$ bag, 1500 psi, subsidiary

· No pay

2. Contractor Quality Control Required

3. Commercial Plant Required

4. Free Footing Concrete for Overbreak in Rock, Structure 3

5. Waterstop

· 6″ rubber—box culvert, wall stems

6. Dampproof

· Applied to box culvert, walls, bridge abutments

· 3-brush application:

primer $^1/_8$ gal/sy
primer $^1/_8$ gal/sy
seal $^1/_{10}$ gal/sy

7. Waterproof

· Applied to walls—2′ strip at each joint

· 2-ply application:

primer	$^1/_{10}$ gal/sy AASHTO-M116[1]
fiberglass fabric	Fed. Spec. HH-C-00466 in 2 layers
asphalt	1.3 gal/sy ASTM D 449[2], Type C in 3 applications

8. Drainage

· Walls require 6″ PVC perforated with outlets at 30′ center to center; also calls for drainage backfill

· 4″ weeps are required in bridge abutments; each weep includes a screen and protective stone ($^1/_2$ cy)

9. Finishes

· Walls: rough board finish

10. Surface Treatments

· Linseed oil on decks

· Mix—$^{50}/_{50}$ linseed oil and mineral spirits

· Application = 2 spray coats

· 1 gal/400 sf

· 1 gal/600 sf

11. Joints

· Expansion dams for Structure 4 included

12. Shoring

· Requires design approval

2.3 COMPUTATIONS

Now with a thorough grasp of the scope of the structural concrete work for Highway I and the specific details involved, the estimator is ready to do the computation of quantities essential to estimating the cost. The format explained in Chapter I will be used in compiling the computations.

The estimator's task described in Section 2.1 is now restated in order to place emphasis on structural concrete components rather than on pay items. These components will each constitute the basis on which cost will be estimated. Each component, with all associated computation data, will also be separated throughout the process of determining the cost.

Component description	Concrete
Footings for walls and bridges	Class C
Pier stems for bridges (wall, 8′+)	Class B
Pier columns for bridges	Class B
Pier beams for bridges	Class B
Abutments for bridges (0–8′)	Class B
Box culvert slabs and footings	Class B
Box culvert walls (0–8′)	Class B
Box culvert roof (slab above grade)	Class B
Decks for bridges	Class A
Sidewalks for bridges	Class A
Parapets for bridges (wall, 0–8′)	Class A

The estimator will recall that this type of breakdown is necessary because of specific differences between the components. As the computations are examined, those differences will begin to become apparent.

Computations of Quantities

Computations of quantities for each structure will be preceded by a summary that describes the structure and points out notable features and assumptions. As the study of the computations progresses, the following practices should be noted.

1. All area computations are rounded up to the nearest 10 square feet.

2. The identity of each computation is established in the left-hand column for clarity and easy return reference. Identity includes the name of the structural component part, the class of concrete involved, and the nature of the computation itself.

3. All computations related to a particular structural component are kept grouped with a component.

4. Chamfer strip is not taken off, since the cost will be incorporated when estimating the cost of the forms.

5. The 2- × 4-inch keyway is not taken off. The cost will be covered by the form material factor and the crew productivity used to estimate form cost. As keyways become larger, their material cost becomes significant enough for additional consideration.

6. Shoring for the box culvert roof is listed. The 8-foot span is not self-supporting with the forms alone.

7. Deductions are not made from the computed pier beam form area for column intrusion, nor are there any similar deductions made in the case of finish or shoring areas. The reason is that such deductions are inconsequential compared to the time and material expended in building the forms, supporting them, and finishing the undersides.

8. Deck form areas include beam flanges, since their cost no more than compensates for the material and effort that go into haunch construction.

9. Float includes only areas such as beam seats that require a disproportionate amount of dry-finishing work.

10. The symbols used in the quantity computation sheets are:

   - BF Board finish   · LO   Linseed oil
   - DB Drainage backfill   · WP   Waterproof
   - DP Dampproof   · WS   Waterstop
   - ED Expansion dam   · 6″ PVC   6″ PVC pipe
   - JS Elastomeric joint seal   · 4″ PVC   4″ PVC pipe

The computations are as follows:

STRUCTURE I—RC BOX CULVERT

Although the box culvert is not large or complex, it does have possibilities for improvement. For instance, there is a good chance that the top longitudinal joint in the walls can be eliminated and the walls and roof poured monolithically. The size of such pours is not prohibitive, and the time and money saved with a good, one-piece internal form is worth considering.

Assuming the three-piece construction as described by the plans, the concrete will be separated into three categories:

· Floor slab, apron, and wing footings (slab on grade)
· Walls and wingwalls (wall, 0–8′)
· Roof (slab above grade)

Further separation would only be academic and would not yield a more meaningful cost.

The computations shown in Figure 2.1a, b, and c, will include the following information:

· Concrete volume   · Large keyway length
· Contact area   · Finish area
· Shored area   · Dampproof area
· Waterstop length

STRUCTURE 2—RETAINING WALLS (TWO EACH)

Traditionally, cost for wall concrete will be figured in two parts:

Footings   Class C concrete
Stems (wall, 8′ +)   Class B concrete

The computation format shown in Figure 2.2a and b, will include the following quantities:

· Concrete volume   · Waterproof area
· Contact area   · Dampproof area
· Large keyway length   · 6″ PVC U-drain length
· Waterstop length   · 6″ PVC weep length
· Architectural finish area   · Backfill quantity

STRUCTURE 3—SIDE ROAD/MAIN LINE

This is a standard 3-span, I-beam bridge of common variety. It holds few secrets. The only thing to watch for is overbreak in the rock foundations under the piers. Any loose rock below grade must be removed and replaced with free concrete. The concrete will be priced in the following categories:

· Footings   · Deck
· Columns   · Sidewalk (deck)
· Abutments, 0–8′   · Parapet (wall, 0–8′)
· Beams

Project _Highway 1, Structure 1_

Location _RC Box Culvert_

QUANTITY ESTIMATE

DETAIL	L	W	H	No. Ea.	Cl. A CY	Cl. B CY	Cl. C CY	Cont. SF	Shore SF	Joint LF	Rub SF	Float SF	Other SF
Floor (SOG) Concrete	72	20	1.5	1	80.0								
"8" "	15	20	1	2	2.2								
"	20	1	1.5	1	2.2								
"	70	1.5	0.5	2	2.2								
"	70	1.8	0.5	2	1.9								
Contact	70		3	2	4.7			420					
"		20	2	2				80					
"		20	3	2				120					
3x6 Key	70			2						3x6 140			
"	23			2						3x6 46			
6" W.Stop	70			2						ws 140			
"	23			2						ws 46			
Float	70	14		1								980	
Damproof	70		1	2									DP 140
Apron (SOG) Concrete	26	10	1	2	19.3								
"8"	35	15	2	2	7.8								
Contact	35		5	2				350					
Float	26	10		2								520	
Wing Foot Concrete	11	4	1.5	4	9.8								
"8" Contact	11		2	8				180					
"		4	2	4				30					
Totals					127.9			1180		3x6 190 / ws 190		1500	DP 140

Figure 2.1(a)   Quantity Estimate – Structure 1, RC Box Culvert (page 1).

31

Project *Highway 1, Structure 1*

Location *RC Box Culvert*

QUANTITY ESTIMATE

DETAIL	L	W	H	No. Eq.	CONCRETE Cl. A CY	CONCRETE Cl. B CY	CONCRETE Cl. C CY	Cont. SF	Shore SF	Joint LF	SURFACE Rub SF	SURFACE Float SF	SURFACE Other SF
Walls, 0-8 Concrete	70	1	5.5	1		143							
"B" "	70	1.5	5.5	2		42.8							
" Contact	70		7	2				980					
"	70		6	4				1680					
"	12		2	4				100					
"	6		1	4				20					
3x6 Key	70			2						3x6 140			
"	12			2						3x6 24			
6" WS	70			2						ws 140			
"	12			2						ws 24			
Rub	6		5	8							240		
Dampproof	70	10		1									DP 700
Wingwalls Concrete	1.5	1	8.5	4		1.9							
(Wall 0-8) "	12	1	6.3	4		11.2							
"B" Contact	13		7	8				730					
"		1	4	4				20					
6" WS			9	4						ws 36			
Rub	13		7	4							360		
"	14		1	4							60		
Dampproof	13		6	4									DP 310
Totals						20.2		3530		3x6 160 ws 200	660		DP 1010

Figure 2.1(b)   Quantity Estimate – Structure 1, RC Box Culvert (page 2).

Project _Highway 1, Structure 1_

Location _RC Box Culvert_

QUANTITY ESTIMATE

DETAIL	L	W	H	No. Eq.	CONCRETE Cl. A CY	Cl. B CY	Cl. C CY	Cont. SF	Shore SF	Joint SF	Joint LF	Rub SF	Float SF	Other SF
Roof (SAG) Concrete	70	20	1.5	1	77.8									
"B"	70	0.5	0.5	2	1.3									
"	20	1	1.5	2	2.2									
Contact	70	8		2				1120	1120					
"	20	20	3					120						
"	20		2	4				160						
3xc key	20		2								3xc 40			
6" ws	20		2								ws 40			
Rub	20		4	2								160		
Dampproof	70	24		1										DP 1680
Totals					81.3			1400	1120		3xc 40 / ws 40	160		DP 1680

Figure 2.1(c)   Quantity Estimate – Structure 1, RC Box Culvert (page 3).

33

Project *Highway 1, Structure 2* Date *1/1*

Location *Retaining Walls (2)* By *JEC* *1 of 2*

QUANTITY ESTIMATE

DETAIL	L	W	H	No. Ea.	CONCRETE Cl. A CY	Cl. B CY	Cl. C CY	Cont. SF	Shore SF	Joint LF	SURFACE Rub SF	Float SF	Other SF		
Footings Concrete	330	15	3.5	2			1288.3								
"C" "	90	13	3	2			260.0								
Contact	330		7	2				4620							
"	90		6	2				1080							
"	15		4	8				480							
"	13		3	4				160							
3×8 Key	420			2						3×8 840					
Totals							1548.3	6340		3×8 840					

Figure 2.2(a) Quantity Estimate – Structure 2, Retaining Walls (page 1).

Project Highway 1, Structure 2

Location Retaining Walls (SC)

QUANTITY ESTIMATE

Date 1/1

By JFC

DETAIL	L	W	H	No. Ea.	CONCRETE Cl. A CY	CONCRETE Cl. B CY	CONCRETE Cl. C CY	Cont. SF	Shore SF	Joint LF	SURFACE Rub SF	SURFACE Float SF	SURFACE Other SF	6" PVC Pipe LF	Drain Bkfill CY
Stem (Walls) Concrete															
"B"	240	2.5	20	2	8869										
Contact	180	2.25	15	2	450.0										
	240		20	4				19,200							
"	180		15	4				10,800							
"		3	20	18				1,080							
"		3	13	12				470							
Board Finish	240		16	2									BF 7680		
"	180		11	2									BF 3960		
3x6 Key	19		18	18						3x6 340					
"	14		8	8						3x6 110					
6" Waterstop	19		18	18						WS 340					
"	14		8	8						WS 110					
2-ply Waterproof		2	19	18									WP 690		
"		2	14	8									WP 230		
Dampproof	240		19	2									DP 9,120		
"	180		14	2									DP 5,040		
6" PVC (thru)	4			28										110	
6" PVC Drain	420			2										840	
Backfill	240	1.5	12	2											320
"	180	1.5	7	2											140
Totals					13369			31,550		3x6 450 / WS 450			BF 11,640 / WP 920 / DP 14,160	950	460

Figure 2.2(b) Quantity Estimate – Structure 2, Retaining Walls (page 2).

The computations (Figure 2.3a, b, c, and d) will include the following quantitative data:

· Concrete volume   · Finish area
· Contact area   · 4″ weep length
· Shore area   · Linseed area
· Large keyway length · Dampproof area

STRUCTURE 4—MAIN LINE/STREAM

This 3-span girder bridge has greater complexity than the other structures due to the topography and the stream it crosses. Reach requirements call for the use of a larger crane or a concrete pump as dewatered pier cofferdams are subject to flooding and access to the piers is difficult. The concrete cost will be categorized as follows:

· Footings   · Beams
· Stems (wall, 8′ +) · Deck
· Columns   · Sidewalks (deck)
· Abutments, 0–8′   · Parapets (wall, 0–8′)

Included in the computations for the preceding are the following quantitative items (see Figure 2.4a, b, c, and d):

· Concrete volume   · Dampproof area
· Contact area   · Expansion dam length
· Shore area   · Class D concrete volume
· Large keyway length · Linseed oil area
· Finish area   · Elastomeric joint length

Summary

The computations were performed in groups identified by structure, and the structural concrete components took a secondary position. It is easier and less confusing for the estimator to compute all quantities for a single structure at one time than it is to try to go from blueprint to blueprint digging out information for a single concrete component. In their present form, the computations would be difficult to use since the cost estimate will be based on pay items and their respective structural components, and those must be arranged accordingly. The solution is to summarize the take-off of quantities in a manner similar to that found in Figure 2.5a, b, c, and d.

2.4 PRELIMINARY PROGRESS SCHEDULE

The quantitative and qualitative take-off is now complete for the Highway I structural concrete work, and the estimator is ready to add

Project Highway 1, Structure 3

Location SR/ML

QUANTITY ESTIMATE

Date 1/1

By See   1 of 4

DETAIL	L	W	H	No. Eq.	CONCRETE Cl. A CY	Cl. B CY	Cl. C CY	Cont. SF	Shore SF	Joint LF	SURFACE Rub SF	Float SF	Other SF
Footings A Concrete	35.5	6	3	2			473.0						
"C" " "	14.5	4	3	2			12.9						
" P "	10	10	3.5	4			51.9						
A Contact	56		3	4				670					
P "	40		4	4				640					
3+8 Key	34			2						3+8 70			
Totals							112.1	1310		3+8 70			
Columns Concrete	3.5	3.5	16.5	4		27.9							
"B" Contact		14	17	4				950					
" Rub	13	14		4							730		
Totals						29.9		950			730		
Beams Concrete	31	4	4	2		36.7							
"B" Contact	31	12	4	2				750					
" "	4	14		4				70					
Rub	31	12		2							750		
Float	31	4		2								250	
Shore	31	4		2					250				
Totals						36.7		820	250		750	250	

Figure 2.3(a) Quantity Estimate—Structure 3, Side Road/Main Line (page 1).

37

QUANTITY ESTIMATE

DETAIL	L	W	H	No. Ea.	Cl. A CY	Cl. B CY	Cl. C CY	Cont. SF	Shore SF	Joint LF	Rub SF	Float SF	Other SF	4"PVC Pipe LF
Abutment o-e Concrete	34.5	3	3	2		23.0								
"B"	34.5	1	2.6	2		6.6								
"	1	2	3	4		0.9								
"	6.5	1	10	2		4.8								
"	8.0	1	9	2		5.3								
Contact	35		6	4				840						
"	2		3	4				30						
"	2		6	4				50						
"	7		10	4				280						
"	8		10	4				320						
v		1	15	4				60						
4" Weeps	3			10										4"PVC 30
Rub	35		3	2							210			
"	2		6	4							50			
"	7		10	2							140			
"	9		10	2							180			
Float	33	2		2								140		
Dampproof	35		6	2									DP 420	
"	7		5	2									DP 70	
"	8		5	2									DP 90	
3x8 Key	34			2						3x8 70				
Totals						40.6		1580		3x8 70	580	140	DP 510	4"PVC 30

Figure 2.3(b) Quantity Estimate—Structure 3, Side Road/Main Line (page 2).

38

Project *Highway 1, Structure 3* Date *1/1*

Location *SR/ML* By *SEC* *3 of 4*

QUANTITY ESTIMATE

DETAIL	L	W	H	No. Ea.	CONCRETE Cl. A CY	Cl. B CY	Cl. C CY	Cont. SF	Shore SF	Joint LF	SURFACE Rub SF	Float SF	Other SF		
Deck Concrete	146	34.5	0.67	1	125.0										
"A" "	28	2.2	0.5	2	2.3										
"	28	2.6	0.5	2	2.7										
"	144	1.4	0.12	5	4.5										
Contact	144	36		1				5190							
"	35		2	4				280							
Rub	144	4		2							1160				
Float	146	28		1								4090			
Linseed	146	28		1									LO 4090		
Totals					134.5			5470			1160	4090	LO 4090		
Sidewalk Concrete	146	4.5	0.67	1	16.3										
(deck) Contact	146		1	2				290							
"A" "	5		1	4				20							
Rub	146		1	1							150				
Float	146	4		1								590			
Linseed	146	4		1									LO 590		
Totals					16.3			310			150	590	LO 590		

Figure 2.3(c) Quantity Estimate—Structure 3, Side Road/Main Line (page 3).

Project _Highway 1, Structure 3_

Location _SR/ML_

QUANTITY ESTIMATE

Date _//_

By _SFC_ _4 of 4_

DETAIL	L	W	H	No. Ea.	CONCRETE Cl. A CY	CONCRETE Cl. B CY	CONCRETE Cl. C CY	Cont. SF	Shore SF	Joint LF	SURFACE Rub SF	SURFACE Float SF	SURFACE Other SF
Parapet Concrete	146	0.75	3.5	1	14.2								
(wall o-e) "	146	1	3.5	1	18.9								
"	146	0.4	1	1	2.2								
"	146	0.25	23	1	3.1								
Contact	146		7	2				2050					
"		1	4	8				30					
"		2	4	8				70					
Rub	146		4	4							2340		40/170
Linseed	146		4	2									40/170
Totals					38.4			2150			2340		40/170

Figure 2.3(d) Quantity Estimate—Structure 3, Side Road/Main Line (page 4).

40

Project __Highway 1, Structure 4__

Location __ML/Stream__

QUANTITY ESTIMATE

Date __//__

By __SLC__   __1 of 4__

DETAIL	L	W	H	No. Eq.	CONCRETE Cl. A CY	Cl. B CY	Cl. C CY	Cont. SF	Shore SF	Joint LF	SURFACE Rub SF	Float SF	Other SF	Class "D" CY
Footings A Concrete	44	7.5	3.5	2			85.6							
"C" A "	5	4	3.5	4			10.4							
A "	47	14	5	2			243.7							
A Contact	60		4	4				960						
A "	8		4	2				70						
P "	61		5	4				1,220						
3x12 key	40			2						3x12 80				
6x18 key	40			2						6x18 80				
Cl. D Conc.	47	14	0.5	2										24.4
Totals							339.7	2250		3x12 80 / 6x18 80				24.4
Stem Concrete	41	6	15	2		273.3								
(Wall B +) Contact	47	6	15	4				2820						
"B" Rub	47	7	7	4							1320			
Totals						273.3		2820			1320			
Columns Concrete	13.7	3.5	3.5	6	37.3									
"B" Contact	14	14		6				1180						
Rub	14	14		6							1180			
Totals					37.3			1180			1180			

Figure 2.4(a)   Quantity Estimate – Structure 4, Main Line/Stream (page 1).

41

Project *Highway 1, Structure 4*　　　　Date *1/1*

Location *ML/Stream*　　　　By *JEC　2 of 4*

QUANTITY ESTIMATE

DETAIL	L	W	H	No. Ea.	CONCRETE Cl. A CY	Cl. B CY	Cl. C CY	Cont. SF	Shore SF	Joint LF	SURFACE Rub SF	Float SF	Other SF		
Abutment, 0-8' Concrete	38	3.5	2.9	2		28.6									
"B" "	38	1.5	4.9	2		20.7									
"	38	1	1	2		2.8									
"	3	1	0.6	4		0.3									
"	2	1	8	4		2.4									
"	6	1	7.8	4		6.9									
Contact	40		9	4				1,440							
"	6		8	8				390							
"	1		5	8				40							
3x6 key	38			2						3x6 80					
Rub	40		3	2							240				
"		1	15	4							60				
"		6	10	4							240				
"															
Float	38	2		2								160			
Dampproof	50		9	2									DP 900		
Totals						61.7		1870		3x6 80	540	160	DP 900		

Figure 2.4(b) Quantity Estimate – Structure 4, Main Line/Stream (page 2).

Project Highway 1, Structure 4

Location ML/Stream

QUANTITY ESTIMATE

DETAIL	L	W	H	No. Eq.	CONCRETE Cl. A CY	Cl. B CY	Cl. C CY	Cont. SF	Shore SF	Joint LF	SURFACE Rub SF	Float SF	Other SF
Beam Concrete "B"	39	4	5.1	2		58.9							
Contact	39	14		2				1,100					
"	4		5	4				80					
Shore	29	4		2					230				
Rub	43	14		2							1,210		
Float	39	4		2								320	
Totals						58.9		1,180	230		1,210	320	
Deck Concrete "A"	248	40	0.75	1	275.6								
"	248	15	0.17	6	14.1								
"	35	13	0.5	2	1.7								
"	35	3.3	0.5	2	4.3								
Contact	248	42		1				10,420					
"	40		2	4				320					
"	35		1	4				140					
Float	248	32		1								7,940	
Rub											1,490		
End Dam										ED 80			
Joint Seal										JS 90			
Linseed													10 / 11,160
Total					295.7			10,880		ED 80 / JS 90	1,490	7,940	11,160

Figure 2.4(c)   Quantity Estimate – Structure 4, Main Line/Stream (page 3).

Project Highway 1, Structure 4

Location ML/Stream

QUANTITY ESTIMATE

Date 1/1

By SEC 4 of 4

DETAIL	L	W	H	No. Ea.	CONCRETE Cl. A CY	Cl. B CY	Cl. C CY	Cont. SF	Shore SF	Joint LF	SURFACE Rub SF	Float SF	Other SF
Sidewalk Concrete	248	4	0.65	2	47.8								
(deck) Contact	248		1	4				1,000					
"A" "		4	1	22				90					
Float	248	3		2								1,490	
Rub	248		1	4							1,000		
Linseed	248	3		2									10 1,490
Totals					47.8			1,090			1,000	1,490	10 1,490
Parapet Concrete	248	1	3.5	2	64.3								
(Wall, o-e) "	6	1	5	4	44								
"A" Contact	248	1	7	2				3,480					
"		1	4	22				90					
"	7		5	8				280					
Rub	248		7	2							3,480		
"	7		5	8							280		
Linseed	248		7	1									10 10,740
Totals					68.7			3,850			3,760		10 10,740

Figure 2.4(d) Quantity Estimate – Structure 4, Main Line/Stream (page 4).

44

Project _Highway 1_

Location _Class A Concrete_

QUANTITY SUMMARY

Date _1/6_

By _Sec 1 of 4_

DETAIL	Form Factor SF/CY	Bid Concrete CY	Actual Concrete CY	Contact SF	Shore SF	Joint LF	SURFACE		
							Rub SF	Float SF	Other SF
Deck 3	40.7		135	5,300			1,200	4,100	LO 4,100
" 4	36.8		296	10,900		ED 80 JS 90	1,500	8,000	LO 1,200
Sidewalk 3 (deck)	18.8		16	300			200	600	LO 600
" 4 (deck)	22.9		48	1,100			1,000	1,500	LO 1,500
Parapet 3 (wall, 0-6')	57.9		38	2,200			2,400		LO 1,200
" 4 (wall, 0-6')	56.5		69	3,900			3,800		LO 1,800
Totals		610	602	23,900		ED 80 JS 90	10,100	14,200	LO 20,400

Figure 2.5(a) Quantity Summary (page 1).

Project __Highway!__

Location __Class B Concrete__

Date __1/1__

By __Sec__   2 of 4

QUANTITY SUMMARY

DETAIL	Form Factor SF/CY	Bid Concrete CY	Actual Concrete CY	Contact SF	Shore SF	Joint LF	Rub SF	Float SF	Other SF	Drain Pipe LF	Drain Mat'l. CY
Box Floor 1 (SOG)	9.4		128	1,200		3x4 700 / ws 200		1,500	DP 2,002		
Abutment 3 (Abut. 0-8')	39.0		41	1,600		3x8 100	600	200	DP 600	4PVC 30	
" 4 (Abut. 0-8')	30.7		62	1,900		3x4 100	600	200	DP 900		
Box Walls 1 (Wall 0-8')	50.7		71	3,600		3x4 150 / ws 200	700		DP 1,000		
Wall Stem 2 (Wall 8'+)	23.6		1339	31,600		3x4 500 / ws 450			BF 11,200 / WP 1,000 / DP 4,200	CPVC 950	DB 460
Pier Stem 4 (Wall 8'+)	10.6		774	2,900			1400				
Pier Column 3	33.3		30	1,000	300		800				
" 4	31.6		38	1,200	300		1200				
Pier Beam 3	24.3		37	900	300		800	300			
" 4	20.3		59	1,200	300		1200	400			
Box Roof 1 (SAG)	173		81	1,400	1,400	3x4 50 / ws 50	200		DP 1,700		

Figure 2.5(b)   Quantity Summary (page 2).

QUANTITY SUMMARY

DETAIL	Form Factor SF/CY	Bid Concrete CY	Actual Concrete CY	Contact SF	Shore SF	Joint LF	SURFACE			Drain Pipe LF	Drain Mat'l. CY
							Rub SF	Float SF	Other SF		
Totals - Class B Conc.		2125	2160	48500	1800	3x6 1,000	7500	2,600	DP 18,600	4PVC 30	DS 460
						3x8 100			BF 11,700	CPVC 950	
						ws 900			WP 1,000		

Figure 2.5(c) Quantity Summary (page 3).

Project __Highway 1__

Location __Class C Concrete__

QUANTITY SUMMARY

Date __1/1__

By __[initials]__   __4 of 4__

DETAIL	Form Factor SF/CY	Bid Concrete CY	Actual Concrete CY	Contact SF	Shore SF	Joint LF	SURFACE Rub SF	Float SF	Other SF
Footings 2	4.1		1549	6,400		3×8 900			
" 3	12.5		112	1,400		3×8 100			
" 4	6.8		340	2,300		3×12 100			
						4×8 100			
Totals		2020	2,001	10,100		3×8 1,000			
						3×12 100			
						6×8 100			

Figure 2.5(d) Quantity Summary (page 4).

the third and very important dimension of time. One of the better ways to do this is through the use of a simple time-scaled arrow diagram, since it expresses logic in a more satisfactory fashion than does a bar schedule. The preliminary schedule for Highway 1 (Figure 2.6) is not a complete project schedule, but it does include the essential project information, and taking normal weather expectations into account, it serves the purpose of assisting the estimator to establish milestones that will affect the cost for structural concrete.

Referring to the preliminary progress schedule for Highway 1, the activity start dates of importance are given below.

ACTIVITY START DATES—HIGHWAY I

- · 4/1   Soldier piles for earth support
- · 4/1   Abutment—Structure 3
- · 4/1   Box culvert—Structure 4
- · 5/1   Piers—Structure 3
- · 5/15   Piers—Structure 4
- · 5/15   Bearing piles—Structure 4
- · 6/15   Abutment—Structure 4
- · 6/15   Walls A and B—Structure 2
- · 6/20   Structural steel—Structure 3
- · 7/15   Deck—Structure 3
- · 8/1   Structural steel—Structure 4
- · 9/5   Deck—Structure 4

In Chapter 6 this schedule will be referred to, and the information found will be used for estimating cost.

2.5 SUPPLIER AND SUBCONTRACTOR

The structural concrete cost estimator depends on materials and subcontractor price quotations. As soon as practical during the take-off period, those suppliers and subcontractors on whom the estimator will depend must be advised of the need, so that they will have ample time to consider and prepare their price packages.

Looking back at the Highway 1 take-off data, it can be seen that it would now be easy to make a *shopping list* for all of the structural concrete cost estimate needs. If made in a comprehensive manner, such a list can be used by a purchasing agent or another estimator. In order to be comprehensive, it must include (1) the description of the item, (2)

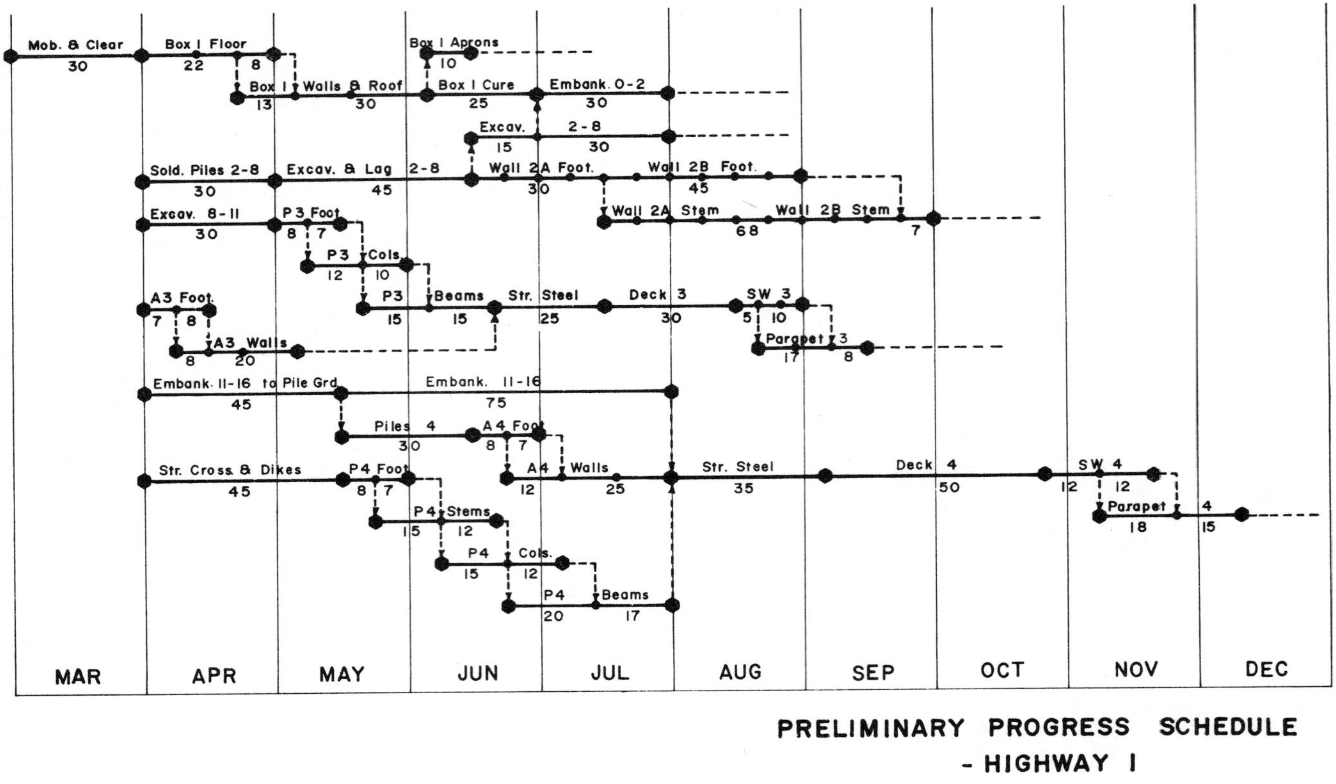

50

MAR APR MAY JUN JUL AUG SEP OCT NOV DEC

Mob. & Clear 30

Box I Floor 22

Box I Walls & Roof 30
Box I Walls & Roof 13
Box I Cure 25
Box I Aprons 10

Sold. Piles 2-8 30
Excav. 8 Lag 2-8 45
Excav. 8-11 30
Embank. 0-2 30
Excav. 2-8 15

Wall 2A Foot. 30
Wall 2A Stem 45
Wall 2B Foot. 68
Wall 2B Stem 7

A3 Foot. 7 8
A3 Walls 8 20
P3 Foot 8 7
P3 Cols 12
P3 10
P3 15
Beams 15
Str. Steel 25
Deck 3 30
SW 3 5 10
Parapet 3 17 8

Embank. 11-16 to Pile Grd. 45
Embank. 11-16 75
Piles 4 30
P4 Foot 8 7
P4 Stems 15 12
P4 Cols. 15 12
P4 20
Beams 17
A4 Foot 8 7
A4 Walls 12
A4 25

Str. Cross & Dikes 45
Str. Steel 35
Deck 4 50
SW 4 12
Parapet 4 18
4 15

PRELIMINARY PROGRESS SCHEDULE
- HIGHWAY I

Figure 2.6 Preliminary Progress Schedule.

the quantity needed, and (3) the schedule for delivery. The materials and subcontractor price needs for Highway 1 are listed below.

MATERIALS AND SUBCONTRACTORS—HIGHWAY 1

Description	Take-off	Schedule
Concrete:		
Class A	602 cy	7/15 to 12/15
Class B	2,160 cy	4/1 to 10/1
Class C	2,001 cy	4/1 to 9/1
Class D	25 cy	5/15 to 6/1
Retarder	for 431 cy, Class A	8/1 to 11/1
Air entrainment	all concrete	4/1 to 12/15
Dimension lumber (2″ and 4″)	as required	4/1 to 12/15
Rough boards (1″ random and 1½″ × 4″)	as required	7/15
¾″ Form plywood (4′ × 8′, 5 ply)	as required	4/1 to 12/15
Form ties	as required	4/1 to 12/15
Expansion dam (Structure 4) (Plan sheet 5 of 6)	80 lf	10/1
Elastomeric joint seal (Structure 4) (Plan sheet 5 of 6)	90 lf	10/1
1″ Premolded joint filler	as required	4/1 to 12/15
6″ Perforated PVC pipe—subc.	850 lf	7/15
6″ PVC pipe	100 lf	7/15
4″ PVC pipe (weeps)	30 lf	4/1
Drainage material—subc.	460 cy	9/1 to 10/15
6″ Rubber waterstop	900 lf	4/1
Linseed oil—subc. (see details)	20,400 sf	9/15 to 12/15
Dampproof—subc. (see details)	14,200 sf (Structure 2)	9/1 to 10/15

(*Continued*)

MATERIALS AND SUBCONTRACTORS—HIGHWAY 1 (Continued)

Description	Take-off	Schedule
	2,900 sf	6/15 to 7/1
	(Structure 1)	
	600 sf	5/15
	(Structure 3)	
	900 sf	8/1
	(Structure 4)	
Waterproof—subc. (see details)	1,000 sf	8/15 to 10/15
15# Felt	as required	6/15
Cure blankets	as required	4/1 to 12/15
Polyethylene sheet	as required	4/1 to 12/15

REFERENCES

[1] American Association of State Highway and Transportation Officials (AASHTO), Standard M116, Washington, D.C. (latest edition).

[2] American Society for Testing and Materials (ASTM), Standard D 449, Washington, D.C. (latest edition).

3 DEVELOPMENT OF COST

3.1 BASIS OF UNDERSTANDING

Cost estimating is an approximation representing an estimator's efforts to produce a monetary illustration of an activity—or a series of activities. It is the art of assembling all anticipated expenses required to accomplish a task.

Estimators everywhere approximate construction cost in various ways. Some project the future using historic cost data obtained from past or ongoing projects. This is an acceptable basis for cost estimating, provided that the historic data used is from well-documented, correct, and appropriately applied information. In the heat of battle, other estimators plug prices: that is, they appear to guess them. A guess is absolutely unacceptable. There must be some knowledge or experience from the past to act as a basis for even the so-called plug or pressure price. Then again, other estimators found their cost estimates on an assembly of carefully gathered facts applied to a myriad of computations. Of course, too much detail can result in a loss of perspective—or even an error. The ability to sensibly evaluate complex construction work, part by part, however, is a definite advantage to the estimator of structural concrete, since the inherent complexity of structural concrete work demands an involved estimating exercise.

Professionals who estimate structural concrete cost should understand as much as possible about the estimating process in general and, in particular, about the variables in labor expense and the basis for equipment expense. Equally important is ample experience best gained through close association with field construction for a period of time long enough to develop an understanding of the needs for labor, equipment, and materials in that type of construction, and long enough to learn what to expect those resources to produce. Without these capabilities, an estimator must rely on the knowledge and judgment of others. This chapter provides the estimator with a basic understanding of the estimating process, and it develops in detail the basis for labor and equipment cost.

3.2 DIRECT AND INDIRECT COST

All total construction cost includes two cost groups known as *direct* and *indirect*. Although this book deals strictly with a method of obtaining the direct cost for structural concrete, it is appropriate at this point to define the difference between the two.

Direct cost is the expense directly associated with the performance of any work, or the provision of any services called for by an owner's plans and specifications. Direct cost activities for a project are often identified by a list of bid items provided by the owner and found in the specifications. Those items describe the project in easily identifiable parts. But many projects are bid in lump sum, in which case an estimator must then *create* a list of direct bid items.

Indirect cost (overhead) is that estimated expense not conveniently identified with any single project activity but necessary for the support of all activities on the project. The expense for a field office and its staff, or the cost for a project manager, is indirect.

There is a gray area between direct and indirect cost where the expenses for certain work or services could fall into either category. For instance, imagine the situation where specifications require the contractor to pay for a flagman to protect the interests of a railroad company at any time work is to be performed near a railroad track. The expense could be viewed as either direct or indirect, depending on whether the contractor wishes to associate it with a specific work activity. Other examples of gray area expenses are insurance premiums and engineering. Usually, a company will develop a pattern of accounting for these expenses, and estimates of cost will follow that established pattern.

Since the estimating profession does vary its practice with respect to gray area expenses, it becomes important that it be understood which of such expenses will be considered as direct in this book. The following expenses will be treated as *direct:*

· Crew foreman and pickup truck
· Equipment ownership
· Small tools and supplies
· Service truck or utility truck
· Taxes on materials
· On-site move of equipment or material
· Certain insurances and taxes based on labor cost
· Electric power sources for the work
· Fringe benefits for labor
· Overtime, lost time, and guaranteed time for labor

Conversely, the following gray area expenses listed will be considered *indirect,* and no future explanation will be provided for them:

· Property taxes on equipment
· Move of equipment to or from the project
· General liability insurance based on volume

· Engineering

· Property damage insurance based on volume

The important thing to remember is to be consistent and responsible for including all expenses in the overall project cost summary.

3.3 THE TOTAL COST PROCESS

When complicated work such as structural concrete construction is to be evaluated, the estimator must have an intelligible means of assembling the many-faceted cost that will result. The procedure used in this book involves the summation of all labor, equipment, material, supply, and subcontract expenses necessary to complete each facet of structural concrete construction and the subsequent summation of the whole. It adapts what is called the *total cost process*. The total cost process relies on the estimator's ability to establish three principal components:

· Quantity
· Cost data
· Productivity

Quantity is a product of the take-off and has been thoroughly discussed in Chapters 1 and 2. *Cost data* are the basis for all monetary input in a cost computation. They represent the unit cost equivalent for labor and equipment, and they define the actual cost for material, supply, or subcontract. *Productivity* is the rate at which a given amount of labor and equipment can perform a given task. Once these components are established, the cost estimating procedure becomes a simple arithmetic exercise best described as follows:

Total cost $= A + B + C + D$

where A = total labor cost

$$= \frac{(\text{crew cost/unit time}) \times \text{total quantity}}{\text{productivity}}$$

B = total equipment cost

$$= \frac{(\text{equipment cost/unit time}) \times \text{total quantity}}{\text{productivity}}$$

C = total material cost

= unit cost of material $\times$ total quantity

D = total subcontract cost

= unit subcontract cost $\times$ total quantity

The advantage of this process as it applies to structural concrete cost is that the estimator can work with any convenient dimensional unit and not be concerned with conversion factors when summarizing. Mathematical errors are reduced with this process, and it is easier for the estimator to cross-reference the cost summary with the individual cost computations.

3.4 LABOR

Determining productive labor cost is much more complex in estimating than many realize. The variables involved in actual practice must be thoroughly understood before attempting to establish a labor cost estimate.

Bid Wage Rate (B)

Labor cost is a function of each of the following factors:

· Basic wage rate   · Time
· Fringe benefits   · Insurances and taxes
· Escalation

By understanding how to find and apply each of these factors, the estimator can develop average unit labor cost rates known as *bid wage rates*. When combined into crews—and subsequently applied to the unit of productive time for a construction activity—these rates will yield sufficient funds to cover all labor cost.

Bid wage rates can be further described as the product of the basic wage rate and numerical factors that represent the impact of escalation, time, and insurance and taxes—plus the product of basic fringe benefits and other numerical factors which describe the effect of escalation and time on present fringe benefits. Analytically, this can be stated as Equation (3.1):

$$B = W (E \times T \times I) + F (E_1 \times T_1) \tag{3.1}$$

where B = Bid wage rate I = Insurance and tax factor
     W = Basic wage rate F = Basic fringe benefits
     E = Wage escalation factor E_1 = Fringe escalation factor
     T = Wage time factor T_1 = Fringe time factor

The following sections will provide the details of bid wage rate determination.

Basic Wage Rate (W)

A basic wage rate (W) is the hourly rate of pay that an employer uses to determine an employee's gross earnings. In a cost estimate, the situation never exists wherein an estimator looks for anything but the lowest rates that can legally, feasibly, and practically apply. The status of the wage rates for each of the various labor classifications involved in construction is usually affected by one or more of the following conditions:

· Specifications include predetermined wage rates
· Collective bargaining agreements are in force
· Local area wage rates prevail
· Established in-house wage rates dominate

An estimator's responsibility is to determine at the outset what conditions apply for the project being appraised.

Predetermined wage rates are often found in project specifications—particularly for federally funded projects. When this is the case, these wage rates are the minimum on which an employer can base computations of an employee's gross earnings, regardless of any other existing wage arrangement. If no conditions exist which set wage rates higher, then they can become the basis on which the estimator develops the labor cost data needed for a cost estimate.

A collective bargaining agreement is the conclusion reached by negotiations of wages and working conditions between the employees, collectively, and the employer. Although they vary considerably, such agreements often include (in addition to specific wage rates and wage increases) employer-paid fringe benefits for medical insurance, life insurance, disability insurance, retirement plans, training programs, etc. They also can include conditions that affect cost for overtime, vacations, holidays, escalation, and efficiency. When working with these agreements, the estimator must understand their entire scope.

Collective bargaining agreements do not always set the highest wage rates. It is possible that an agreement will be in force, but the specified predetermined wage rates will be higher than those in the agreement or some other condition will exist that requires higher rates. For example, the payrolls of any construction company will reveal that certain employees are paid higher wage rates than the norm. Often, the reason is that the employee is a particularly skilled worker and has therefore earned recognition. Such recognition also stems an employee's desire to migrate to other companies who often try to spirit good talent away. Another reason for higher in-house wages is longevity. Long-established companies very often have a number of employees who over the years have established themselves as loyal, dependable, and effective workers, and it behooves a company to do a bit more for those with these characteristics.

When a project is to be bid in the absence of predetermined wage rates or collective bargaining agreements, the question arises as to what wage rates to use as the basis for labor cost. This is a significantly important question to answer in a heavily labor-oriented industry such as structural concrete construction. The answer is to use local area wage rates or open-shop rates appropriate to the nature of the project.

Local area wage rates are those rates paid that do not have as their basis any fixed or contracted guidelines. Their derivation is extremely complex, and in an unfamiliar area, they are difficult to determine. They are influenced by the presence of nearby union shop work, competitor recruitment, local market conditions, local skill availability, and other subtle factors.

Although local area wage rates can be reasonably determined at any given time, it is difficult to know what the future will bring because of the many influencing variables. It is recommended that an estimator learn as much as possible of the market trends and plans in order to best judge the future.

Fringe Benefits (F)

Insurance (life, health, and disability), profit sharing programs, training programs, and other benefits are often provided for the employees of a construction company through a plan activated by the company alone or by the employees and the company jointly. Such benefits are intended to provide the employee with protection, security, and the incentive to work productively. The cost is significant, and labor rates used in estimating must reflect this cost.

Usually, information about the cost for fringe benefits can easily be obtained from a company accountant, an insurance broker, or whoever administers the program on behalf of the employees. If a collective bargaining agreement is involved, the fringes are probably clearly defined in that agreement. At times, benefits will be included with predetermined wages.

Escalation (E)

Escalation is both a byword and a nemesis to the estimator. The obscurity of spiraling inflation, variable market trends, seesaw labor supply, and unpredictable competitors make it extremely difficult to determine, in advance, the effects of escalation in the construction field. However, there are a number of things that an estimator can consider that will help overcome this difficulty.

When establishing labor rates, the estimator naturally considers inflation and how much effect it will have on the employee's cost of living and the subsequent need for periodic increases in wages to meet rising costs.

If the project is not locked-in to a collective bargaining agreement wage structure, the judgment an estimator makes can be based on current inflation projections combined with a view toward the probable market activity. For instance, a depressed market will tend to make workers available who would be reluctant to demand too great an increase as long as there are other workers available to replace them. This situation assumes, of course, that the ranks of unemployed have among them sufficient skills to meet the project's needs. However, when there is a shortage of certain skills, the degree of unemployed becomes irrelevant and escalation becomes a greater factor.

In short, determination of escalation in wages is a balancing process between the demands of the existing labor market and the contractor's needs. Another consideration is the strong presence of unions with fixed wage increase agreements. The open-shop contractor finds that the nearby, or adjacent, union-shop project wage structures often force a close matching of open-shop wages with increases to the union wages and periodic increases provided for by collective bargaining in order to stem attempts by union representatives to organize the labor force or to entice workers to leave.

Determination of escalation is never exact, but in the long run, an estimator's projections will be best if they are based on a continued awareness of industry labor supply and market conditions.

A wage escalation factor (E) is a multiplier that represents the average amount by which a basic wage rate will increase (or decrease) over the duration of the project. The multiplier can, and does, vary between labor classifications on any given project. Again, predetermined wages, union influence, and the availability of skilled labor are among the reasons. To find a wage rate adjusted for escalation, simply multiply the basic wage rate (W) by the escalation factor (E).

Escalation of fringe benefits is not necessarily affected by the same conditions that affect wages. Instead, changes in premium cost or fund administration cost are usually the basis for escalation. Since fringe benefits are a significant portion of labor cost, they must be recognized as they escalate.

Time (T)

The effect of time on labor cost is extremely difficult to pin down because of the many variables involved. However, variations in premium time, paid vacations, paid holidays, paid show-up time, and other time benefits are the considerations that must be made by the estimator.

In order to best describe the influence of time on labor cost, time itself—as it relates to labor—must be defined. Time consists of two basic parts:

· Premium time (P)

· Lost Time (L)

Premium time (or overtime) is the time worked in any given day or week over the basic amount of time established. The basic workday is usually 8 hours long, and the basic workweek is usually 40 hours long. Basic time is paid for at straight-time rates. Premium time is paid for at some established premium wage rate: usually, one and one-half times the straight-time rate.

A time factor (T), is a multiplier that represents the influence of both premium time and lost time on the escalated basic wage rate. When applied, this multiplier will adjust the rate so that it represents an average paid wage per labor hour per hour of production.

Premium Time

Premium time pay is a commonly recognized construction expense. It is best described as the bonus a worker receives for working in excess of the regular business hours.

A contractor finds it impossible to avoid premium time expense even with a rigid 40-hour-week policy, particularly in structural concrete construction. Finishers must occasionally remain to complete the finishing of a bridge deck long after the concrete has been placed; concrete placing crews at times find they must work overtime in order to complete the placing of a large volume of concrete; contractors sometimes permit crane operators to work an extra amount of time each day to ensure that critically needed cranes are always maintained and available; and Saturdays are utilized to accelerate work if a schedule demands it.

To establish the average premium time that each labor classification will have on a proposed project, an estimator may either refer to historic data from present or past projects or resort to experience and judgment. Regardless of the basis, the important thing to remember is that the planned premium time cost must suit the nature of the work proposed and its time related needs.

In order to establish the effect that premium time has on the hourly cost of an employee, an estimator must understand how to develop a premium time factor (P). When this factor is applied to the average wage rate, it will yield an average adjusted wage rate that represents the average hourly cost for the employee, including premium pay. This factor can best be described by Equation (3.2):

$$P = \frac{\text{straight-time cost} + \text{premium cost}}{\text{straight-time cost}} \tag{3.2}$$

This concept can be further explained by the following example:

> Assume a worker put in 52 hours per week at a basic hourly rate of $9.00 per hour, with time-and-one-half pay for overtime. Computation of the premium time factor (P) would be
>
> $$P = \frac{52 \text{ hr} \times \$9.00/\text{hr} + 0.5 \times 12 \text{ hr} \times \$9/\text{hr}}{52 \text{ hr} \times \$9/\text{hr}}$$
>
> $$= \frac{522}{468}$$
>
> $$= 1.115$$
>
> The average wage rate is then adjusted:
>
> Average wage rate = $9.00/hr × 1.115 = $10.04/hr

Close examination of the forgoing example shows that premium time expense is a function of time and the premium time factor (P) can be stated in terms of time only. If H equals the hours worked and H_p equals the premium time hours worked, the premium time factor can be stated as follows:

$$P = 1 + \frac{H_p}{2H} \quad \text{(time-and-one-half)} \tag{3.3}$$

and

$$P = 1 + \frac{H_p}{H} \quad \text{(double time)} \tag{3.4}$$

Premium time affects employees on fixed wages or salaries, if the basis for the hourly value of a salaried employee is viewed as being a

40-hour week. A longer workweek would reduce the hourly value of the salary.

$$P = \frac{\text{basic hours}}{\text{hours worked}} = \frac{40}{H} \quad \text{(salary)} \tag{3.5}$$

Table 3.1 provides the premium time factors for the even premium hours (up to and including 20 hours per week for hourly situations), with the 40-hour workweek used as the basis.

Hourly fringe benefit rates can also be affected by premium time, depending on whether their cost is based on a fixed amount or on fixed rates paid for each hour worked. If the total cost is fixed, an adjustment similar to that used for salaried employees must be applied. If the hourly rate is fixed, then no adjustment is necessary. There have been cases where fringe benefit rates were treated exactly as wage rates. This would require handling the cost for overtime hours worked in the same manner as were hourly wages.

Lost Time

Lost time is that time for which an employee is paid even though no work has been performed. Holidays, vacations, rain days, and sick days are lost time days—if they are paid for. Show-up time, travel time, guaranteed time, and other nonproductive periods of time, if compensated, are also lost time. These lost time periods can be estimated and a factor developed for adjusting the hourly cost of an employee to suit the hours actually worked.

Within the time frame of the hours actually worked are brief periods of nonproductive time, or work stoppages, for which an employee's pay continues. Coffee breaks, safety meetings, on-site travel, brief inclement weather stoppages, equipment failures, and other situations are a significant cause for an accumulation of lost time of this kind. This time loss, being extremely variable and difficult to isolate, is best reflected in productivity. (See Section 3.6, "Productivity.")

A lost time factor (L), is defined as that amount by which a wage rate can be multiplied so that it will include the effect of lost time. This factor is expressed as

$$L = \frac{\text{gross wages}}{\text{earned wages}}$$
$$= \frac{\text{cost for hours worked} + \text{cost for lost hours}}{\text{cost for hours worked}} \tag{3.6}$$

The hours are usually based on a period of time long enough to establish an average occurrence. A full year, or construction season, is best for these purposes. Using an example:

Assume a worker earns $9.00 per hour and works a 40-hour week. During the year, the employee is paid for a total of 220 days, including 6 holidays. In addition, an average of 40 hours of pay each year for show-up time on rainy days is received. The lost time factor (L) is computed as follows:

Hours worked $= (220 - 6)$ days $\times$ 8 hr/day $= 1712$ hr

Lost hours $=$ holidays $\quad$ 6 $\times$ 8 hr/day $= 48$ hr

$\qquad\qquad = $ show-up $\qquad\qquad\qquad = \underline{40\ \text{hr}}$

$\qquad\qquad\qquad\qquad\qquad\qquad\qquad\quad 88\ \text{hr}$

$$L = \frac{1712\ \text{hr} \times \$9.00/\text{hr} + 88\ \text{hr} \times \$9.00/\text{hr}}{1712\ \text{hr} \times \$9/\text{hr}}$$

$$= \frac{16{,}200}{15{,}408}$$

$$= 1.051$$

The adjusted wage rate for lost time based on a 40-hour week is

Adjusted wage rate $= \$9.00/\text{hr} \times 1.051 = \$9.46/\text{hr}$

It can be seen from this example that the lost time factor is also a function of time and can be expressed as Equations (3.7) and 3.8):

$$L = \frac{\text{hours worked} + \text{lost hours}}{\text{hours worked}} \quad \text{(40-hour week)} \qquad (3.7)$$

or

$$L = 1 + \frac{H_l}{H} \quad \text{(40-hour week)} \qquad (3.8)$$

where $H_l =$ compensated lost time hours

When premium time is introduced, the lost time factor is affected to some extent. This is demonstrated by the following example:

Assume that the same employee works 52 hours per week. The total number of days worked and the lost time will remain the same:

Hours worked $= (220 - 6)$ days $\times$ 10.4 hr/day $= 2226$ hr

Lost time $= 88$ hr

$$L = \frac{2226 \text{ hr} \times \$9.00/\text{hr} \times 1.115 + 88 \text{ hr} \times 9.00/\text{hr}}{2226 \text{ hr} \times \$9.00/\text{hr} \times 1.115}$$

$$= \frac{23130}{22{,}338}$$

$$= 1.036$$

The adjusted wage rate for lost time is now found to be

Adjusted wage rate = $9.00 × 1.036 = $9.32/hr

Expressing the lost time factor (L) in terms of hours, again we have

$$L = \frac{\text{hours worked} \times P + \text{lost hours}}{\text{hours worked} \times P} \qquad (3.9)$$

or

$$L = 1 + \frac{H_l}{HP} \qquad (3.10)$$

All this seems rather complicated for the bit of difference that lost time makes in the productive hourly cost of a worker, but when dealing with a labor intensive business such as the construction of structural concrete, it is best to completely understand the variables so that when choices are made, they are well-founded.

It was mentioned earlier that lost time for an employee was best determined by considering a long enough period of time to establish an average occurrence of lost hours versus the average hours worked. Usually, a complete construction season provides the best measure of lost time, because many conditions occur once in a season or at specific times during the season. If an estimator is to establish a lost time factor, it is necessary to know something of the days most likely to be worked, so that the effect can be easily judged. One way to do this is to establish a construction calendar appropriate to the conditions for the general location involved and contractor concerned.

Table 3.2 is a Construction Calendar appropriate for structural concrete work in the mid-Atlantic area. It assumes a year-round season, and it displays the range of possibilities for many workers employed outside in heavy structural concrete construction in that general area, based on experience and locally reported weather data.

The Time Factor

Factors for premium time (P) and lost time (L) have heretofore been described as individual multiples applied to wage rates separately.

Since they are both related to the common denominator of time worked, a single factor can be derived from them. This factor is known as the time factor (T), and it is expressed analytically as Equation (3.11):

$$T = P \times L \tag{3.11}$$

Assuming that H equals actual hours worked, H_p equals premium hours paid, and H_l equals lost time hours paid, and referring to Equations (3.3) and (3.10), we can express the time factor as

$$T = \frac{H + \frac{1}{2}H_p}{H} \times \frac{HP + H_l}{HP} \tag{3.12}$$

When this combination is reduced, we have the formula for the time factor as in Equations (3.13) and (3.14):

$$T = 1 + \frac{H_p}{2H} + \frac{H_l}{H} \quad \text{(time and one-half)} \tag{3.13}$$

or

$$T = 1 + \frac{H_p}{H} + \frac{H_l}{H} \quad \text{(double time)} \tag{3.14}$$

These formulas are the basis for all time factor determinations.

Figure 3.1 displays an example of a time factor determination, using a format that includes all the necessary and applicable considerations. Table 3.3 is a convenient vehicle for choosing lost time factor when the basic time data is known. (Again, the data used are based on general experience from construction in the mid-Atlantic area. The estimator should verify all factors to assure that they apply appropriately to factual conditions.)

It was explained earlier that premium time had a negative effect on hourly cost for salaried employees, if a 40-hour week was considered the base. Actually, in some cases, the easiest way to describe the overall effect of time (whether premium or lost), is to make a comparison between the gross earnings and the estimated hours worked. Determination of the hours worked can be made through the use of the Construction Calendar (Table 3.2), or by any other means chosen by the estimator. For example:

> Assume that a foreman who works a 45-hour week year-round, at a weekly salary of $400, at the end of the year will have worked 200 days. The hourly productive wage is as follows:

WEEKLY PREMIUM TIME

Hours per week, 5 days	$H_1 =$	_48_
Average hours per day	$H_1/5 =$	_9.6_
Weekly premium hours	$H_p =$	_8_

ANNUAL PRODUCTIVE TIME

Days per year			_365_
Weekend days		(−)	_104_
Holidays	6 to 12	(−)	_6_
Vacation days	0 to 10	(−)	_0_
POTENTIAL WORK DAYS, "A"			_255_
Weather days	14% X "A"	(−)	_36_
Days ill	5% X "A"	(−)	_13_
Days absent	2.5% X "A"	(−)	_6_
ACTUAL WORK TIME		_200_ days x _9.6_ hrs/day =	_1920_ hrs.
Saturday makeup, 7% X "A"		_0_ days x ___ hrs/day =	_0_ hrs.
ANNUAL PRODUCTIVE TIME,		$H_2 =$	_1920_ hrs.

ANNUAL PAID LOST TIME

Holidays	0 to 12	_6_ days x 8 hrs/day =	_48_	hrs.
Vacation	0 to 10	_0_ days x 8 hrs/day =	_0_	hrs.
Showup time	7% X "A"	_18_ days x 2 hrs/day =	_36_	hrs.
Guaranteed time			_0_	hrs.
ANNUAL PAID LOST TIME		$H_L =$	_84_	hrs.

TIME FACTOR DETERMINATION

$$T = 1 + \frac{H_p}{2H_1} + \frac{H_L}{H_2} = 1 + \frac{8}{2 \times 48} + \frac{84}{1920} = 1.127$$

Figure 3.1 Time Factor Determination.

$$\text{Rate} = \frac{\$400/\text{week} \times 52.14 \text{ weeks/year}}{200 \text{ days} \times 9 \text{ hours/day}}$$
$$= \$11.59/\text{hour}$$

The effect of lost time on fringe benefits (as was the case with premium time) is very much dependent on the terms under which they are paid. Adjustment of fringe benefits, therefore, must be in accordance with the principles discussed for wages.

Insurance and Taxes (*I*)

All construction firms pay substantial amounts for insurance and taxes on behalf of each employee, based on the employee's earnings. These insurances and taxes protect the employee from total loss of income due to injury on the job, layoff, or retirement. They are as follows:

FICA Federal Insurance Contributions Act (or Social Security; retirement)

SUI State Unemployment Insurance (layoff)

FUTA Federal Unemployment Tax (layoff)

WCI Worker's Compensation Insurance (job injury)

Each of these is expressed as a percentage of wages earned. Their value will vary with the year of the estimate and with the location, nature, and inherent risks of the work. Since these are the determining factors, it is suggested that the estimator stay constantly aware of the current rates and any pending changes. When the rates of insurance and taxes are determined, they can then be applied directly to the employee's gross earnings.

Summary of Labor Rates

As the reader can easily see, labor cost determination can be a complex matter. Understanding the concept is imperative to correct cost estimating. Chapter 6 presents a uniform procedure for establishing bid wage rates that will be particularly convenient to the estimator.

3.5 EQUIPMENT

Construction cost estimators frequently use equipment rates that are based on well-thought-out, calculated financial considerations and cost data covering all ownership and operating expenses. The determination of these rates is of great importance to the preparation of a cost estimate, since equipment cost can, for many construction activities, be composed of as much as two-thirds of the total activity cost. Although equipment rate determination may not always be the estimator's direct responsibility, for the sake of expediency, something should be known about how the rates are derived, because there are occasions when rates must be determined.

Equipment rates are derived from two distinct and separate considerations:

1. Ownership expense
2. Operating expense

Ownership expense is defined as all fixed expense necessary to purchase, deliver, and assemble the equipment and to pay for all interest, taxes, insurance, and storage cost. It is considered a fixed expense directly related to the investment made in purchasing the machine.

Operating expense represents the cost for fuel, oil, grease, filters, and other expendables, plus the cost for labor, equipment, parts, and services necessary to maintain the machine in good operating condition. This includes all major repair and overhaul expense, but does *not* include the cost for the operator or oiler assigned to run the equipment on the job. Operating expense is directly related to use.

For purposes of estimating, each of these equipment expenses is expressed in terms of the cost per hour of use. This requires a determination of both the economic life of the machine and its annual application.

Equipment Life

The economic, or useful, life of equipment is difficult to predict. It is a function of the type of work the machine does and the care that it receives. Generally, a contractor will establish the economic life of equipment based on the company's experience. There are, however, authoritative publications, such as the Caterpillar Tractor Company's *Caterpillar Performance Handbook,*[1] that provide average economic life projections for all types of construction equipment under certain stated conditions. In lieu of the use of such publications, an estimator can obtain economic life information directly from most equipment manufacturers. In any case, all predictions are speculative.

Average economic life of equipment is a measure of the total number of hours a machine functions economically. Once known, it is possible to predict the economic life span of a machine in years by determining the annual hourly use. Annual hourly use of equipment is found in much the same way as it was for labor. The important goal is to predict this time as accurately as possible. The following factors are considered in determining annual use hours.

Workweek   In structural work, contractors throughout the United States tend to limit working hours to a 40-hour week, reasoning that structural work is often labor-oriented and the wage scales are on the high side of the overall construction wage spectrum. This makes working overtime uneconomical for any reason other than emergency or absolute need. In the case of structural concrete, therefore, a 40- to 44-hour week can be considered suitable for equipment use determination.

Seasonal Limitation   Seasonal conditions affect equipment use. The influence of weather on construction progress depends significantly on geographic location. For example, in the north a contractor can expect to shut down for 3 to 4 months during the winter, while southern locations offer the possibility of working year-round.

Lost Time   Holidays, rain days, mechanical failure, and other work stoppages affect equipment use. There are usually 6 to 12 holidays observed each year. Rain days must be predicted as they were for labor. Mechanical failure and other lost time factors must also be predicted as seen by the individual contractor.

An example of annual equipment use determination is as follows:

Assume it is required to establish the average number of hours an 80-ton truck crane will be used on a project. The project works 40 hours per week.

Total days per year	365	
Days not worked:		
Weekends		104
Holidays		7
Winter shutdown		
8 weeks @ 5 days/week		40
Other		24
Total		$\overline{365 - 175}$
		= 190 Total days worked/yr

Actual average hours worked is over 40, or say, 42. Total annual use, therefore, is:

$$190 \text{ days} \times \frac{42}{5} \text{ hr/day} = 1556 \text{ hr}$$

Ownership Expense

Ownership of equipment includes the following initial expenditures:

· Purchase price   · Unloading expense
· Sales taxes   · Assembly expense
· Delivery charges

The sum of these expenditures is known as the *total investment*.

As equipment is used, it depreciates in value until, in time, it is no longer economical to own and operate. In other words, it has reached the end of its economic life. At any time in its life, including the end, a machine has some residual value. That value is known as *salvage value*. Salvage value is the amount received for a machine when it is sold. The total investment, less the salvage value, will yield the *depreciable cost* of the machine. Depreciable cost represents the loss of equipment value over a period of time due to age, wear, and obsolescence.

$$\text{Depreciable cost} = \text{total investment} - \text{salvage value} \qquad (3.15)$$

Hourly ownership expense is, in part, dependent on the prediction of the average economic life of a machine. A uniform hourly depreciation expense can be found by dividing the average economic life of a machine into the depreciable cost. This is known as the straight-line method of depreciation.

$$\text{Hourly depreciation} = \frac{\text{depreciable cost}}{\text{economic life}} \qquad (3.16)$$

The initially determined hourly rate of depreciation may not continue to be realistic throughout the life of a machine if there is a high rate of inflation or deflation. Contractors can compensate for such changes by applying inflation or deflation indices annually, thereby adjusting the hourly depreciation rate.

Hourly ownership expense is also associated with time related expenses, such as interest, taxes, insurances, storage, and all expenses incurred at the place of storage. Normally, such expenses are expressed as a percentage of the *average investment*.

$$\text{Average investment} = \frac{\text{total investment} + \text{salvage value}}{2} \qquad (3.17)$$

Interest Interest on an investment is simply the amount paid for borrowing money to purchase equipment. If money is not borrowed, it can be viewed as the earnings not obtained through other investments because the money is tied up in equipment. Interest rates are currently high because of inflation. An estimator must use caution in setting an interest rate for equipment rate determinations.

Taxes Property taxes and other periodic local levies on equipment vary with location. An estimator must decide on the location of a machine's *tax home* and determine what that location's tax structure is so that a rate can be established.

Insurance Insurance coverage, or protection against fire, theft, liability, and damage, must also be paid for. The estimator can obtain information regarding this expense from a company accountant or from an insurance company representative.

Storage Storage expense covers the cost for rent, maintenance, and the overhead involved in maintaining a place to unload, store, and protect equipment for the idle periods between jobs.

It can now be said that the total hourly ownership expense for a machine is the sum of the hourly uniform depreciation and all other time related hourly expenses. Equation (3.18) is an analytical expression of this expense.

$$C = \frac{P - S}{L_1} + \frac{P + S}{2L_2} \times I \tag{3.18}$$

where $\dfrac{P - S}{L}$ = hourly depreciation

$\dfrac{P + S}{2}$ = average investment

$\quad\quad C$ = hourly equipment ownership cost

$\quad\quad P$ = total investment

$\quad\quad S$ = salvage value

$\quad\quad L_1$ = economic life in hours

$\quad\quad L_2$ = average annual use in hours

$\quad\quad I$ = interest, tax, and storage expense in percentage of the average investment

Operating Expense

Today more than ever before, equipment operating expenses are of great importance in establishing rental rates. The radical fuel, oil, labor, equipment, and parts cost increases of the seventies and early eighties have served to make even the short-term considerations sensitive. Understanding this problem is a responsibility in estimating—just as is understanding any other quoted materials or subcontractor price.

The expense for operating equipment is identified in three categories: repair expense, fuel and lubricating expense, and tire expense.

Repair Repair expense, usually expressed in terms of a percentage of the depreciable cost, includes all expenditures for parts, mechanics, equipment, tools, shop facilities, and outside services necessary to repair, overhaul, and otherwise maintain equipment in good running condition. Because of its importance, most construction firms are deliberate in keeping comprehensive cost records for this expense.

$$\text{Hourly repair} = \frac{\text{depreciable cost}}{\text{economic life}}$$
$$\times \text{ repair factor} \quad \text{(percent)} \tag{3.19}$$

Fuel and Lubricating This expense is directly related to the owner's or manufacturer's historic records of consumption. It includes the cost for fuel, oils, grease, filters, and other consumables. To determine these expenses, an estimator must obtain the equipment records of consumption and apply them to the current or projected value of those consumables involved.

$$\text{Hourly fuel and lubrication} = \frac{\text{total consumption}}{\text{economic life}} \tag{3.20}$$

Tire Tire expense is treated in different ways, depending on the equipment application and the job circumstances. Tires delivered with a new machine are often included as part of the initial investment. Replacement tires, if worn through ordinary use, are an operating expense. If a specific job application is such that tires are worn or destroyed quickly, the contractor may choose to charge replacement expense to the job. However, tire replacement expense is ordinarily considered an operating expense and is based on the normally anticipated life and cost of the tires.

$$\text{Hourly tire cost} = \frac{\text{total tire replacement cost}}{\text{economic life}} \tag{3.21}$$

Total hourly equipment operating expense can be expressed analytically as in Equation (3.22).

$$EOE = \frac{R + F + T}{L} \tag{3.22}$$

Where EOE = equipment operating expense

$\quad\quad R$ = repair expense,

$\quad\quad F$ = fuel and lubricating expense,

$\quad\quad T$ = tire expense

$\quad\quad L$ = economic life in years

Equipment Rate Determination

Hourly equipment expense, as described in the preceding section, can be expressed as a single hourly rent by adding ownership expense and operating expense. That is,

$$\text{Hourly rent = ownership + operating} = C + EOE \quad\quad (3.23)$$

If the contractor is successful in predicting annual use and overall economic life, the rental charges will return the correct amount necessary to cover all expenses. In estimating, however, it is often more convenient to leave the two expenses separated so that a check can be made to assure that all ownership expense has been covered for the duration that a machine is on the job. The procedure for working such a check is discussed later.

Figure 3.2 demonstrates typical data and the computations for an 80-ton truck crane. This method is applicable to most types of equipment. Note that the expense for an operator is not included here.

Publications such as the *Rental Rate Bluebook*,[2] by Equipment Guide Book Company, or *Operating Cost Guide*,[3] by the Power Crane and Shovel Association, provide detailed information related to equipment expense. These publications contain convenient and vital information and should be carefully read and absorbed.

There are many other good publications that explain equipment expense in detail, and it is suggested that an estimator have sufficient reference data of this type available.

3.6 PRODUCTIVITY

Sections 3.4 and 3.5 detailed the development of labor and equipment rates that represent the cost for each hour worked. Overtime, holidays, vacation, show-up time, escalation, insurance and taxes, freight costs, and many other factors that affect cost are incorporated into the rates. It was assumed in developing these rates that every worker or machine actually works all the time assigned. The fact is, they do not.

There is a subtle loss of time from within the work period, for which the employee is paid and for which equipment rent is paid, that no work is done at all. This loss of effort is called *efficiency loss*. Its causes are mechanical failure, coffee breaks, on-site moves, rain inter-

INFORMATION	Equipment Description	_80 Ton Truck Crane_		
	Annual Use (L_2)		_1500_	hrs
	Economic Life (L_1)	_8_ yrs	_12000_	hrs
	Interest Rate		_12_	%
	Tax Rate	(I)	_4_	%
	Insurance Rate		_2_	%
	Storage Rate		_1_	%

OWNERSHIP	Total Cost, FOB Factory		$ _400,000_	
	Sales Tax	_5_ %	$ _20,000_	
	Delivery Charge		$ _3,000_	
	Unload Expense		$ _500_	
	Assembly Expense		$ _1,500_	
	TOTAL INVESTMENT (P)		$ _425,000_	
	Salvage Value (S)	_20_ %	$ _85,000_	
	DEPRECIABLE COST (P−S)		$ _340,000_	
	AVERAGE INVESTMENT ($\frac{P+S}{2}$)		$ _255,000_	
	Depreciation ($\frac{P-S}{L_1}$)		$ _28.33_ / hr	
	Interest, etc. ($\frac{P+S}{2L_2}$)×(I) I = _19_ %		$ _32.30_ / hr	
	HOURLY OWNERSHIP EXPENSE		$ _60.63_ / hr	

OPERATE	Repairs _45_ % x ($\frac{P-S}{L_1}$)		$ _12.75_ / hr
	Fuel _5.0_ gal/hr x $ _1.20_ /gal		$ _6.00_ / hr
	Oil _0.3_ gal/hr x $ _1.70_ /gal		$ _0.51_ / hr
	Grease _0.1_ lbs/hr $ _0.35_ /lb		$ _0.04_ / hr
	Filters & other expendibles		$ _0.10_ / hr
	Tires $ _4000_ /yr ÷ _1500_ hrs/yr		$ _2.67_ / hr
	HOURLY OPERATING EXPENSE		$ _22.07_ / hr

Figure 3.2 Equipment Rate Determination.

ruption, hot weather slow-up, poor supervisory direction, late material deliveries, labor disputes, safety meetings, injuries, and many other circumstances attributable to both deliberate and involuntary acts of the workers or their supervisors, as well as to unpredictable equipment availability. Since this loss of efficiency affects productivity, it is necessary to compensate for the loss by setting productivity rates at levels based on the elapsed time taken to complete an activity.

Another factor that is not considered in the development of labor and equipment rates is time involved in crew and equipment preparation for an activity and the subsequent time for demobilization after the activity is completed. At times, the estimator may evaluate setup and dismantling expense separately, but there are many operations for which the estimated cost must include this expense and the average productivity rate must be adjusted accordingly to suit the need. A simple example follows.

A concrete placing crew, using a pump, is to place 100 cubic yards of concrete. Productivity time begins when the crew and their equipment are moved in and set up. The pump must be positioned, slick lines and vibrators must be placed, etc. Time stops after the concrete is poured; but the pump is cleaned, and tools and slick lines are gathered and cleaned before all is ready to move out. Although the 100 cubic yards were placed in 2 hours, the elapsed time was 3 hours. Therefore, the rate of production was 33 cubic yards per hour.

With these factors in mind, productivity can now be defined as the rate at which a given amount of labor and equipment can perform a specific task; it includes all associated losses due to inefficiency, setup, and dismantling. Simply, productivity rates must consider elapsed time and its cost, not just the immediate capability of the crew or its equipment.

As the various aspects of structural concrete construction have been developed in this book, applicable productivity rates have been introduced.

Table 3.1   Premium Time Factor (P)

Work hours (H)	Premium time hours (H_p)	Premium time factor		
		Half-time (P_1)*	Full-time (P_2)†	Salary (P_3)‡
40	0	1.000	1.000	1.000
42	2	1.024	1.048	0.952
44	4	1.046	1.091	0.909
46	6	1.065	1.130	0.870
48	8	1.083	1.167	0.833
50	10	1.100	1.200	0.800
52	12	1.115	1.231	0.769
54	14	1.130	1.259	0.741
56	16	1.143	1.286	0.714
58	18	1.155	1.310	0.690
60	20	1.167	1.333	0.667

* $P_1 = 1 + (\text{premium hours}/2 \times \text{hours worked}) = 1 + H_p/2H$.
† $P_2 = 1 + (\text{premium hours}/\text{hours worked}) = 1 + H_p/H$.
‡ $P_3 = (\text{basic hours}/\text{hours worked}) = 40/H$.

Table 3.2   Construction Calendar

	Total days	Week-end days	Holi-days (range)*	Vacations (range)†	Weather days‡	Ill days§	No-show days§	Work days (range)
5-DAY WEEK¶								
Jan.	31	8	1–1	0–0	5	2	1	14–14
Feb.	28	8	0–1	0–0	3	1	0	16–15
Mar.	31	10	0–0	0–0	4	2	1	14–14
Apr.	30	8	1–1	0–0	3	1	0	17–17
May	31	10	0–2	0–0	2	0	0	19–17
June	30	8	0–1	0–0	2	1	1	18–17
July	31	8	1–1	0–5	2	0	0	20–15
Aug.	31	10	0–0	0–5	1	0	0	20–15
Sept.	30	8	1–1	0–0	2	1	1	17–17
Oct.	31	8	0–2	0–0	3	1	1	18–16
Nov.	30	10	1–1	0–0	3	1	0	15–15
Dec.	31	8	1–1	0–0	3	2	1	16–16
Totals	365	104	6–12	0–10	33	12	6	204–188
6-DAY WEEK¶								
Jan.	31	4	1–1	0–0	6	2	1	17–17
Feb.	28	4	0–1	0–0	3	1	0	20–19
Mar.	31	5	0–0	0–0	5	2	1	18–18
Apr.	30	4	1–1	0–0	3	1	0	21–21
May	31	5	0–2	0–0	3	1	1	21–19
June	30	4	0–1	0–0	3	1	1	21–20
July	31	4	1–1	0–5	3	1	1	21–16
Aug.	31	5	0–0	0–5	3	1	1	21–16
Sept.	30	4	1–1	0–0	3	1	0	21–21
Oct.	31	4	0–2	0–0	4	1	1	21–19
Nov.	30	5	1–1	0–0	4	1	0	19–19
Dec.	31	4	1–1	0–0	3	2	1	20–20
Totals	365	52	6–12	0–10	43	15	8	241–225

* Varies depending on policy, union agreements, etc.
† Choice for vacation planning is arbitrary.
‡ Will vary with geographical location.
§ An estimate based on historic information.
¶ Table based on Central Atlantic States experience.

Table 3.3   Time Factor (T)*

| Paid lost time (hr/yr, H_l) | Hrs/wk (H_1): | 40 | 42 | 44 | 46 |
	Hrs/yr (H_2):	1600	1680	1760	1840
0		1.000	1.024	1.045	1.065
10		1.006	1.030	1.051	1.071
20		1.013	1.036	1.057	1.076
30		1.019	1.042	1.063	1.082
40		1.025	1.048	1.068	1.087
50		1.031	1.054	1.074	1.092
60		1.038	1.060	1.080	1.098
70		1.044	1.065	1.085	1.103
80		1.050	1.071	1.091	1.109
90		1.056	1.077	1.097	1.114
100		1.063	1.083	1.102	1.120
110		1.069	1.089	1.108	1.125
120		1.075	1.095	1.114	1.130
130		1.081	1.101	1.119	1.136
140		1.088	1.107	1.125	1.141
150		1.094	1.113	1.131	1.147
160		1.100	1.119	1.136	1.152
170		1.106	1.125	1.142	1.158
180		1.112	1.131	1.148	1.163
190		1.119	1.137	1.153	1.168
200		1.125	1.143	1.159	1.174
210		1.131	1.149	1.165	1.179
220		1.138	1.155	1.171	1.185
230		1.144	1.161	1.176	1.190
240		1.150	1.167	1.182	1.196

$$* \ T = 1 + \frac{H_p}{2H_1} + \frac{H_l}{H_2}$$

48	50	52	54	56	58	60
1920	2000	2080	2160	2240	2320	2400
1.083	1.100	1.115	1.130	1.143	1.155	1.167
1.089	1.105	1.120	1.134	1.147	1.160	1.171
1.094	1.110	1.125	1.139	1.152	1.164	1.175
1.099	1.115	1.130	1.143	1.156	1.168	1.179
1.104	1.120	1.135	1.148	1.161	1.172	1.183
1.109	1.125	1.139	1.153	1.165	1.177	1.188
1.115	1.130	1.144	1.157	1.170	1.181	1.192
1.120	1.135	1.149	1.162	1.174	1.185	1.196
1.125	1.140	1.154	1.167	1.179	1.190	1.200
1.130	1.145	1.159	1.171	1.183	1.194	1.204
1.135	1.150	1.163	1.176	1.188	1.198	1.208
1.141	1.155	1.168	1.181	1.192	1.203	1.213
1.146	1.160	1.173	1.185	1.197	1.207	1.217
1.151	1.165	1.178	1.190	1.201	1.211	1.221
1.156	1.170	1.183	1.194	1.205	1.216	1.225
1.161	1.175	1.188	1.199	1.210	1.220	1.229
1.167	1.180	1.192	1.204	1.214	1.224	1.233
1.172	1.185	1.197	1.208	1.219	1.228	1.238
1.177	1.190	1.202	1.213	1.223	1.233	1.242
1.182	1.195	1.207	1.218	1.228	1.237	1.246
1.187	1.200	1.212	1.222	1.232	1.241	1.250
1.193	1.205	1.216	1.227	1.237	1.246	1.254
1.198	1.210	1.221	1.231	1.241	1.250	1.258
1.203	1.215	1.226	1.236	1.246	1.254	1.263
1.208	1.220	1.231	1.241	1.250	1.259	1.267

REFERENCES

[1] *Caterpillar Performance Handbook*, 10th ed., Caterpillar Tractor Company, Peoria, Ill., 1979.

[2] *Rental Rate Blue Book*, Equipment Guide Book Company, Palo Alto, Calif., 1980.

[3] *Operating Cost Guide*, Power Crane and Shovel Association, Milwaukee, Wis., 1976.

4 FORMWORK

4.1 FORMWORK OBJECTIVES

The word *formwork* describes all those functions affiliated with the use of the forms, or molds, that give shape to concrete and hold it in place until it has hardened and become self-supporting. Form building, erection, stripping, maintenance, planning, and design are all functions of formwork. Together, their cost often exceeds 50 percent of the total concrete cost. In an industry where concrete cost frequently represents a significant portion of the total construction dollar value, it is obvious that a very important factor involves an estimator's capability to evaluate formwork accurately.

The forming of concrete will always produce a need for the strengths inherent in the many available commercial forms and form support systems that employ various combinations of steel, aluminum, plastic, wood, fibers, and fiberglass. These commercial systems are usually designed to withstand many repeated applications and, where needed, to perform structural tasks that might otherwise be very difficult. Generally, commercial systems are expensive to use. Their economic use is often restricted to applications involving repetitive use, or special conditions. In the long run, the purchase of commercially manufactured forms may be an economical move if the contractor is willing to amortize them over a long period of time involving several projects. To partially overcome some of the restrictions, commercial producers rent forms and form support systems. Rentals require that the contractor find a frequent and continuous need during the period of rental, since the rent is usually based on time and not on the number of uses. Rentals also often involve custom fabrication of parts that must be purchased at full price and may never be of any further use.

There is no material used more extensively than wood in the construction and support of forms. (See Figure 4.1.) Wood is an inexpensive, strong, flexible, versatile, durable, light, and workable material. It is particularly adaptable to forming concrete surfaces of unique shape in unique locations. Its lower cost often suits the limited needs found in construction. An estimator capable of evaluating formwork of wood will be capable of making sound comparisons to alternative systems. This capability is in line with the objective of developing an ability to evaluate all significant aspects of a project without relying on outside sources for interpretation of requirements.

4.2 FORM COMPONENTS

Heavy construction involves using wood forms in an infinite number of sizes, shapes, and strengths, each serving a unique purpose at a dif-

Figure 4.1 Wood Forms for a Bridge Pier. (Richmond Screw Anchor Co., Inc.)

ferent cost, depending on the quality of materials chosen, the number of uses planned, the maximum loads planned, the physical location of use, and the degree of complexity in construction. In order to reach a reasonable level of understanding in form cost estimating, it is necessary to understand some of the variations found in the formwork for each of the structural concrete components. Load conditions and form types, for instance, are pertinent to isolating data for the components. The estimator will recognize that even though classified, formwork will always have similarities between components and differences within the components. The following headings describe the forms for each of the structural components in some detail.

Footing

Footings are generally the least expensive to form because they involve uniformly sized form panels that are of low-cost material and are easy to build and erect using a small, less-skilled crew. Handling footing forms seldom requires a large lifting crane, since the panels are often light and are always placed at, or below, grade where workers have relatively safe and easy access with a minimum of climbing.

Footing forms have the potential to survive many more uses than do other forms. Concrete surface tolerance and texture requirements seldom restrict the use of forms with considerable surface deterioration. Often, form panels that are no longer satisfactory for use in other components continue to be suitable for footing forms.

The necessity for using form ties in footing form assembly is reduced because the dimensional requirements are, at times, such that the use of timber crossties and external blocking against earth excavation side walls is sufficient to hold the form in place.

Slab on Grade

Forming of a slab on grade is not, in the true sense, always formwork when the form is simply a plank held by steel stakes that contain the edge of the concrete slab. A form of this type can often be installed by a relatively small labor crew with very little fabrication skill. At times, however, the form for a slab on grade resembles a footing form with similar depths and dimensions. A slab on grade form may also include added and complex features such as hanging haunches, keyways, box outs, and anchorage templates that distinguish the slab on grade as different from other components.

Abutment, 0 to 8 Feet High

A bridge abutment is unique in that there is no other structural component that involves as many variables in form application. Abutment formwork can at times be viewed as if it were for a wall, beam, column, or footing. Most often, however, as with bridge abutments, the formwork is constructed of a series of interconnecting walls and pedestals. Forming these contiguous parts is usually the task of a single crew working on one or more of the parts simultaneously. This explains why the abutment is considered as a single component. (See Figure 4.2.)

The cost for forming abutments is often quite high because of the custom fabrication of intersecting forms and the installation of many bulkheads and keyways. Formwork also includes the setting of bolt templates and beam pedestal forms and the forming of utility box outs. These forming responsibilities require quality workmanship and greater effort. Abutments of 8 feet or less in height do not involve much climbing or working from ladders or scaffolds. A smaller lifting crane is needed for setting and removing forms and sometimes for

Figure 4.2   Bridge Abutment Forming. (John Driggs Co., Inc.).

transferring tools and equipment to the workers. In stripping abutment forms, a certain amount of material is lost each time, which is attributable to necessary destruction in dismantling.

Wall, 0 to 8 Feet High

Wall forms commonly consist of two flat form panels erected, facing each other, on a vertical or near vertical plane. They are held together by a system of internal form ties extending between panels, and they are held in position by a system of braces, or guys, that support the assembly against wind or working loads. A wall form is usually simple to build and erect as long as the materials used are of proper quality to suit the concrete surface finish requirements and sufficient care is taken in their erection and alignment to maintain dimensional and aesthetic qualities. Some wall forms, such as those for curved or warped surfaces, are not so simple, and often require greater skills and more time to build. For instance, a curved wall form may cost six times that of a straight wall of the same height. It is up to the estimator to recognize such variations.

Wall forms 8 feet or less in height are considered easy to handle and require little hazardous climbing. Scaffolding is seldom necessary with these forms. A small lifting crane will usually handle all formwork lifting needs. (See Figure 4.3.)

Abutment, over 8 Feet High

Abutment forms over 8 feet in height are similar in fabrication to those for low abutment forms, but there is a great difference in the require-

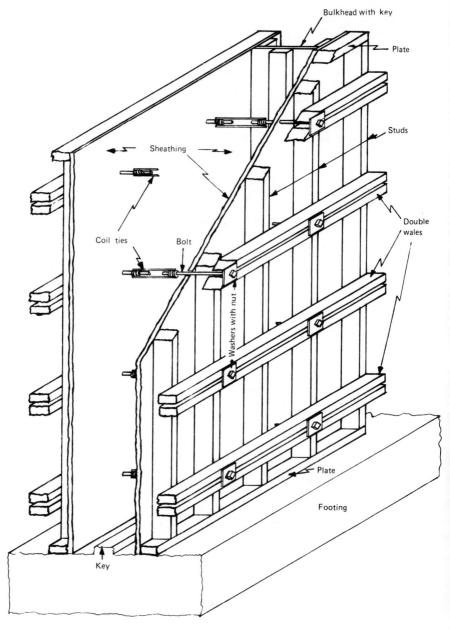

Figure 4.3 Wall Form.

ments for strength and erection. These forms are subject to greater pressures because of their height and are therefore built much stronger. Erection usually requires a larger lifting crane to handle the heavier and more cumbersome form panels. The use of scaffolding and the necessity for climbing on these forms is common. As hazards increase, crew productivity is reduced.

Wall, over 8 Feet High

Wall forms over 8 feet in height always increase the potential for hazardous climbing and the use of scaffolding. Form strengths must be greater in order to resist greater lateral concrete pressures. The greater weights and panel sizes require the use of a larger lifting crane. When there is potential for repeated use of large wall form sections, the panels are often assembled into *gangs*. Gang forms are an assembly of smaller form components bolted together and then stiffened and kept intact through the use of stiffbacks. Gang forms reduce erection cost by speeding up the recycling process, but a larger lifting crane is required for handling.

Column

Column forms differ from others because of the need for greater strength to withstand higher concrete placing pressures. The relatively small horizontal cross section of a column permits the rapid rise of concrete within the form and a corresponding rapid rise of liquid pressure. Specified alignment and dimensional tolerances usually require care and skill in erecting a column form. These forms can be prefabricated and erected in sections or in a fully assembled configuration. The use of scaffolds, external bracing, and guys is common, and the equipment needs are similar to those for walls over 8 feet in height.

Commonly, column forms are held together by a system of clamps, or yokes, that encircle the form at vertical intervals. These yokes must be of sufficient strength to resist all lateral pressure from within the form. Column forms of larger horizontal dimension may also require the use of internal form ties in combination with the yoke system. (See Figure 4.4.)

Beam

Beam form construction involves the installation of both vertical wall and horizontal floor forms to shape the sides and bottom of the beam

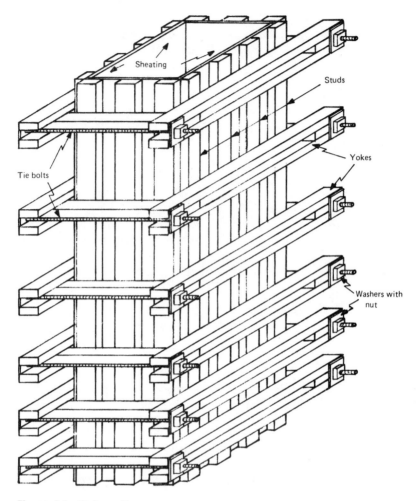

Figure 4.4   Column Form.

mold. The side forms are simply wall forms in the way that they resist lateral pressures from rising concrete. The bottom, or floor, forms are subject to vertical loads created by the weight of the concrete, workers, equipment, and materials. This total load often requires added support from beneath. The beam form must be fabricated and erected by skilled workers capable of paying particular attention to the compensating factors required for vertical settlement that occurs as the form is loaded. Tolerances are usually such that quality materials must be used in order to obtain the concrete surface uniformity and texture required. Figure 4.5 shows a bridge beam form being sup-

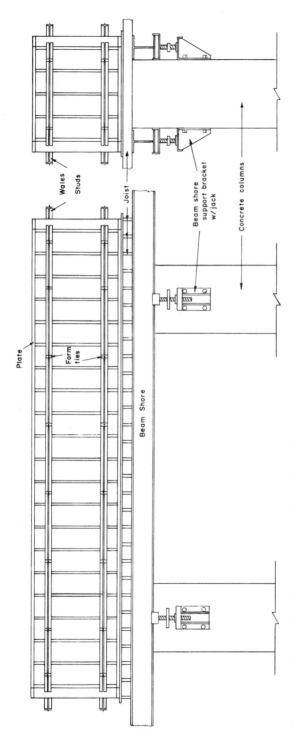

Figure 4.5 Bridge Pier Beam Form with Steel Beam Shoring.

91

ported by steel beams resting on brackets that are anchored to the supporting columns.

Deck

Deck forms are supported by the steel or concrete beams on which the finished concrete deck will rest permanently. There is no external support system employed in deck forms since they are held in place by deck form hangers that attach to the main carrying beams. Deck forming includes the installation of any cantilever forms, bulkheads, box outs, haunch forms, keyways, joint materials, and screed rails that must be installed prior to placing the concrete. At times, an estimator may consider the forms for bridge sidewalks and parapets as an integral part of the deck form system, since the same fascia deck form panels often serve both—and the same crew erects them.

Deck form crews are usually larger because of the usually larger contact areas involved. They must be skilled, since careful installation and close tolerances are necessary. (See Figure 4.6.)

Slab above Grade

The form for a slab above grade is always associated with added support from beneath, since the spans involved always exceed the practical capability of the form system to support itself under loading. Typical are forms for some box culvert roofs or those for a rigid frame bridge. The amount of form prefabrication is dependent on the nature of the structure and the possibilities it lends to stripping and recycling.

Erection of slab above grade forms often requires extreme care to compensate for settlement under loading. The range of required crew skills will vary greatly with the nature of the slab above grade form involved. (See Figure 4.7.)

4.3 LOADS ON FORMS

Concrete forms must always meet the minimum standards for safety and strength necessary for their intended use. Although contractors continue to build and use forms without the benefit of design, and without mishap, there is a growing trend in construction toward requiring specific professional design and approval of all critical forms to ensure their quality and strength. The expense involved may be well worth it if the design yields better economy in form construction as well as safety.

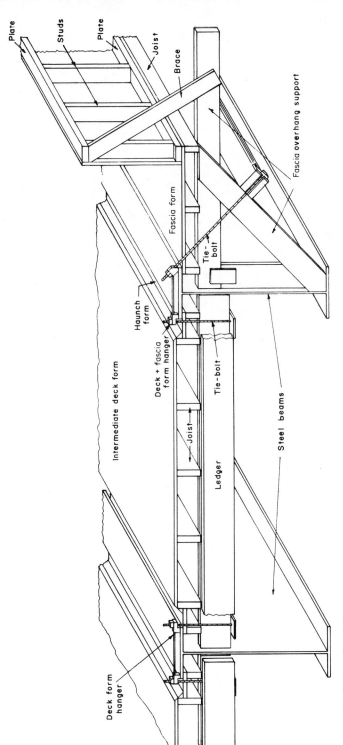

Figure 4.6 Bridge Deck Form.

93

Figure 4.7 Box Culvert Form with Shoring. (Photo by Jerry L. Smith, *Construction Magazine.*)

In estimating form cost, there is seldom time or need for dealing with the complexities of form design. However, there is a need to quickly establish the form type and the related cost factors for a given forming situation. To accomplish this, the estimator must have some knowledge of the basic factors that influence form design.

Since a form must remain firmly in place without excessive deflection or deformation when subjected to a load, the principal basis for establishing form strength is the form load. Form loads fall into one of two categories: they are either *dead loads* or *live loads*. Dead loads are those full static loads created by the weight of the concrete and the weight of the forms. Live loads are those loads that change or move and are considered for their maximum effect. Lateral concrete pressures, workers, equipment, and the placing of materials all impose live loads.

Dead Loads

Standard concrete mixes are considered to weigh 150 pounds per cubic foot. Variations in the density of the concrete ingredients will affect this weight, but for most practical applications 150 pounds per cubic foot is acceptable. When concrete is placed on a deck form, for instance, it exerts a vertical load that is the direct result of this unit of concrete weight.

Wood forms themselves will generally vary in weight from 5 to 15 pounds per square foot, with the variation being a function of the size and spacing of the form frame members combined with the type and thickness of the sheathing.

Live Loads

When fresh concrete is placed into a vertical form such as that for a wall, it exerts a lateral pressure against the form in much the same manner that a liquid would. The amount of pressure caused by fresh concrete is a function of the rate at which it rises against the form, its temperature, the method of compaction used, its slump, and the height of the form. The American Concrete Institute, Committee 347, has done extensive research in form design and has established formulas in its *Recommended Practice for Concrete Formwork* (ACI 347–78)[1], for use in determining the pressure against vertical forms. Those formulas assume the use of 150-pound concrete using Type I cement, no additives, a 4-inch slump, and internal vibration. They are as follows:

For column forms with a maximum of 3000 pounds per square foot, or 150h, whichever is less:

$$P = 150 + \frac{9000\,R}{T} \tag{4.1}$$

For wall forms limited to a rise of concrete of 7 feet per hour or less with a maximum of 2000 pounds per square foot, or 150h, whichever is less:

$$P = 150 + \frac{9000\,R}{T} \tag{4.2}$$

For wall forms for use when rise of concrete is from 7 to 10 feet per hour, with a maximum of 2000 pounds per square foot, or 150h, whichever is less:

$$P = 150 + \frac{43{,}400}{T} + \frac{2800\,R}{T} \tag{4.3}$$

For wall forms for use when rise exceeds 10 feet per hour

$$P = 150h \tag{4.4}$$

where P = the lateral pressure in pounds per square foot (psf)

T = temperature of concrete in degrees Fahrenheit (°F)

R = rate of concrete rise against form in feet per hour (ft/hr)

h = height of fresh concrete in form in feet (ft)

These formulas were used to produce Tables 4.1 and 4.2, which show the maximum lateral concrete pressures exerted on a vertical form for various rates of concrete rise and concrete temperatures in walls and columns. As concrete is placed, it begins to stiffen. The pressures derived represent the maximum that concrete will exert laterally before it stiffens and is no longer affected by the fluid concrete placed above it. Figure 4.8 demonstrates this condition by showing a section of a wall form, 20 feet high, against which concrete at 60 degrees Fahrenheit, rises at a rate of 7 feet per hour. In this case, the maximum fluid pressure against the form reaches 1200 pounds per square foot, and then the concrete stiffens enough to become self-supporting. The pressure never reaches the maximum of 1200 pounds per square foot near the top because it can never exceed the fluid pressure of 150h.

For horizontal forms, ACI Committee 347 recommends that a minimum live load of 50 pounds per square foot be used for workers and their equipment, and if motorized concrete buggies are used, it rec-

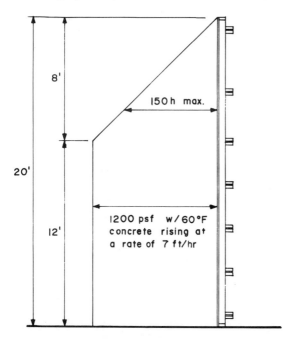

Figure 4.8 Lateral Concrete Pressure.

ommends that this minimum be raised to 75 pounds per square foot. ACI also sets 100 pounds per square foot (125 pounds per square foot with motorized concrete buggies) as the minimum combined live load and dead load on horizontal forms, regardless of concrete thickness.

Deck or slab above grade forms are subject to concentrated impact loading from such causes as falling concrete or the starting and stopping of concrete buggies. Loads created from these causes can become critical. The interested reader can refer to *Formwork for Concrete Structures*, by R. L. Peurifoy,[2] published by McGraw-Hill Book Company, in which the effect of these types of loads and other form design considerations are discussed in some detail.

Wind and other external forces create the need for design of bracing for exposed vertical forms. ACI Committee 347 recommends that a form of less than 8 feet in height be considered subject to wind load of 15 pounds per square foot if it is exposed, and if greater than 8 feet in height, it be considered subject to a wind load of 15 pounds per square foot, with a minimum equivalent load acting at the top of the form of 100 pounds per lineal foot. Forms of 8 feet or more that are not exposed to wind are also considered to be loaded at 100 pounds per lineal foot along the top. Table 4.3 shows the minimum lateral forces along the top of a wall for various intensities of wind.

4.4 QUALITY OF MATERIALS

The choice of materials used in the construction of wood forms governs the form's strength, durability, and cost. Familiarity with those materials is important to the estimator since the choice is extensive and should be made with an understanding of the need when estimating cost. For instance, there would be no point in estimating the use of an expensive plywood sheathing for a form that is to be used one time, when a sheathing material of sufficient strength but of lower quality and cost would suffice.

This section focuses on a few of the commonly used form materials and their qualities, but the estimator is reminded to recognize that there is a wider choice for wood forms and considerable information about them is available in many of the referenced publications given in this book.

Lumber

All sawn wood form materials must meet those standards appropriate to the safe casting of concrete that will meet the specified qualities established by the designer. Although quality and strength requirements for concrete forms will vary considerably with the nature of the structural component involved and the manner in which the form is loaded, a contractor will generally use lumber of a constant quality and strength and depend on form design to account for all variations. Even though any reasonably strong, straight lumber can be used, it is doubtful that a contractor will find more than one or two species of lumber in a given location that are both suitable and economical for use. The choice is important in that productivity can be affected by the general quality of the lumber used.

Specifically, form lumber can be of any wood species that is uniformly dimensioned and of predictable strength. Most often, form lumber is of a softwood, such as southern yellow pine or Douglas fir, that is fairly light, easy to work, and quite strong. Lumber can be purchased and used in rough sawn condition or dressed on as many sides as desired. Most frequently, the lumber used in formwork is dressed on all four sides and, as such, is designated as S4S (surfaced four sides). The dimensions of dressed softwood lumber have been set by the U.S. Department of Commerce in the *American Softwood Lumber Standard*, PS 20–70,[3] in which the nominal size and actual size of both dry and green lumber are given. Dry lumber, that with 19 percent or less moisture, is considered partially cured. Green lumber has a moisture content in excess of 19 percent. Rough lumber is lumber that has not been dressed by a planing machine and is 1/8 inch greater in thickness and in width. Table 4.4 provides dimensional properties of standard lumber and unit weights for each size that approximate those of southern pine or Douglas fir (approximately 35 pounds per cubic foot).

Strength in lumber is a function of species, grade, size, moisture content, and direction of load. For those interested, the properties of strength for visually graded structural lumber are fully described in the *National Design Specification for Wood Construction*,[4] published by the National Forest Products Association. This authority, it is noted, holds that when the duration of the full maximum load does not exceed 7 days, the normal strength values of wood members and fastenings may be increased by 25 percent. It also points out that when moisture content exceeds 19 percent, the strength must be reduced. In many form applications, the duration of a load is quite short, and lumber that contains in excess of 19 percent moisture is seldom used. Therefore, form lumber can possibly be considered in the 25 percent stronger category, so long as practical reasoning is used. Certainly, consideration must be given to the effects of lumber deterioration.

Plywood

Plywood, a popular and cost-effective wood form sheathing material, comes in 4- × 8-foot sheets that offer lower form assembly and dismantling costs and better quality concrete surfaces. The user may choose the most suitable of a variety of grades made in several thicknesses. Any plywood can be used in form construction, but exterior plywood, or plywood made with waterproof glue to bond the veneer layers, is considered best. Waterproof glue will resist long periods of exposure to moisture. Exterior plywood products are available in combinations that include the smooth surfaces, durability, and strength that are best in formwork.

The U.S. Department of Commerce has published a voluntary *Product Standard*, PS 1–74,[5] which establishes nationally recognized requirements for the principal types and grades of construction and industrial plywood and provides a basis for common understanding among producers, distributors, and users of plywood. This publication, in part, covers wood species, veneer grading, and glue bonds. In so doing, it describes the five groups of wood species, each of which have differing strength characteristics, with Group I being the strongest. It also defines the grades of veneers, A through D, with A having the least surface defects. An exterior plywood particularly designated for use in concrete forms is described in this standard as a Class I, or Class II plywood, each of which must have face veneers not less than Grade B and inner plys not less than Grade C. Class I is the stronger of the two, whereas the face veneers are of Group 1 species. Class II face veneers may be of Group 1 or 2 species, and under certain conditions, of the Group 3 species. The American Plywood Association calls this plywood *Plyform*. Plyform is a proprietary term applied only to specific products which bear the APA grade trademark. Plyform sheets are sanded on both sides and are oiled at the mill. The sheets may require further oiling in the field before use. It is common for Plyform to be used 10 times.

Another plywood product that meets the same standards set for Plyform Class I and Class II is called High Density Overlaid Plyform Class I and Class II, or *HDO Plyform*. HDO Plyform has a hard, smooth semiopaque surface of thermosetting resin-impregnated materials that form a durable, abrasive-resistant surface that does not necessarily require oiling. HDO Plyform is often used where very smooth surfaces are required. With care, HDO Plyform can survive as many as 50 uses.

Still another proprietary plywood product called *Structural I Plyform* is manufactured for special engineered applications that require stronger and stiffer panels. Structural I Plyform contains all Group I wood species and can be obtained with high-density overlay materials as used in HDO Plyform.

For those interested in a greater understanding of the applications for plywood as a form sheathing material, the American Plywood

Association publishes *Plywood for Concrete Forming*[6] and *Plywood Design Specifications*,[7] which thoroughly explain qualitative and strength characteristics of plywood.

Hardware

In estimating structural concrete cost, hardware is a general term used to describe all hardware, or metal devices, employed in the assembly and erection of forms, exclusive of any external support devices such as steel shoring, posts, or braces. Hardware includes the nails, straps, and anchors used, as well as the commonly known form tie systems. The predominant expense, however, is in the form tie system.

Form Ties

A form tie system is simply a device, or an assembly of devices, that when correctly employed will hold a concrete form firmly in place under maximum loading until the concrete becomes self-supporting. Estimating the cost for a form tie system can be somewhat obscure, since the forms for each structural concrete component are assembled differently, and the choice of the system in each case is quite broad. Forms for footings, for example, may be held with coil ties or with no ties at all, if they can be (as is often the case) held with a series of external wood struts, wood ties, and wood spreaders. Abutment and wall forms are often adaptable to the use of snap ties, coil ties, taper ties, or she-bolts, and the choice is a matter of preference as well as physical strength requirements. (See Figure 4.9.) Column forms are often held by yokes or clamps. (See Figure 4.10 or 4.4.) Beams, depending on shape and size, may require the use of the systems similar to those used in walls, or they may require none at all. Deck forms are held by metal hangers (see Figure 4.11), and slab above grade forms are largely dependent on an external support system, with minimal use of ties. The tie systems used for demonstration in this book will be confined to the use of snap ties, coil ties, bolts, and deck hangers of the following capacities:

Snap Ties	3000 and 5000 lb
Coil Ties and Bolts	6000, 9000, and 10,000 lb
Deck Hangers	6000, 8000, and 12,000 lb

Although there is a much wider choice in kind and strength, it is felt that these ties are representative of a common usage.

Form tie systems consist of working parts and expendable parts.

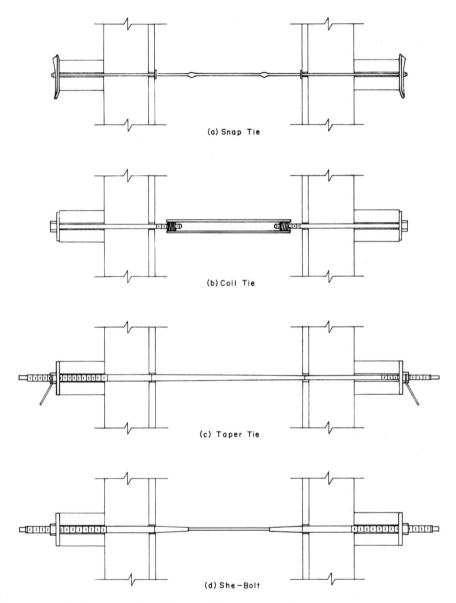

(a) Snap Tie

(b) Coil Tie

(c) Taper Tie

(d) She—Bolt

Figure 4.9 Wall Form Ties. (Richmond Screw Anchor Co., Inc.)

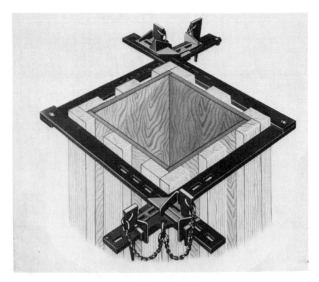

Figure 4.10 Column Clamps. (Symons Corporation.)

Figure 4.11 Bridge Deck Construction. (Patent Scaffolding Co.)

Working parts are those parts of the system such as the nuts, bolts, washers, and plates that can be recovered and reused. Expendable parts are those parts of the system that remain embedded in the concrete, or are otherwise lost to use more than one time. The proportional value of the working part to the whole system varies with the choice of system. For instance, a snap tie is entirely expendable except for the two locking clamps used at each end. (See Figure 4.9.) On the other hand, the taper tie is entirely retrievable. More will be said about the effect these factors have on the overall form tie cost later in this chapter and in Chapter 6.

Nails

Nails are an absolute need in wood form construction. Although their cost represents a small portion of the overall hardware expense in forms, nails do contribute greatly to form strength and durability. Common wire nails are used most extensively for the construction of forms, because they retain their holding capability through repeated use of the form. Usually, 5/8- or 3/4-inch sheathing is held to the form panel frame with 6d nails. The frame itself is assembled using nails of sufficient length to meet design loads. This is a variable that depends on the dimensions, specific gravity, and condition of the lumber, as well as the direction of load and the diameter of the nail. A reasonable, average use would involve from 0.05 to 0.10 pounds per square foot of form. For form design, the basis for nail holding capability is best defined by the National Forest Products Association in its publication, *National Design Specification for Wood Construction.*[4] Table 4.5 provides the diameters, lengths, and number of nails per pound for common and box nails and for spikes.

4.5 MATERIAL FACTORS

The contact areas for a structural concrete component are a measure of the neat concrete surfaces to be shaped and supported by forms. These contact areas are used to determine all neat form material quantities. A total neat form material requirement is computed by multiplying the total contact area by a unit quantity of material per square foot of contact. This unit quantity of material is called a *material factor.* Material factors are primarily used to estimate quantities for lumber, sheathing, and form ties. A neat form material factor is an exact unit measure of a specific material used to build a form that will fit the contact area perfectly and will resist the maximum load applied. As such, it is a function of design. Although form design is not within the scope of this book, all of the neat material factors presented are the product of design. Form design is governed by economy, preference, form loads, and the strength qualities of the lumber, plywood, and hardware used. In order to establish comprehensive and workable neat material factors, some of the variables involved must be eliminated. To that end, all neat material factors in this book are based on designs using Douglas fir–larch, Grade No. 2 lumber, Plyform Class I sheathing, form ties of both the snap-off and coil type, and standard deck hangers.

Determining the neat material factors for various form types does not fulfill the estimator's need. Job conditions will affect certain losses or will require the use of added materials through breakage, waste, maintenance, and form oversize. These losses must be added to the neat material quantities so that the total cost will be correct. Form material losses are vague and subject to varying conditions. They can be quantified only from experience, as are the losses that are later described in this chapter.

Form Conditions

The involvement in determining neat material factors for forms is great. Estimators interested in developing their own factors must consider many conditions. The factors developed in this book are based on average construction conditions, using commonly available materials as described.

Form Categories

Most forms for structural concrete components will fit into one or more of the following five categories, three vertical and two horizontal.

Vertical	Horizontal
Wall form, 0 to 8 feet high	Deck form
Wall form, over 8 feet high	Slab above grade form
Column form, 20 feet high	

The vertical wall form of 8 feet or less is subject to limited lateral pressures because of its height. As the wall form exceeds 8 feet in height, the potential for higher lateral pressures increases. These pressures, or loads, affect the required material strength and therefore affect the amount of material used. The column form, as explained in Section 4.2, is subject to even higher lateral pressures and thereby requires even greater material use.

The deck form involves the vertical loading of a relatively thin concrete slab. The identifying characteristic of a deck form is that it is entirely self-supporting and hangs from existing beams or headers by a metal deck hanger system similar to that shown in Figure 4.11. The slab above grade form serves the needs for all slab thicknesses and requires added temporary support. Added support, however, is not considered in the development of form material factors, but is handled separately.

Load Conditions

To simplify the development of load expectations in forms for various structural concrete components, a few representative conditions are chosen.

It is assumed all concrete mixes will weigh 150 pounds per cubic foot, and will be placed at a temperature of 60 degrees Fahrenheit, with a 4-inch slump. The weight of forms, where applicable, will be between 5 and 15 pounds per square foot of form area. Personnel and equipment will impose a live load of 75 pounds per square foot of horizontal form. The duration of loads will be 7 days or less. (See Section 4.3.)

Vertical forms generally rest on previously established foundations and are primarily designed to withstand lateral pressures. Lateral pressures are (as was explained in Section 4.3) a function of the rate of vertical rise of the concrete against the form. Five rates of rise are chosen as representative for all vertical forms: 4, 7, 10, 15, or 20 feet per hour.

Horizontal forms are designed to withstand the combined loading of concrete forms, workers, and equipment as the concrete is placed. The concrete is usually the predominant load, and the thickness of the concrete is the variable. Eight slab thicknesses were chosen to represent conditions for horizontal forms: 8, 12, 24, 36, 48, 60, 72, 84, or 96 inches.

Sheathing

The sheathing used in determining form material factors were as follows:

Wall Forms	5/8- and 3/4-inch Plyform, Class I
Column Forms	3/4-inch Plyform, Class I
Deck Forms	5/8- and 3/4-inch Plyform, Class I
Slab above Grade Forms	5/8- and 3/4-inch Plyform, Class I

All Plyform is loaded with the surface grain parallel to the span (the strong way).

Lumber

The lumber used for form frame work is of Douglas fir–larch, Grade No. 2, with 19 percent or less moisture. In those cases where practical, material factor tables will include the related lumber dimensions.

Form Ties

The form tie factors established were deliberately kept to a minimum to maintain simplicity. They are based on certain data from Richmond Screw Anchor Company, Inc., catalogs and are as follows:

Wall Forms	3M (3000 pound) and 5M snap ties
	6M coil ties
Column Forms	6M coil ties or bolts
Deck Forms	6M, 8M, and 12M deck hangers
Slab above Grade Forms	Various

Neat Material Factors

The form conditions described, when applied in design, will yield useful neat material factors. Tables 4.6 to 4.10 cover the neat material needs for forms for each of the structural concrete components. It must be remembered that these factors do not take into consideration the material losses and excesses that are common in form construction and use, nor do they include materials for large keyways or special stiff-backs and shoring. However, they do include commonly used bracing, blocking, and spreaders.

Nails and Miscellaneous Hardware

Not yet mentioned is the measure of the nails and miscellaneous items of hardware used in the assembly of forms. A wall form, for instance, may employ from 0.05 to 0.10 pounds of nails per square foot, and at $0.30 per pound, the form cost is affected minutely. Wall holders, straps, clamps, and other fabricated steel devices made to hold forms together may cost from $1.00 to $2.00 per pound, but their density is not high and their potential for many other uses is quite probable. It is noted that the material factors presented here are sufficient to encompass the small added cost for nails and miscellaneous hardware.

4.6 MATERIAL LOSS AND EXCESS USE

The neat material factors for forms describe the exact quantities of material sufficient to build forms that will cover the contact area computed in the take-off. Although these neat factors will be applied in the estimate of form material cost, they alone are not sufficient to account for all form material needs on the project. They must be adjusted to account for the material losses and excessive uses that are a reality in the industry.

A material loss can be measured by comparing the actual material cost to that of the neat material called for. The difference in cost represents the loss from material breakage, waste in form fabrication, construction of oversized forms, and maintenance. A record of this comparison, however, is not always possible to obtain, and the estimator must consider using another basis for estimating the cost. Certainly it is important to understand why the lumber factor, for instance, is 3.5 board feet per square foot of contact rather than the neat 2.5 board feet per square foot as derived by design.

Lumber and Plywood

The losses and excessive uses of dimension lumber and plywood sheathing materials for forms are similar. The following paragraphs explain the nature of those losses and provide an estimate of their effect on the form materials used for structural concrete construction.

Breakage

Careless handling, poor storage practices, and theft are a reality in construction. With care, a contractor can reduce losses from these causes by instilling in employees the need for good handling techniques and proper storage practices—and by keeping the exposure of material stored in the field to an absolute minimum. Even with due care, it is reasonable to expect a 5 percent loss. This loss is total and without salvage or residual benefit.

Fabrication

Fabrication loss in formwork is quite normal and necessary. Forms cannot always be built in sizes or shapes that utilize full dimension lumber lengths or full sheets of plywood. Consider the odd shapes of forms for abutment seats, wing walls, deck haunches, and bulkheads that all require custom shaping and cutting. Construction of these forms necessitates the loss of material.

Fabrication losses differ with different types of forms. For example, the loss in fabrication of footing forms would, on the average, be much less than the loss in fabrication of abutment forms. In other words, fabrication losses are a function of the form's complexity. The following are estimated lumber and plywood losses created in form fabrication as identified by structural component.

Loss	%	Loss	%
Footing	2	Column	3
Slab on Grade	2	Beam	5
Abutment	8	Deck	5
Wall	4	Slab above Grade	4

Oversize

A form is always at least as large as the concrete surface it supports. Often it is larger, since a form is usually built to serve more than a single time. Also, since concrete surfaces vary in size, the form must be large enough to serve the largest contact area involved. A form also employs added lumber for keyways, chamfer strips, or blocking. In order to account for oversize and normal added use of materials, a determination of an average form oversize must be made.

Form oversize loss is determined by making several assumptions: (1) the take-off of contact areas is sufficiently accurate to represent neat form needs; (2) the vertical dimension of a vertical form 8 feet or less in height will be constructed to within one foot of the top of the finished concrete surface; (3) the vertical dimension of a vertical form over 8 feet high will be constructed to within $1\frac{1}{2}$ feet of the top of the finished concrete; and (4) the horizontal length of any form will extend beyond the supported surface by as much as $1\frac{1}{2}$ feet. Applying the average of these limits to a sampling of form sizes for each structural concrete component yields the following losses attributable to oversize.

Loss	%	Loss	%
Footing	14	Wall, over 8 feet	6
Slab on grade	11	Column	10
Abutment, 0 to 8 feet	12	Beam	15
Wall, 0 to 8 feet	11	Deck	7
Abutment, over 8 feet	7	Slab above grade	10

Maintenance

Maintenance loss in form lumber and plywood is the result of damage and wear. Damage occurs when stripping crews are careless in removing, handling, and stacking forms, or when they fail to properly clean, oil, and maintain them. Wear is a function of the repeated exposure of a form to the deteriorating effects of water, concrete, vibration, and weather. Damage and wear will be greater for those forms that require a larger amount of dismantling and reassembly each time they are used.

The following are estimated cyclical maintenance losses for structural concrete forms and must be repeated each time a form is used.

Loss	%	Loss	%
Footing	2	Wall, over 8 feet	2
Slab on grade	2	Column	3
Abutment, 0 to 8 feet	5	Beam	4
Wall, 0 to 8 feet	3	Deck	5
Abutment, over 8 feet	4	Slab above grade	4

Summary of Lumber and Plywood Loss

Table 4.11 summarizes all the lumber and plywood material losses given as caused by breakage, fabrication, oversize, and maintenance, and it projects the effect of these losses on forms that will be recycled up to 10 times. To determine the total quantity of material required for a given contact area, multiply the contact area by the neat material factor times the appropriate loss.

Form Ties

Form ties are affected by losses and overuse on the job just as lumber and plywood are. The losses differ, however, and the difference is in the nature of the materials and their storage, handling, and use. The following subsections explain the basis for estimated losses in tie systems for the forms for all structural concrete components; included are considerations for the added hardware used.

Breakage

Breakage loss in form tie materials can result from insufficient planning, careless handling, poor storage management, and theft. Losses in shipment are usually minimal, and theft is not ordinarily a problem with form tie parts. Once tie materials are on the job and are placed in storage, however, other losses can—and do—occur.

Most contractors with a sizable backlog of formwork will maintain a ready supply of form tie parts to meet every anticipated need. This in itself may result in an over-expenditure, especially if the needs change as they often do. If they don't change, there is still the problem of loss and damage while in storage. A sufficient supply of form tie parts for a large formwork project, for instance, could include every conceivable configuration, size, and strength of form ties, along with a varied assortment of nuts, bolts, washers, hooks, clips, anchors, and wedges. If those parts are not kept sorted and identified, or if workers are permitted to indiscriminately rummage through the supply, a definite loss will result. Parts will not be found when needed, or they will be damaged and replacement will become necessary to meet immediate needs. It is estimated that losses due to breakage can result in a 5 percent increase in total form tie expense.

Fabrication

Form tie materials are often overused. It is not uncommon to find that in practice, tie spacing is closer than necessary, or that extra ties are used to hold a complex form assembly together. In most forming situations, form ties exceed the design strength requirements in favor of form erection convenience and practicality. Therefore, it is reasonable to estimate 5 percent for this overused to be included in the cost.

Oversize

Although actual form areas may exceed the contact areas, the use of ties will remain unaffected since tie use is a function of the load rather than of form panel size.

Maintenance

Maintenance losses in form systems involve only the working parts. Working parts can survive many uses, but during their repeated use, workers will bend bolts, drop washers in the mud, or leave extra parts unattended or forgotten at the work site. This loss is an ongoing problem that the contractor must constantly attend to, as each form cycle produces added loss. It is estimated that a working part will survive an average of 15 uses. The value of the working part for each use would therefore be $1/15$ of the cost for the part.

Summary of Form Tie Loss

Form tie loss due to breakage and fabrication is held at a constant 10 percent for all form applications. This loss applies to both working parts and expendable parts. In addition, the survival of working parts is limited to 15 uses, after which their entire value is considered consumed. Table 4.11 includes these factors.

4.7 FORM CONSTRUCTION AND USE

Labor and equipment cost for form construction and use is by far the largest portion of the total form cost. As in any estimate, the cost to build, erect, or strip forms is based on the estimated crew productivity. Since productivity, as explained in Chapter 3, is a variable influenced by many conditions in the labor market as well as by various acts of management, any stated crew size or any productivity rate given is subject to adjustment to suit the particular case involved. Table 4.12, "Form Construction—Crews and Productivity," lists average crews and their anticipated productivity as viewed by the author. This table is useful if it is thoroughly understood.

All form labor and equipment expense is incorporated into three form activities identified as *build, erect,* and *strip.* These identities are self-explanatory, but it is important to know more of the details involved with each. For instance, referring to Table 4.12, the estimator should understand that one-half of a foreman means that a crew foreman is not needed solely for the supervision of that activity and could carry on other responsibilities at the same time, the cost for which would be included elsewhere. The same practice applies to the workers or to equipment. It should also be noted that oilers are not included for cranes in all cases, because in many instances, the hydraulic crane with only an operator is utilized. Knowing fully what the terms build, erect, and strip really encompass, and what the crew responsibilities are under those terms, will help the estimator to perform comprehensive estimates of cost.

Build

Building of forms prior to use (or, prefabrication), is a common practice with many form types. Some forms, such as those for a bridge deck, cannot be prefabricated and must be assembled in place and totally dismantled each time they are used. Other forms will require a lesser degree of dismantling and rebuilding for each use. In this case, building forms refers only to the initial prefabrication of the form, and all further expenses are considered to be covered under erection or stripping.

Prefabrication of forms is usually done under somewhat ideal conditions. That is, the form sections are built on the ground at a location where materials and power tools are readily available and where smaller crews with less need for heavy supporting equipment can work effectively.

Erect

The average crew productivity rates for erection of forms as shown in Table 4.12 are sufficient to cover the installation of all forms, templates, hardware, keyways, joint materials, chamfer strips, stiffbacks, braces, guys, and screed rails. These productivity rates also consider the fabrication and assembly of forms in place where commonly required. Not included is the installation of external support systems, such as sectional shoring, beam shores, or post shores; nor is the installation of such items as scuppers, expansion dams, or conduit included.

Strip

Stripping for forms involves the removal, dismantling, cleaning, oiling, storage, and repair of the forms after use so that they will be ready for the next planned operation. The stripping crew is also responsible for the removal of all concrete fins and the plugging of all tieholes.

4.8 METHODS OF FORM SUPPORT

Thus far, quantities of lumber, plywood, and ties for forms and the construction and use of forms have been thoroughly explained. The factors developed, however, have not included consideration for any of those materials and devices used to supply added support for forms, and the crew productivity rates have covered only the installation of selected form supports.

Form support is necessary for maintaining the alignment and stability of a form. For example: Beam forms often lack the strength to resist the usual heavily concentrated load involved and will either deflect excessively or fail unless supported from beneath; wall forms must be braced, or guyed, to prevent toppling from wind or working loads; and cantilevered deck forms must be supported by overhang brackets or jacks. These, and other means of form support, are an important and integral part of a form system. Their material cost is always estimated separately and may either be added to the form material cost or be itemized separately under Common Concrete Cost (see Section 5.7), whichever is preferred. Installation cost may or may not be included with the form erection cost, depending on the system used.

The following form support systems are in common use, and their installation cost is covered as shown.

Type support	Location of installment cost
Sectional shoring	Separate
Beam shores	Separate
Post shores	Separate
Braces	With form erection and stripping
Guys	With form erection and stripping
Stiffbacks	With form erection and stripping
Deck overhang brackets	With form erection and stripping

Before actual use, a form support system requires careful design. For estimating purposes, however, the extent of support can be approximated by referring to load tables or other sources of information specifically directed to the application. These aspects will now be discussed in some detail.

Sectional Shoring

Sectional shoring is a commonly used method of support. It consists of tubular steel frames connected by steel cross braces to form a rigid, trusslike structure beneath the form. The height, length, and width of a form will not limit the use of sectional shoring so long as each leg in the system is founded on a sufficient footing. The weight of the loaded form governs the required strength and spacing of the shoring legs. Figure 4.12 shows sectional shoring in use for the support of a concrete grider bridge.

Sectional shoring can be erected easily with a relatively small and unskilled crew. No fabrication is necessary, and adjustments are simply made by using built-in jacks located at the top and bottom of each leg. The frames normally used have leg capacities of as much as 25,000 pounds and are available in sizes from 2 to 5 feet wide, and 3 to 6 feet high. They can be spaced nearly any distance apart to accommodate load conditions. Frames of greater capacity are available for spe-

Figure 4.12 Sectional Shoring. (Patent Scaffolding Co.)

cial applications. Three or four workers can prepare for and erect most sectional shoring. The rate at which erection takes place is a function of the existing jobsite conditions.

Beam Shores

Many form support tasks are met through the use of beam shores. A beam shore is any beam that is used as added support for a horizontal form.

The advantage of beam shores is that they are quickly erected while keeping the area beneath the form clear of obstructions, facilitating simultaneous passage of workers, equipment, or traffic. There is a variety of beam types to choose from, the choice depending on the load application and the best available type beam for that particular operation.

Depending on job conditions, beam shores can be supported in several ways. They may bear on a bracket or a clamping device that is attached to a permanent column, or they may rest on an existing beam or header. They may also be supported by posts or sectional shoring. Figure 4.5 demonstrates the application of beam shoring for a bridge pier beam.

Wood Beam

Wood beams are continually in use as form support in heavy concrete construction. Their load carrying capacity is not particularly adaptable to extremely heavy loads over great spans, but they serve well for the shorter spans between vertical supports. Once the load requirements are determined, the estimator can quickly approximate the necessary beam size by referring to load tables for wood, such as those found in *Wood Structural Design Data,*[8] published by the National Forest Products Association, or *Formwork for Concrete,*[1] published by the American Concrete Institute.

Steel Beam

Steel beams are available in many sizes and capacities, exceeding the capability of wood beams in every respect. Load tables are available from steel handbooks such as the *Manual of Steel Construction,*[9] published by the American Institute of Steel Construction.

Patented Beams

There are a number of patented beam shore systems available that offer a variety of advantages. Although they are, for the most part, limited to lighter loads, they are flexible and inexpensive to install. Many systems are telescopic and can be used for varied spans. It is recommended that the estimator obtain load tables from several patented beam manufacturers so that their use can be considered when applicable. Figure 4.13 demonstrates the use of the telescopic system for support of a slab above grade form. The system shown is a product of the Spanall Company, a Division of Patent Scaffolding Company.

Post Shores

Post shores are a commonly used means of form support. They are versatile in that they can be used as a single unit or as a part of a group of posts working together. When two or more posts are employed as a form support, diagonal and horizontal cross braces are often added to increase their load carrying capacity. Post shores can be made from wood timbers, steel columns, or patented shores. As with beams, the same publications previously mentioned have load tables for posts or columns.

Figure 4.13 Beam Shores-Support a Slab above Grade. (Patent Scaffolding Co.)

Wood Posts

Wood posts shores (Figure 4.7) are relatively simple, light, and strong and are inexpensive to install. They are difficult to adjust to grade because of their fixed length and require the use of wedges for such adjustments. Bracing of wood post shores is simplified because the braces can be quickly nailed to the post.

Patented Posts

Patented post shores have many advantages. Available for all heights in various capacities up to 10,000 pounds, they are easily adjusted, quick to install, and strong enough to survive many applications. Although relatively expensive to purchase, the estimator may find that there is enough demand to justify the investment.

Braces and Guys

Forms for columns and walls are usually held in place and kept from becoming misaligned or toppled by construction loads or winds with a system of braces or guys. The size and frequency of use of these systems is a function of the form height and of those external loads on the form that are to be resisted. Table 4.3 gives the minimum lateral forces acting along the top of a wall for various wind pressures. These forces, once determined, along with the physical conditions that govern support length and direction of load, will be used to estimate the size and the nature of support. The installation cost for braces or guys is considered to be equal and has been considered in establishing the form erection and stripping productivity factors provided in Table 4.12. The material cost can be estimated on a separate basis or with the regular form material cost. Tables 4.6 to 4.8 include factors sufficient to cover ordinary requirements for braces.

Stiffbacks

Stiffbacks used with a wall form improve the form's strength, rigidity, and alignment qualities, particularly with larger panels or gang forms. In repeated use, stiffbacks are an advantage, since they make handling and erection easier and cause less damage to the form. Stiffbacks are attached to the form through use of form ties and specially made holding devices. They can be of any type and size material that will supply the strengths and rigidity required. The cost for materials is extra. Installation and removal cost is considered a part of form erection and stripping cost.

Deck Overhang Brackets

Figure 4.14 is a photograph of a deck overhang bracket, and Figure 4.15 shows how it is applied in supporting the deck form that cantilevers along a bridge fascia beam. The installation and removal cost for these brackets was taken into consideration in the form erection and stripping factors established for decks as shown in Table 4.12. The cost for the material is extra and is based on similar losses due to breakage, fabrication, and maintenance, as was described for form tie working parts. A commonly used bracket has a total capacity of 3000 pounds and is spaced along the fascia beam a distance that is governed by the loaded form weight plus any added load imposed by a screeding device or a finishing machine.

4.9 FORM ACCESS

Form access is any means used to afford safe and convenient access for workers to the forms for any of the structural concrete components. Safe and convenient access is achieved through the use of sectional scaffolding, bridges, walkways, platforms, power lifts, elevators, towers, or ladders. Figure 4.16 is a sketch of a job-built scaffold of the

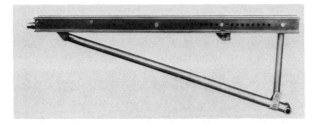

Figure 4.14 Bridge Deck Overhang Bracket. (Richmond Screw Anchor Co., Inc.)

Figure 4.15 Bridge Deck Overhang Form. (Richmond Screw Anchor Co., Inc.)

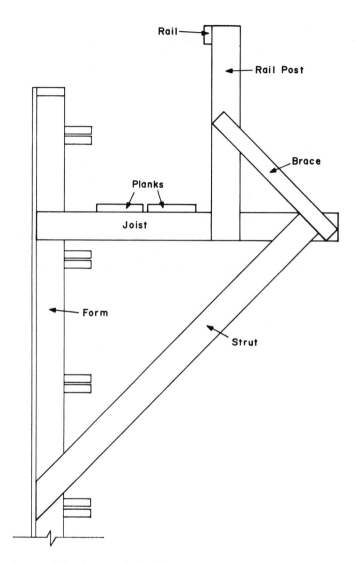

Figure 4.16 Access Scaffold.

type that is often employed as access along the forms for walls, decks, beams, and columns. Every project has unique access requirements, and there are any number of ways to fill them. When estimating cost, the point is to remember that form access can be of considerable consequence and is not to be overlooked. As will be explained in Chapter 5, the entire expense for the labor, equipment, and materials involved in providing ramps and scaffolding for form access is a Common Concrete Cost.

Table 4.1   Maximum Lateral Pressure on Wall Forms (Due to concrete)*

Rate of rise (ft/hr)	Maximum lateral pressure, P (lb/sf)					
	40°F	50°F	60°F	70°F	80°F	90°F
1	375	330	300	279	262	250
2	600	510	450	407	375	350
3	825	690	600	536	488	450
4	1050	870	750	664	600	550
5	1275	1050	900	793	712	650
6	1500	1230	1050	921	825	750
7	1725	1410	1200	1050	938	850
8	1795	1466	1247	1090	973	881
9	1865	1522	1293	1130	1008	912
10	1935	1578	1340	1170	1043	943

* Based on ACI Committee 347 pressure formulas for placement at 10 ft/hr or less. No pressure to exceed 150 h.

Table 4.2   **Maximum Lateral Pressure on Column Forms** (Due to concrete)*

Rate of rise (ft/hr)	Maximum lateral pressure, P (lb/sf)					
	40°F	50°F	60°F	70°F	80°F	90°F
1	375	330	300	278	262	250
2	600	510	450	407	375	350
3	825	690	600	536	488	450
4	1050	870	750	664	600	550
5	1275	1050	900	793	712	650
6	1500	1230	1050	921	825	750
7	1725	1410	1200	1050	938	850
8	1950	1590	1350	1178	1050	950
9	2175	1770	1500	1307	1163	1050
10	2400	1950	1650	1436	1275	1150
12	2850	2310	1950	1693	1500	1350
14	3000	2670	2250	1950	1725	1550
16		3000	2550	2207	1950	1750
18			2850	2464	2175	1950
20			3000	2721	2400	2150
22				2979	2625	2350
24				3000	2850	2550
26					3000	2750
28						2950
30						3000

* Based on ACI Committee 347 pressure formulas for placement in lifts not exceeding 18 ft. No pressure to exceed 150 h.

Table 4.3 Minimum Lateral Forces on Wall Forms (Due to wind)*

Wall height, h (ft)	ACI (15 psf or 100 lb/ft)	Other (psf)			
		10	20	25	30
4	30	20	40	50	60
6	45	30	60	75	90
8	100	100	100	100	120
10	100	100	100	125	150
12	100	100	120	150	180
14	100	100	140	175	210
16	120	100	160	200	240
18	135	100	180	225	270
20	150	100	200	250	300
22+	$7.5\,h$	$5.0h$	$10.0h$	$12.5h$	$15.0h$

* Based on ACI Committee 347 design criteria for design of bracing for walls above grade. Forces used must conform to local codes when greater than ACI Committee 347 minimum. For walls below grade use 100 lb/ft for forms of more than 8 ft height. Lower forms may be braced as required. Forces act at top of wall form.

Table 4.4   Standard Rough and Dressed (S4S)* Lumber

Nominal size (in)	Actual size Rough (in)	Actual size S4S* (in)	Section area Rough (sq in)	Section area S4S* (sq in)	Lumber content (bf/ft)	Average weight† (lb/ft)
1 × 4	$^7/_8$ × 3$^5/_8$	$^3/_4$ × 3$^1/_2$	3.17	2.62	0.33	0.64
6	5$^5/_8$	5$^1/_2$	4.92	4.12	0.50	1.00
8	7$^3/_8$	7$^1/_4$	6.45	5.44	0.67	1.32
10	9$^3/_8$	9$^1/_4$	8.20	6.94	0.83	1.69
12	11$^3/_8$	11$^1/_4$	9.95	8.44	1.00	2.05
2 × 4	1$^5/_8$ × 3$^5/_8$	1$^1/_2$ × 3$^1/_2$	5.89	5.25	0.67	1.28
6	5$^5/_8$	5$^1/_2$	9.14	8.25	1.00	2.00
8	7$^3/_8$	7$^1/_4$	11.98	10.88	1.33	2.67
10	9$^3/_8$	9$^1/_4$	15.23	13.88	1.67	3.37
12	11$^3/_8$	11$^1/_4$	18.48	16.88	2.00	4.10
3 × 4	2$^5/_8$ × 3$^5/_8$	2$^1/_2$ × 3$^1/_2$	9.52	8.75	1.00	2.13
6	5$^5/_8$	5$^1/_2$	14.77	13.75	1.50	3.34
8	7$^3/_8$	7$^1/_4$	19.36	18.12	2.00	4.40
10	9$^3/_8$	9$^1/_4$	24.61	23.12	2.50	5.62
12	11$^3/_8$	11$^1/_4$	29.56	28.12	3.00	6.84
4 × 4	3$^5/_8$ × 3$^5/_8$	3$^1/_2$ × 3$^1/_2$	13.14	12.25	1.33	2.98
6	5$^5/_8$	5$^1/_2$	20.39	19.25	2.00	4.68
8	7$^3/_8$	7$^1/_4$	26.73	25.38	2.67	6.17
10	9$^3/_8$	9$^1/_4$	33.98	32.38	3.33	7.87
12	11$^3/_8$	11$^1/_4$	41.23	39.38	4.00	9.57
6 × 6	5$^5/_8$ × 5$^5/_8$	5$^1/_2$ × 5$^1/_2$	31.64	30.25	3.00	7.35
8	7$^5/_8$	7$^1/_2$	42.89	41.25	4.00	10.03
10	9$^5/_8$	9$^1/_2$	54.14	52.25	5.00	12.70
12	11$^5/_8$	11$^1/_2$	65.39	63.25	6.00	15.37
8 × 8	7$^5/_8$ × 7$^5/_8$	7$^1/_2$ × 7$^1/_2$	58.14	56.25	5.33	13.67
10	9$^5/_8$	9$^1/_2$	73.39	71.25	6.67	17.32
12	11$^5/_8$	11$^1/_2$	88.64	86.25	8.00	20.96
10 × 10	9$^5/_8$ × 9$^5/_8$	9$^1/_2$ × 9$^1/_2$	92.64	90.25	8.33	21.94
12	11$^5/_8$	11$^1/_2$	111.89	109.25	10.00	26.55
12 × 12	11$^5/_8$ × 11$^5/_8$	11$^1/_2$ × 11$^1/_2$	135.14	132.25	12.00	32.14

* Surfaced on all four sides.
† Weight based on 35 lb/cf.

Table 4.5 Nails and Spikes

Size (d)	Length (in)	Common Gauge	Common Diam. (in)	Nails/lb
2	1	15	0.072	876
4	1½	12½	0.099	316
6	2	11½	0.113	181
8	2½	10¼	0.131	106
10	3	9	0.148	69
12	3¼	9	0.148	63
16	3½	8	0.162	49
20	4	6	0.192	31
30	4½	5	0.207	24
40	5	4	0.225	18
50	5½	3	0.244	14
60	6	2	0.263	11

Table 4.6A Neat Material Factors*—Wall Forms
(Using ⅝-inch plywood sheathing)

Component	Form ht. (ft)	Conc. rise (ft/hr)	Max. press. (psf)	Lumber (bf/sf) Neat	Brace	Total	Ties (T/sf)† 3M	5M	6M
Footing	4	7	600	2.65	0.05	2.70	0.08		
	8	7	1200	2.85	0.10	2.95	0.15	0.11	
Slab on grade	2	4	300	3.00	0.05	3.05	0.08		
	4	4	600	2.65	0.05	2.70	0.08		
Abutment,	4	10	600	2.65	0.05	2.70	0.08		
0–8′	8	10	1200	2.85	0.10	2.95	0.15	0.11	
Wall, 0–8′	4	10	600	2.65	0.05	2.70	0.08		
	8	10	1200	2.85	0.10	2.95	0.15	0.11	
Abutment,	8	7–10	1200	2.85	0.10	2.95	0.15	0.11	
8′ +	16+	7	1200	2.65	0.20	2.85	0.22	0.13	0.13
	16+	10	1340	2.75	0.20	2.95	0.24	0.14	0.13
Wall, 8′ +	8	7–10	1200	2.85	0.10	2.95	0.15	0.11	
	16+	7	1200	2.65	0.20	2.85	0.22	0.13	0.13
	16+	10	1340	2.75	0.20	2.95	0.24	0.14	0.13
Beam (sides)	4	7	600	2.65	0.05	2.70	0.08		
	8	7	1200	2.85	0.10	2.95	0.15	0.11	

* Factors are based on use of Douglas Fir–Larch, Grade No.2, and concrete at 60°F.
† Tie factors are for one-half tie, assuming a two-sided wall form.

Box			Spike		
Gauge	Diam. (in)	Nails/lb	Gauge	Diam. (in)	Spikes/lb
15½	0.067	984			
14	0.080	459			
12½	0.099	237			
11½	0.113	145			
10½	0.128	94	6	0.192	41
10½	0.128	86	6	0.192	38
10	0.135	71	5	0.207	30
9	0.148	50	4	0.225	23
9	0.148	45	3	0.244	17
8	0.162	34	2	0.263	13
—	—	—	1	0.283	10
—	—	—	1	0.283	9

Table 4.6B   Neat Material Factors*—Wall Forms
(Using ³/₄-inch plywood sheathing)

Component	Form ht. (ft)	Conc. rise (ft/hr)	Max. press. (psf)	Lumber (bf/sf)			Ties (T/sf)†		
				Neat	Brace	Total	3M	5M	6M
Footing	4	7	600	2.50	0.05	2.55	0.08		
	8	7	1200	2.65	0.10	2.75	0.15	0.11	
Slab on grade	2	4	300	2.90	0.05	2.95	0.08		
	4	4	600	2.50	0.05	2.55	0.08		
Abutment,	4	10	600	2.50	0.05	2.55	0.08		
0–8'	8	10	1200	2.65	0.10	2.75	0.15	0.11	
Wall, 0–8'	4	10	600	2.50	0.05	2.55	0.08		
	8	10	1200	2.65	0.10	2.75	0.15	0.11	
Abutment,	8	7–10	1200	2.65	0.10	2.75	0.15	0.11	
8' +	16+	7	1200	2.50	0.20	2.70	0.22	0.13	0.12
	16+	10	1340	2.50	0.20	2.70	0.22	0.13	0.13
Wall, 8' +	8	7–10	1200	2.65	0.10	2.75	0.15	0.11	
	16+	7	1200	2.50	0.20	2.70	0.22	0.13	0.12
	16+	10	1340	2.50	0.20	2.70	0.22	0.13	0.13
Beam (sides)	4	7	600	2.50	0.05	2.55	0.08		
	8	7	1200	2.65	0.10	2.75	0.15	0.11	

* Factors are based on use of Douglas Fir–Larch, Grade No.2, and concrete at 60°F.
† Tie factors are for one-half tie, assuming a two-sided wall form.

Table 4.7 Neat Material Factors*—Column Forms
(Using ³/₄-inch plywood sheathing)

Column size	Form ht. (ft)	Conc. rise (ft/hr)	Max. press. (psf)	Size studs (b × h × 2)	Lumber (bf/sf) Neat	Yokes	Brace	Total	Ties 6M (T/sf)
2' × 6'	20	15	2400	2 × 4	1.70	2.70	0.50	4.90	0.30
		20	3000	4 × 2	2.00	3.30	0.50	5.80	0.30
3' × 3'	20	15	2400	2 × 4	1.60	2.00	0.45	4.05	0.30
		20	3000	2 × 4	1.80	2.00	0.45	4.25	0.30
4' × 4'	20	15	2400	2 × 4	1.50	2.00	0.35	3.85	0.25
		20	3000	6 × 2	1.50	2.30	0.35	4.15	0.30

* Factors are based on use of Douglas Fir–Larch, Grade No. 2, and concrete at 60°F. All yokes are of double 2 × 6 lumber.

Table 4.8 Neat Material Factors*—Beam Forms

Beam size, b × h (ft)	Floor span (ft)	⅝" plywood sheathing Lumber factor (bf/sf)	Tie factor (T/sf) 3M	5M	³/₄" plywood sheathing Lumber factor (bf/sf)	Tie factor (T/sf) 3M	5M
4 × 4	4	2.30	0.05		2.20	0.05	
	6	2.55	0.05		2.55	0.05	
	8	3.25	0.05		3.05	0.05	
	10	3.25	0.05		3.05	0.05	
4 × 6	4	2.60	0.08		2.60	0.08	
	6	2.95	0.08		2.75	0.08	
	8	3.45	0.08		3.20	0.08	
6 × 6	4	2.55	0.08		2.60	0.08	
	6	3.00	0.08		2.80	0.08	
	8	3.65	0.08		3.40	0.08	
4 × 8	4	2.90	0.12	0.09	2.70	0.12	0.09
	6	3.10	0.12	0.09	2.95	0.12	0.09
	8				3.25	0.12	0.09
6 × 8	4	2.95	0.11	0.08	2.70	0.11	0.08
	6	3.20	0.11	0.08	3.05	0.11	0.08
	8				3.45	0.11	0.08
8 × 8	4	2.95	0.10	0.07	2.70	0.10	0.07
	6	3.30	0.10	0.07	3.15	0.10	0.07
	8				3.60	0.10	0.07

* The factors are a composite of those found in Tables 4.6 and 4.10.

Table 4.9   Neat Material Factors*—Deck Forms

Detail	Form span (ft)	Joist size, $b \times h$ (in)	Ledger size, $2b \times h$ (in)	Lumber factor (bf/sf)	Tie factor (T/sf)		
					6M	8M	12M
5/8″ Plyform Class I							
8-inch slab	4	2 × 6	2 × 6	1.10	0.04		
	6		2 × 8	1.30	0.03		
	8		2 × 12	1.45		0.02	
	10		3 × 12	1.70			0.02
12-inch slab	4	2 × 6	2 × 6	1.20	0.05		
	6		2 × 10	1.55	0.04		
	8		2 × 12	1.70		0.03	
	10		3 × 12	1.95			0.02
3/4″ Plyform Class I							
8-inch slab	4	2 × 6	2 × 6	1.10	0.04		
	6		2 × 8	1.20	0.03		
	8		2 × 12	1.40		0.02	
	10		3 × 12	1.70			0.02
12-inch slab	4	2 × 6	2 × 6	1.20	0.05		
	6		2 × 10	1.40	0.04		
	8		2 × 12	1.60		0.03	
	10		3 × 12	1.95			0.02

* Based on use of Douglas Fir–Larch, Grade No. 2. Weight of concrete at 150 lb/cf. Weight of forms at 5 to 15 lb/sf. Live load of 75 lb/sf. Includes deck overhang without overhang bracket.

Table 4.10 Neat Material Factors—Slab above Grade Forms

Clear span (ft)	Joist, $b \times h$ (in)	Lumber (bf/sf) Thickness (in)							
		12	24	36	48	60	72	84	96
5/8″ plywood deck									
4	2 × 6	0.75	0.90						
	2 × 8			1.35	1.45				
	3 × 6					1.80	2.00		
	3 × 8							2.65	3.00
6	2 × 8	1.00							
	3 × 6		1.40	2.00					
	3 × 8				2.20				
	3 × 10					3.00	3.35		
	4 × 8							3.55	4.00
8	3 × 8	1.50	1.85						
	3 × 10			2.50					
	6 × 8				4.35	4.80	5.35		
10	3 × 10	1.90	2.30						
	6 × 8			4.00	4.35				
3/4″ plywood deck									
4	2 × 6	0.65	0.80						
	2 × 8			1.15					
	3 × 6				1.50				
	3 × 8					2.20	2.40	2.40	2.65
6	2 × 8	0.90							
	3 × 8		1.60	1.70					
	3 × 10				2.50	2.75	3.00		
	6 × 6							3.60	4.00
8	3 × 8	1.35							
	3 × 10		2.00						
	4 × 8			2.30					
	6 × 8				4.00	4.35	4.80	4.80	5.35
10	4 × 8	1.80							
	6 × 8		3.20	3.45	4.00				

Table 4.11 Form Material Loss Factors

Form component	Material loss (%)				Material loss factors (per cycle)					
	Break.	Fab.	O'size	Maint.	1	2	4	6	8	10
Footing	5	2	14	2	1.23	1.25	1.29	1.33	1.37	1.41
Slab on grade	5	2	11	2	1.20	1.22	1.26	1.30	1.34	1.38
Abutment 0–8	5	8	12	5	1.30	1.35	1.45	1.55	1.65	1.75
Wall 0–8	5	4	11	3	1.23	1.26	1.32	1.38	1.44	1.50
Abutment 8' +	5	8	7	4	1.24	1.28	1.36	1.44	1.52	1.60
Wall 8' +	5	4	6	2	1.17	1.19	1.23	1.27	1.31	1.35
Column	5	3	10	3	1.21	1.24	1.30	1.36	1.42	1.48
Beam	5	5	15	4	1.29	1.33	1.41	1.49	1.57	1.65
Deck	5	5	7	5	1.22	1.27	1.37	1.47	1.57	1.67
Slab above grade	5	4	10	4	1.23	1.27	1.35	1.43	1.51	1.59
Hardware —all forms	5	5	—	—	1.10	1.10	1.10	1.10	1.10	1.10

Table 4.12 Form Construction—Crews and Productivity

Component	Average Production (sf/hr)	Foreman	Carpenter	Carpenter helper
Build				
Foot	60–70		1	1
Abutment 0–8'	40–50	1/2	1	1
Wall 0–8'	50–60	1/2	1	1
Abutment 8'+	40–50	1/2	2	1
Wall 8'+	50–60	1/2	2	1
Column	50–60	1/2	1	1
Beam	40–50	1/2	1	1
Erect				
Foot	60–70	1	2	1
Slab on grade	50–60	1	2	1
Abutment 0–8'	30–40	1	2	1
Wall 0–8'	40–50	1	2	1
Abutment 8'+	30–40	1	3	1
Wall 8'+	40–50	1	3	1
Column	30–40	1	2	1
Beam	20–30	1	2	1
Deck	40–50	1	4	1
Slab above grade	20–30	1	4	1
Strip				
Foot	150–170	1/4	1	1
Slab on grade	120–140	1/4		1
Abutment 0–8'	60–80	1/4	1	1
Wall 0–8'	100–120	1/4	1	1
Abutment 8'+	60–80	1/2	1	1
Wall 8'+	100–120	1/2	1	1
Column	100–120	1/4	1	1
Beam	80–100	1/4	1	1
Deck	130–150	1/2	1	1
Slab above grade	60–70	1	1	1

Crew and equipment					
Laborer	Crane	Service truck	Generator	Bench saw	Welder
1	$1/4$	$1/4$	1		
1	$1/4$	$1/4$	1	1	
1	$1/4$	$1/4$	1	1	
1	$1/2$	$1/4$	1	1	
1	$1/2$	$1/4$	1	1	
1	$1/4$	$1/4$	1	1	
1	$1/4$	$1/4$	1	1	
2	$1/2$	$1/4$	1		
2	$1/4$	$1/2$	1		
2	$1/2$	$1/2$	1	1	$1/4$
2	$1/2$	$1/4$	1	1	$1/4$
2	$3/4$	$1/2$	1	1	$1/4$
2	$3/4$	$1/4$	1	1	$1/4$
2	$1/2$	$1/2$	1	1	$1/4$
2	$3/4$	$1/2$	1	1	$1/4$
3	$3/4$	$3/4$	2	1	$1/2$
3	1	$3/4$	2	1	$1/4$
2	$1/2$	$1/2$	1		
2	$1/4$	$1/2$	1		
2	$1/2$	$1/2$	1		
2	$1/2$	$1/2$	1		
3	$3/4$	$1/2$	1		
3	$3/4$	$1/2$	1		
2	$3/4$	$1/2$	1		
2	$3/4$	$1/2$	1		
4	$1/2$	1	1		
4	$1/2$	1	1		

REFERENCES

[1] *Formwork for Concrete,* SP4, 4th ed., American Concrete Institute, Detroit, Mich., 1979.

[2] R. L. Peurifoy, *Formwork for Concrete Structures,* 2d ed., McGraw-Hill Book Company, New York, 1976.

[3] *American Softwood Lumber Standard,* PS 20–70, U.S. Department of Commerce, National Bureau of Standards, Washington, D.C., 1970.

[4] *National Design Specification for Wood Construction,* National Forest Products Association, Washington, D.C., 1977.

[5] *U.S. Product Standard, PS 1-74, for Construction and Industrial Plywood,* U.S. Department of Commerce, National Bureau of Standards, Washington, D.C., 1974, amended 1978.

[6] *Plywood for Concrete Forming,* American Plywood Association, Tacoma, Wash., 1979.

[7] *Plywood Design Specifications,* American Plywood Association, Tacoma, Wash., 1980.

[8] *Wood Structural Design Data,* National Forest Products Association, Washington, D.C., 1978.

[9] *Manual of Steel Construction,* 7th ed., American Institute of Steel Construction, Inc., New York, 1973.

5 CONCRETE

5.1 CHARACTERISTICS

Concrete can be described as an artificial stone cast into a preformed shape. The basic ingredients in concrete are a selected mixture of cement, water, and fine and coarse aggregates, which when first combined, form a near liquid or plastic mass that can be poured into forms of any shape.

When water and cement combine in a concrete mix, a paste is formed that fills nearly all voids between the aggregate particles. Within a relatively short period of time, the paste transforms itself (through a chemical process called *hydration*) into a hard material of great strength. During this transformation, the paste begins to stiffen, losing its plastic quality. This stiffening is called *set*. Once set, concrete can no longer be disturbed. The time required for a concrete mix to set can be adjusted by adding accelerators or retarders to the mix, or it can inadvertently be affected by weather conditions. Almost always, set occurs within a very few hours of the time water and cement are combined.

Through the continuing process of hydration, concrete gains in strength until it reaches its designed strength. This is generally considered to take 28 days, with about 60 percent of designed strength being reached within 7 days.

Reinforcing steel placed strategically within the concrete casting adds further to the structural capability of concrete, and thereby affords the use of concrete in a greater number of structural applications.

The design of a concrete mix is not necessarily important to an estimator. What is important is to understand the processes involved with concrete—from manufacture to completed product. These processes affect cost. They begin with the proportioning of the concrete ingredients and continue with the mixing and delivery of the concrete, the placing of the concrete in forms, and the curing and finishing of the hardened concrete. This chapter discusses each of these involved steps.

5.2 CONCRETE MIX PROPORTIONS

The situation requiring an estimator to design a concrete mix is improbable. Nevertheless, an estimator should know enough about concrete mix proportioning to permit an approximation of material needs when necessary, provided that the mix design criteria are available.

In the United States, concrete is most often purchased, placed, and paid for by the cubic yard measure. But, at the concrete batch plant, all ingredients are bought and dispensed by weight. The relationship, therefore, between volume and weight of ingredients must be understood. This relationship is described as follows:

$$\text{Absolute volume} = \frac{\text{bulk weight}}{\text{specific gravity} \times \text{unit weight of water}} \quad (5.1)$$

Absolute volume means solid volume or volume without voids. Any ingredient in a concrete mix for which the weight and specific gravity are known can be translated into terms of the volume it proportionately fills in the mix. Therefore, if the proportional weights of all ingredients are known, the volume of each can be computed and the total volume of the mix can be determined by summation.

Each ingredient in a concrete mix has its own physical characteristic. Most often it is found that the characteristics of cement and water are constant:

    1 cubic foot cement (sack) = 94.00 lb
    1 cubic foot water   = 62.40 lb
    1 cubic foot water   = 7.48 gal
    Specific gravity cement   = 3.15
    Specific gravity water   = 1.00

Aggregates usually vary in composition and must be tested for specific gravity before a mix can be designed and batch weights established for the batch plant. Once the specific gravities of the aggregates are known, a reasonable approximation can be made of the total material requirements for a project using specified mix parameters. For example:

Assume that 15,000 cubic yards of concrete must be manufactured for a project. Specifications provide the following information relative to the concrete mix.

    Maximum water per sack cement = 5.5 gal
    Cement per cubic yard   = 6 sacks
    Fine aggregate, percent by
    weight of total aggregate   = 40 percent

Determine the total amount of each ingredient required to batch the entire 15,000 cubic yards of concrete.
Tests indicate the specific gravity of the aggregates is

Fine aggregate   2.65
Course aggregate   2.70

The absolute volume of one cubic yard of mix is found as follows:

$$\text{Absolute volume (27 cf)} = +\frac{6 \times 94 \text{ lb/sack}}{3.15 \times 62.4 \text{ lb/cf}} \quad \text{(cement)}$$

$$+\frac{40\% \times W \text{ lb}}{2.65 \times 62.4 \text{ lb/cf}} \quad \text{(fine aggregate)}$$

$$+\frac{60\% \times W \text{ lb}}{2.70 \times 62.4 \text{ lb/cf}} \quad \text{(coarse aggregate)}$$

$$+\frac{5 \text{ gal} \times 6 \text{ sacks} \times 8.34 \text{ lb/gal}}{1.00 \times 62.4 \text{ lb/cf}} \quad \text{(water)}$$

Solving for W (weight of aggregates) we find,

$$W = \frac{27 - 2.87 - 4.01}{0.00598} = 3365 \text{ lb}$$

Therefore, the neat material requirements for batching 15,000 cubic yards of concrete will be:

Fine Aggregate	$15,000 \times 40\% \times 3365/2000 =$	10,085 tn
Coarse Aggregate	$15,000 \times 60\% \times 3365/2000 =$	15,142 tn
Cement	$15,000 \times 6 \times 94/2000$ $=$	4,230 tn
Water	$15,000 \times 5 \times 6$	$= 450,000$ gal

Usually a waste quantity would be added to these quantities to compensate for losses on the ground or for other factors associated with the site and the plant used.

5.3 PRODUCTION AND DELIVERY OF CONCRETE MIX

Concrete mix is often supplied to a project by a commercial concrete producer who coordinates deliveries with the contractor to ensure that the correct amount of a specified mix arrives from the batch plant at the right time and at a manageable rate. When this is the case, the estimator need only be concerned with obtaining prices from qualified competing producers. Here, the important thing to remember is to examine each quotation very carefully. Commercially produced concrete cost will vary greatly with add-on charges for periodic escalation, heat or ice, additives, extended truck unloading time, less than minimum loads, or overtime (over 8 hours) for a truck driver.

It is the estimator's obligation to thoroughly understand the project needs and how they will relate to the quotations received. Occasion-

Figure 5.1   Mobile Batch Plant. (The Vince Hagan Company.)

ally, an estimator is faced with the need to find the cost for manufacturing a concrete mix at the jobsite, using a mobile batch plant (Figure 5.1). This situation usually arises from economic considerations associated with large volume and high rate demands or remote project locations, weighed against the possibilities from a commercial producer. Mobile, on-site batch plants of every description and capacity can be found in use. Their configuration may vary due to specific mix requirements or other factors, but basically the cost involved in the manufacture of concrete mix with a mobile batch plant is founded on the following:

Fixed Expenses (Lump sum)

Site Acquisition   Rent, lease, or purchase of land

Site Preparation   Construct ramps, access roads, install fences and utilities, remove same

Move and Set up Plant   Also dismantle and remove

Plant Ownership   Depreciation for all plant, including mixer, storage bins, elevators, conveyors, generators, washers, etc.

Operating Expenses (Cubic yard)

Plant Operation To operate mixers, storage facilities, elevators, conveyors, generators, washers, etc.

Feed Aggregate to Plant For use of cranes, loaders, trucks, or other means to charge the plant with aggregates from the stockpile

Utilities The use of utilities for power, heat, refrigeration, water supply, or other services

Repairs Mechanic, parts, and supplies used to maintain plant, and other associated equipment

Material Expenses (Delivered)

Cement	Barrel or ton
Fine aggregate	Ton
Coarse aggregate	Ton
Water	Gallon
Ice	Cubic yard
Other	Cubic yard

Haul Expenses (Cubic yard)

Mix or Batch Trucks   A function of distances or time
Haul-Road Maintenance

Note that many of the operative units are in terms of common use. Their relationship to the cubic yard of concrete must be understood as explained earlier.

5.4 PLACING CONCRETE

When considering the cost for a construction activity, an estimator strives to find the best and least expensive way to do the job and, within the boundaries of the method chosen, must judge the labor and equipment requirements and their productive capability. This is not always so simple, particularly when many variables are involved as is the case with placing concrete into forms. Fortunately, all the variables that can influence the placing of concrete do not occur at one time, and it is possible to reasonably establish average concrete placing needs and predict productivity.

The factors that influence concrete placing fall into two categories: those that can be controlled and those that can only be anticipated.

1. Factors to Control
    · Type of equipment   · Access to pour
    · Capacity of equipment   · Communications

- Capacity of batch plant
- Sufficiency of labor skills
- Sufficiency of haul units
- Dimension of pour
- Form capacity
- Rate of pour
- Physical proximity of pour to grade

- Need for additives
- Supply of aggregates
- Supply of cement
- Supply of water
- Concrete mix overrun
- Crew preparation and cleanup time

2. Factors to Anticipate
   - Weather
   - Temperature of air
   - Temperature of concrete
   - Equipment failure
   - Plant failure

   - Early concrete set
   - Low slump
   - High slump
   - Workability of concrete
   - Truck driver failure

With these factors in mind, the estimator's principal need is the capability to, in some manner, relate the possibilities to the known conditions. Certainly, in performing an estimate of cost, one introduces those controllable factors proven to be effective and efficient; but beyond that, the estimator must anticipate the average effect of such elements as weather, equipment failure, or human failure on productivity.

Component Characteristics

Structural concrete was categorized in Chapter 1 by significant component parts. Each component involved differences requiring individual evaluation which might relate to variations in formwork, concrete placing techniques, finishing, or other construction features— individually or combined. The main point is that considering all the factors that affect cost, the best way to conclusively estimate their value is to keep the components separated throughout the estimation process.

The cost for placing concrete in heavy construction is a function of the series of conditions that exist at the time of placing. As previously mentioned, these conditions can be either controlled or anticipated. The estimator who can adeptly predict the needs for any concrete placing situation will, to a great extent, have fulfilled the purpose. To assist the estimator toward meeting this end, the structural concrete components are again listed and briefly described, and the placing characteristics for each are amplified.

Component	Description
Footing	Abutment support Pier (column or stem) support Wall support
Slab on grade	Box culvert invert Bridge approach slab Culvert apron Floor slab
Abutment 0 to 8 feet high	Backwall Beam seat Endwall Parapet Wingwall
Wall 0 to 8 feet high	Barrier Box culvert wall Grade beam Parapet Pier stem Retaining wall
Abutment over 8 feet high	Backwall Beam seat Endwall Wingwall
Wall over 8 feet high	Barrier Box tunnel wall Pier stem Retaining wall
Column	Beam support Floor support
Beam	Beam support Floor support
Deck	Bridge deck on beams Bridge sidewalk Floor slab on beams
Slab above grade	Arch Box culvert roof Box tunnel roof Heavy floor slabs

Footing

A footing pour generally involves a relatively large volume of concrete placed into an accessible form. Most often, a footing is located at or below grade and with fair access. Productivity can be high.

Footing pours can be made using any crew and equipment array so long as their size and capability are appropriate. The opportunity to pour concrete directly from the mix truck is greatest in many footing pours, but regardless of the method of concrete transferal, this type pour offers the best productivity.

Because footings are always placed on a graded subgrade and require only minimum dimensional tolerances, the yield (theoretical concrete measure versus concrete used) is often poor. The tendency to overexcavate is quite common, carpenters do not have to place footing forms with great dimensional care so long as the minimum requirements are met, and the strike-off of top surfaces is not so critical.

Slab on Grade

A slab on grade pour involves placing concrete over a large area of relatively thin section on a graded subgrade. Some applications are as follows:

· Inverts for box culverts   · Aprons at culvert ends

· Floor slabs for tunnels   · Floor slabs in buildings

· Approach slabs for bridges   · Pavements

Any of these applications requires care in setting forms to proper line and grade and great care in subgrade preparation as well as in surface strike-off and finishing.

The access to a slab on grade pour is usually good, and productivity should be relatively high regardless of the placing method used. When placing concrete, particular attention must be paid to set and workability of the mix. Mix ingredient design is extremely important in placing and wet surface finishing of the slab on grade. The concrete must be compacted, struck-off with a mechanical or hand screed, and finished before it sets. High air temperatures or rain can become a detriment and cause insurmountable problems to finishing.

Yields can vary greatly in a thin slab since very small dimensional variations make great volume differences. Most often owners concern themselves with minimum thicknesses, and there is a tendency to undergrade the subgrade in order to ensure the required thickness. The result is a somewhat poor yield. A good yield is a trade-off between the cost for good grade control and the cost for added concrete mix.

Abutment and Wall, 0 to 8 Feet High

In placing concrete, a bridge abutment is a series of interconnected walls forming what are known as bridge seats, wingwalls, backwalls, and parapets. To this extent an abutment pour is often similar to any wall pour of equal height, and therefore it is classified as one. The difference between the separately identified structural components lies primarily in their formwork. This category covers all wall pours up to and including 8 feet in height.

Wall pour access can be at, below, or above grade. When not otherwise restricted, concrete can be placed directly from the mix truck into the forms, using a chute or a combination of chute and hoppers. If direct placement is impossible, nearly any other available means can be used, recognizing that placing concrete into wall forms is often restricted by the narrow opening at the top of the form. There is seldom a concern for segregation of the concrete mix due to the height dropped or for pressures due to the rise of the mix against the forms, since these problems do not develop significantly in low profile wall pours.

Low walls are usually founded on a previously poured foundation. Because of the height, there is little need for erection of scaffolding to gain access. These conditions afford greater crew efficiency and productivity. High volume is not a factor in a low wall pour, but weather can be—particularly cold weather that requires heated aggregates and/or preheated forms.

Abutment and Wall, over 8 Feet High

In placing concrete, abutments and walls over 8 feet in height are similar to each other, just as are the lower abutments and walls. Their greater height affects concrete placing cost to an extent great enough to justify separate categories by height. Certainly, if a crew can no longer work from the ground, and all tools, equipment, and materials must be hoisted, the productivity will be affected.

The restrictions most affecting productivity when pouring concrete for high walls are: (1) staging, scaffolding, and ladders must be used as access; (2) materials must be hoisted, thus eliminating direct placement of concrete mix from a mix truck; (3) the rate of placing concrete into forms must be controlled so that the pressures against the forms do not exceed design capacity; and (4) tremies or elephant trunks may be necessary to transfer the mix to the bottom of the form without segregation. Obviously, good planning can overcome some of these restrictions. If the contractor plans on equipment with sufficient hoisting capacity, provides enough hoppers, builds safe and convenient access, and recognizes the formwork needs and capabilities, optimum productivity can be attained.

Column

In many ways, a column pour is the same as a wall pour in that the access and conveniences are similar and the crew and equipment applications are identical. The horizontal cross section of a column is relatively small compared to its height, with 6 feet usually being considered the maximum horizontal dimension. The height will vary greatly depending on the overall structure design.

Productivity in placing concrete into column forms is affected primarily by limited access and by the rise of the plastic mix in the forms. Access involves a single hopper or entrance point, and a rapid rise of plastic mix can create excessive pressures on the forms. Again, it takes good planning to realize optimum results. Yield in a column is usually very good, since the forms are constructed and held to close tolerances.

Beam

Beam pours differ slightly from wall or column pours in that form pressures do not usually reach critical stages. If a beam form support system design is adequate and planning is proper, placing the concrete mix is limited only by the form's location and the methods used.

Most often, dimensional tolerances for beams are such that a good yield is possible. Also, on bridge beams, the wet finishing of the beam seats is important, requiring very close tolerances.

Deck or Slab above Grade

Pouring an aerial slab of concrete encompasses nearly all of the same needs and cautions required for a slab on grade. The conditions are identical, except that the bottom surface is formed and supported above ground, and placing of mix directly from a truck is not possible.

With sufficient crew and good planning, however, productivity can be high.

Again, premature set and rain are to be avoided and sufficient finishing capability is most important. Yields are a direct function of closely held tolerances.

Placing Methods

A significant number of those controlled factors listed at the beginning of this section are associated with the very important matter of choosing a method for placing concrete. The choice, of course, will be a direct result of the estimator's knowledge and planning. The five most commonly applied methods for placing concrete into forms in heavy construction are the *direct, crane, conveyor, pump,* and *buggy* methods. A variation of one of these methods may at some point be the only choice for placing concrete, but more often than not, concrete can be placed by any one of several methods. It is left to the estimator to appraise the situation and recognize the importance of reasonable applications. For example, estimating the use of a concrete pump while an adequate crane sits idly by or figuring a crane that is inadequate for the job simply doesn't make sense. The most commonly applied methods will now be briefly described.

Direct

Direct placement of concrete mix from the transit mix truck (Figure 5.2) into the forms most often involves footings, slabs on grade, or low walls. Conditions must be such that the mix truck can be moved close to and above the forms to allow flow of mix from the discharge via a chute into the forms. The maximum horizontal distance that a mix can usually be transferred in this manner is 25 to 30 feet, with the average rate of discharge being $^3/_4$ to $1^1/_2$ cubic yards per minute, depending on mix consistency, rate of compaction, and many other possible constraints. Productivity is usually high.

Crane

Placing concrete mix with a crane and concrete bucket is probably the most commonly applied method in heavy construction. The reason, of course, is that cranes are versatile and available. Cranes lift heavy loads to great heights and can reach distances. Their use in handling heavy form panels and steel reinforcing and other materials is universal. It is only natural that they are also employed in the transfer of con-

Figure 5.2 Transit Mix Truck. (Construction Machinery Company.)

crete mix from the mix truck to the forms. This application may not, in every instance, seem to be the most practical or convenient, but utilization of equipment already on rental and on the project should certainly be a consideration. Generally, as long as the pour lies within the reach and lifting capacity of a crane, this method can be used.

The economy of using cranes in placing concrete is a function of the crane's ability to lift and transfer concrete mix at a satisfactory rate. Many cranes can swing concrete at a rate of 40 to 60 cubic yards per hour, depending on the size crane and bucket. There must be an assimilation of equipment and project needs. For instance, a 35-ton crane may reach and place concrete mix using a half-cubic-yard bucket, but economically, perhaps an 80-ton crane with a 2-cubic-yard bucket should be used, thereby saving considerably in crew and equipment time through increased productivity. When establishing concrete placing costs, an estimator will do well to recognize the broad scope of equipment applications for the project.

Cranes most commonly used for placing concrete mix in heavy construction are truck cranes (mechanical, truck mounted), crawler cranes (mechanical, track mounted), and hydraulic cranes (hydraulic, truck mounted, or self-contained, rubber tire unit).

Lifting and reaching capabilities for nearly all the normally expected applications can be had in any of these three types. With any
given crane capacity, the rental cost will vary, with crawler cranes
generally costing the least and hydraulic cranes the most. Each has
characteristics that are considered an advantage or a disadvantage—
depending on job conditions.

Truck Cranes Truck cranes (Figure 5.3) range in all sizes from 15 to
over 200 tons, and in boom length from 20 to over 200 feet. However,
except for special lifting applications, a truck crane of over 150-ton
capacity is seldom needed. These lifting and reach capabilities, combined with their mobility, fast swing and hoisting ability, make the
truck crane an ideal choice for many construction applications, including the placing of concrete. A truck crane does have some draw-
backs, in that a second person is often needed to drive the truck when
the machine is moved, and often the gantry must be lowered in order
to get under bridges or low, overhead wires. Long moves usually require removal of a portion of the boom.

Figure 5.3 Truck Crane. (Clark Equipment Company.)

Crawler Cranes These cranes (Figure 5.4) have an even broader range of sizes than do truck cranes, but again, capacities of over 150 tons are not commonly required. As with truck cranes, crawler cranes can hoist and swing a concrete bucket with good control, quickly and safely. One unique advantage with crawler cranes is that they can be operated from locations inaccessible to any other type crane. With laterally extended, long marine tracks and wide pads, a crawler crane can operate on very soft ground with considerable stability. Crawler cranes cannot be economically *walked* long distances since they are slow-moving. Often, long moves require that a crawler crane be loaded onto a lowboy truck and hauled. Larger cranes sometimes require complete disassembly in order to meet legal size and weight regulations for moving.

Hydraulic Cranes These cranes (Figure 5.5) have come into popular use in heavy construction for a very good reason: they are extremely mobile. Such features as the telescopic boom, hydraulic outriggers,

Figure 5.4 Crawler Crane. (Koehring Corporation.)

Figure 5.5 Hydraulic Crane. (Koehring Corporation.)

and low profile, combined with quick maneuverability, often override the fact they are slower to hoist or swing. The range of capacities available in hydraulic cranes is nearly as great as with mechanical cranes. Sizes of from 12 to 80 tons are in common use. For pouring concrete, a hydraulic crane is often too slow and expensive, but its use for this purpose is often overridden by its many positive features.

Conveyor

Conveyors have come into popular use in placing concrete because they are mobile, relatively inexpensive to purchase and operate, and capable of transferring concrete mix as rapidly as by any other method. They are used both independently and in conjunction with other placing equipment such as cranes or buggies; however, ideally they are best suited to direct feed from a mix truck.

There are three types of conveyors used in placing concrete today: portable, feeder, and spreader.

Portable Conveyors These conveyors (Figure 5.6) are independently powered, self-driven machines capable of short lift, short reach applications; they are usually limited to lengths of not more than 60 feet and heights of up to 35 feet. The average rate at which concrete can be transferred with a 16-inch portable conveyor can range (depending on belt speed and power) from 15 to 90 cubic yards per hour. Productivity is usually limited by such factors as availability of mix trucks, capacity of forms, slump, and interruptions for moves. As a result, the average productivity seldom reaches above the level of 40 cubic yards per hour. With proper access, the setup time for a portable conveyor is short and can be accomplished without towing or other assistance. Since reach is limited, it is often necessary to move the portable conveyor several times during a pour. Such moves will cause no appreciable interruption to the pour if surface conditions adjacent to the pour are good and the conveyor can propel itself to a new location. Portable conveyors are equipped with discharge hoppers and chutes or tremies that assist the spotting of concrete mix.

Feeder Conveyor Systems These systems (Figure 5.7) consist of a series of belt conveyors which, working together, can transfer high volumes of wet concrete mix over a long distance without segregation. They are most frequently employed to pour bridge decks or other large components where the uninterrupted flow of concrete can be had. The system's conveyors, each 30 to 40 feet long, travel on a track and are so interconnected that the overall system can be shortened or lengthened while in use—and without interruption of concrete flow. A feeder conveyor system may be charged directly from the mix truck

Figure 5.6 Portable Conveyor. (Morgen Manufacturing Company.)

Figure 5.7 Feeder Conveyor. (Morgen Manufacturing Company.)

or by other means. The discharge is usually into some type of spreading conveyor. The average transfer rate of a feeder conveyor will vary from 50 to 125 cubic yards per hour. In terms of elapsed time, however, the productivity is usually much less than that.

Spreader Conveyors These conveyors (Figure 5.8) carry out the function of distributing the concrete mix discharged from the principal placing conveyor or other placing equipment. There are two types of spreader conveyors: radial and side discharge.

The *radial spreader conveyor* distributes concrete over an area of up to 30 feet in radius. It is simply a swinging, cantilevered belt conveyor capable of extending or retracting itself to suit reach requirements. It is limited in that it is not easily moved during a pour, and it cannot always be positioned to reach all points in a pour.

The *side discharge spreader conveyor* is particularly useful for placing concrete over large areas such as bridge decks, pavement slabs, or other massive structural components, since it distributes the mix evenly to the entire area of the pour. It operates by means of a traveling diverter that discharges the concrete mix over the side of the belt. Any method can be employed to feed the spreader. They are available in lengths up to 100 feet and with belt sizes of 16 and 24 inches.

Pump

The pumping of concrete mix is growing in popularity as new and improved pumps are developed. Three types of concrete pumps are in general use: the piston pump, the squeeze pump, and the pneumatic pump. The piston pump is by far the most popular because of its ability to handle stiff mixes with larger aggregate sizes.

Concrete pumps have a great advantage when distance, height, or access are a problem. They are invaluable in tunnel work. They can also be invaluable for pouring long, unreachable bridge decks. Installation of a long *slick line (feed pipeline)* in such applications is somewhat cumbersome, but setup of a pump is fairly simple and quick. The major problem with concrete pumps is that they are expensive to maintain in good repair. They are also highly vulnerable when subjected to improperly mixed concrete or concrete that has stiffened because of too slow delivery or too many trucks waiting. A inexperienced operator who does not stay in touch with the placing crew needs and plant delivery rate can also create problems. The operator

Figure 5.8 Spreader Conveyor. (Morgen Manufacturing Company.)

Figure 5.9 Truck-Mounted Piston-Type Concrete Pump. (Morgen Manufacturing Company.)

must also be aware that if the mix doesn't remain consistent, friction in the pipeline may stop the flow.

Piston Pumps These pumps (Figure 5.9) operate by pushing concrete from a filled cylinder into a pipeline (4 to 8 inches in diameter), thereby forcing the concrete toward the discharge end with each repeated stroke and cylinderful. Distances of up to 1500 feet horizontally or 500 feet vertically have been reached with a piston pump. With two pistons (as with most pumps), a steady flow of concrete can be had at the discharge. If fed steadily, and if all other conditions are

Figure 5.10 Truck-Mounted Squeeze-Type Concrete Pump. (Challenge-Cook Bros., Inc.)

proper, a 5-inch pump can produce 100 cubic yards per hour through a 200-foot line, but on the average, a production of from 40 to 50 cubic yards per hour is more realistic.

Squeeze Pumps These pumps (Figure 5.10) have similar capabilities, except that they do not handle as harsh mixes as the piston pump. The pump actually squeezes concrete mix into the discharge pipeline (3 to 5 inches in diameter) by passing hydraulically pressured rollers over a flexible hose filled with concrete mix.

Both the piston and squeeze pump can be obtained in truck-mounted, trailer-mounted, or skid-mounted models. The truck-mounted units are generally equipped with folding hydraulically operated booms, which allow the operator to spot concrete at distances exceeding (in some cases) 100 feet vertically or horizontally.

Pneumatic Pumps Pneumatic pumps employ compressed air that forces the mix from a receiving chamber to a discharge chamber from which it is deposited. Pneumatic pumps are more likely to be applied to special jobs, such as gunite work, shotcrete, or other fine-mix applications.

Buggy
Concrete buggies of two types have been used in construction for many years: hand operated or powered. The choice is a function of the contractor's need.

Hand Operated Buggies These buggies are useful for low production at short distances. If walkways are level and smooth, an 8-cubic-foot buggy can be used to transfer as much as 5 cubic yards of concrete per hour to forms as far as 100 feet away. If the distance is doubled, the transfer rate is 3 cubic yards.

Gasoline Powered Buggies These buggies (Figure 5.11) also available in diesel or propane powered models, come in sizes ranging from 10 to 28 cubic feet. They are more suited to greater productivity and to greater distances. The 28-cubic-foot power buggy, for instance, can move as much as 20 cubic yards per hour a distance of 500 feet, or 15 cubic yards per hour a distance of 1000 feet. The power buggy can negotiate some slight grades, but generally it would be most suited to a relatively good, level travel way as would be the case with a bridge deck pour.

Figure 5.11 Powered Concrete Buggy. (The Prime-
Mover Company.)

Placing Crews

Labor is the greatest cost factor in placing concrete. Estimating the cost for labor requires a clear understanding of crew needs and the realities of productivity in any given situation.

From a cost viewpoint, a crew begins placing concrete at the time it moves to the site of a pour to set up, and finishes when it has dismantled, cleaned its tools, and is ready to move on to the next assignment. The cost is, therefore, based on the elapsed time—or, all time from beginning to end of their involvement. Since elapsed time is real, and the resulting crew cost is real, the hourly productivity applied to any hourly crew cost must be based on performance, adjusted for elapsed time, if the unit cost is to be real.

Another point is that, in estimating the cost for labor to place concrete, it is difficult at times to imagine the many people needed for the required work. That is, it is easy to forget the laborer who is always running after spreaders or looking for another extension cord. It is also easy to forget that the service truck driver spends time moving in tools, concrete buckets, and other equipment for the pour.

With the foregoing points in mind, it is obvious that the cost estimating process must include both an average hourly crew makeup that reflects all time spent, as well as a comparative productivity that reflects the elapsed time taken. To assist in understanding this concept, refer to Table 5.1, which lists each of the structural components and the concrete placing methods that may apply to each component. With each method, preparatory time is given along with an average hourly productivity rate. From these, a productivity rate based on elasped time is determined and listed, along with the average makeup for a crew.

In general terms, a crew for placing concrete consists of: a foreman who is in charge of placing operations; a carpenter who ensures form stability and can do any necessary form repairs while the pour is underway; and laborers, who are the backbone of a concrete placing crew, and whose duties include the following:

· Spot the concrete chute
· Place crane hook on concrete bucket
· Dump concrete bucket

· Operate vibrators
· Shovel concrete in the forms

· Clean conveyors
· Clean buckets
· Clean tools

· Operate buggy
· Spot concrete pump discharge
· Guide concrete mix truck into position
· Unload and carry supplies and tools
· Shovel concrete along a chute
· Place any curing protection applied at time of pour
· Move scaffolds and walkways
· Move conveyors

In addition, there are finishers to perform wet finishing of exposed concrete surfaces; truck drivers to haul necessary buckets, tools, parts, equipment, and other supplies to the placing crew; and equipment operators to operate cranes, conveyors, pumps, etc.

Support Equipment

There is a substantial array of important supportive concrete placing equipment from which a placing crew must draw if it is to satisfactorily complete the pouring, compaction, and wet finishing of structural concrete. The contractor may or may not choose to amortize this expensive equipment, but the cost is to be recognized and included directly or indirectly in the total cost estimate.

Concrete Buckets

There are two basic types of concrete placing buckets: standard (bottom dump or upright) and laydown.

Standard Buckets These buckets (Figure 5.12) are the most commonly used type. They are round in shape and discharge the concrete mix through a single or double gate at the bottom. The gate may be equipped with pneumatic controls, or it may be operated manually. Sizes range from ½ to 8 cubic yards, but it is seldom that a bucket larger than 4 cubic yards is called for.

Laydown Buckets These buckets (Figure 5.13) are rectangular in shape; they lay down when being charged and hang upright when being discharged. They offer advantages in that the bucket is easily accessible for charging from a mix truck, regardless of bucket size, and the side discharge gate is easy to view and aim when pouring into narrow openings at the tops of walls or columns. Similar sizes and gate operating options are available as for upright buckets.

For concrete pours of great size, two buckets of either type are generally applied: one being dumped while the other is being filled. This procedure requires moving the crane hook from one bucket bail to the other. Automatic hooks are available for use with the larger bucket sizes to facilitate moving the hook.

Figure 5.12 Upright Concrete Bucket.
(Erie Strayer Company.)

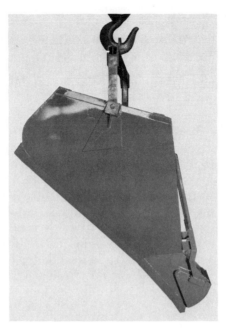

Figure 5.13 Laydown Concrete Bucket.
(Erie Strayer Company.)

Vibrators

Vibrators (Figure 5.14) are used to compact concrete, to displace trapped air, and to otherwise assist the filling of all voids in the form. The number and size of vibrators required for any one application is in part a function of the rate at which the concrete is placed, the size of the aggregate, and the concrete slump. Generally, small one-operator vibrators ($3/4$ to $1 1/2$ inches) will compact from 5 to 15 cubic yards of concrete per hour. Larger vibrators ($1 1/2$ to 6 inches), handled by one or two operators, can compact 15 to 70 cubic yards per hour.

Three types of vibrators are in popular use: *electric, gasoline (or diesel)*, and *air operated*. The electric vibrator is most popular for its versatility: domestic or portable power sources can be chosen. Gasoline power vibrators are second in popularity. Their reliability is not always as satisfactory, but they are portable and effective, and do not depend on any other outside source for power. Air vibrators depend on a compressor, which may or may not always be cost-effective. Larger-size air vibrators are particularly effective with massive, high rate pours.

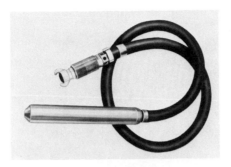

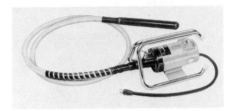

**Figure 5.14 Vibrators (a) Air; (b) Electric; (c) Gaso-
line.** (Wacker Corporation.)

Mechanical Finishers

A finisher (Figure 5.15) strikes-off the concrete at exactly the right grade and then finishes and seals the surface, leaving a minimum amount of hand-finishing.

Mechanical finishers are widely used today for bringing concrete surfaces to within the strictest of dimensional tolerances. The several

Figure 5.15 Mechanical Finisher. (Bid-Well Corporation.)

models available on the market are adept at finishing bridge decks, pavement slabs, or floor slabs. Some are even capable of finishing sloped paving. Usually, mechanical finishers can be adjusted to fit crown dimensions or other nonplaned surfaces.

5.5 CURING CONCRETE

Curing impedes the loss of water and sustains hydration, thereby assuring that the concrete will reach its greatest strength. It is very important that concrete be properly cured, particularly during the first 7 to 10 days after being poured, when strength increases so rapidly. Initial application of curing protection generally takes place immediately after concrete sets or immediately after forms are removed. Therefore, placing the protection is often the responsibility of either the concrete placing crew or the form stripping crew. Continued maintenance of protection is a specifically assigned task; therefore, it can be said that the cost for curing includes all materials used, plus any continued maintenance expense. There are a number of methods used for curing concrete, some of which are described next.

Liquid Curing Compound

A 100 percent resin-base liquid membrane–forming compound is in common use as a curing protection for all types of concrete structures.

Usually, a single application of 1 gallon per 150 to 200 square feet is required; at times, a second application may be required.

Liquid curing compounds are convenient because, once applied, there is no further maintenance or removal cost. Some caution is warranted, however, if surfaces are soon to receive another application of concrete—as would be the case with a construction joint. Unless cleaned off, the curing compound would act as a bond-breaker. Cleaning might involve wire brushing or sandblasting.

Water

From a quality point of view, a continuous application of water over concrete is an ideal curing protection. If the concrete cannot be flooded, sprinklers or soakers may be installed. Often, regardless of cure method chosen, owners require the contractor to wet the exposed surfaces with an atomized spray of water until the concrete becomes sufficiently hard.

Burlap Blanket

Using burlap blankets in conjunction with a water application is another effective means of protection. A blanket is generally bound in two or more layers and can hold moisture well, requiring wetting down only one or two times a day, depending on the atmospheric conditions. If burlap blankets are to last very long, they must be kept clean and dry when not in use.

Polyethylene Sheet

A polyethylene sheet properly applied can create an airtight seal that will prevent the evaporation of moisture from concrete. There is little maintenance cost with this application if installation is done with care. However, polyethylene is very susceptible to wind damage and to deterioration from prolonged sun exposure and will therefore require some maintenance and replacement.

Combined Polyethylene and Burlap Blanket

These blankets cost more, but offer the moisture retaining benefits of both burlap and polyethylene.

Straw

Straw, kept moist, is another effective way to protect concrete. Straw, however, is a fire hazard and is susceptible to wind damage. Straw can be used in combination with polyethylene, reducing the need for continued wetting down.

Sand Cover

A wet layer of sand 2 to 3 inches thick is yet another cure protection method that may be effective. Sand is not always readily available or inexpensive, and there is the cost of placing and removal to consider.

Insulated Blanket

During the winter months when temperatures go below 40 degrees Fahrenheit, it is often a requirement that concrete be protected. If external heaters are not in use, a commonly applied method of protecting exposed surfaces is the insulated curing blanket. These blankets are expensive to purchase and maintain, but they will hold in moisture and the heat of hydration.

5.6 FINISHING CONCRETE

Finishing concrete can involve one of many possible requirements, as explained in Chapter 1. Each of these finishing requirements entails a cost that can vary, depending on contractor planning and the nature and location of the surface to be finished. For instance, if a rubbed finish is required, a contractor would be wise to plan on doing the finishing immediately after the forms are stripped because, as the concrete surface gets harder, the effort required becomes greater and, therefore, more expensive.

In general, finishing can be identified in two categories: wet finishing and dry finishing. These two categories are now explained.

Wet Finishing

Wet finishing means that the concrete surface is finished before it finally sets. This refers to the usually horizontal surfaces of a pour such as a bridge deck surface, the top of a wall, or a beam seat. Wet finishing is performed by finishers who work with the concrete placing crew. Their cost is usually included with the concrete placing crew cost. Except in cases of very close tolerance requirements, there is seldom further dry finishing work to be done on a wet finished sur-

Figure 5.16 Rotary Finisher. (Whiteman Manufacturing Company.)

face; when there is, it is usually corrective work or close tolerance grinding.

Wet finishing of small surfaces involves the use of small hand tools such as a float, bull float, screed, trowel, or edger. The large surfaces of bridge decks or floor slabs are often finished with a combination of small tools and large machines, such as the mechanical finisher described earlier, or a rotary finisher.

A rotary finisher is a gasoline operated machine that turns three or four trowel blades in a circular motion, thereby finishing the surface. It is used after the concrete surface achieves initial set and can support the operator, and before it has hardened. The cost for rotary finishing may be considered separately and not part of the placing cost. (See Figure 5.16.)

Dry Finishing

Dry finishing of concrete takes place after the concrete has set and hardened. Usually it involves surfaces that will be exposed to view and must take on a uniform, specified appearance. Dry finishing involves one of the following:

· Float finishing   · Sandblast finishing
· Rub finishing   · Tooled finishing
· Burlap finishing

Each of these finishes involves an expenditure of labor, equipment, and material, the amount of which depends on the degree of difficulty of the finishing job. Rub finishing a bridge pier beam, for instance, is much more expensive than rubbing a low wall that can be reached entirely from the ground.

Although there are innumerable cost possibilities, the principal differences in finishing cost depend on whether or not the work is being done from the ground. When working from a ladder, scaffold, staging, or lift, a person is cautious, less dexterous, and therefore, significantly slower. Table 5.2 provides a listing of labor and equipment expectations for the various listed finishes, as well as the applications and productivity for each.

5.7 COMMON CONCRETE COST

Structural concrete construction cost, regardless of component or pay item, always involves expenditures for items that are not easily identified with any single component or phase of work but are necessary and supportive to all concrete work. It also involves a number of small expenditures for items such as additives or special treatments that are often too insignificant to evaluate by separate component or phase. These expenditures are treated as common to all concrete work and they are each evaluated under the single identifying item called *Common Concrete Cost (CCC)*. The expenses incurred under the heading of Common Concrete Cost are now briefly described.

Cure

Estimators often find that the cost for curing concrete (described in Section 5.5) does not warrant a breakdown by individual component and is evaluated with greater ease as a single, all-encompassing task. The cost includes expenses for all maintenance and materials.

Joints

This item includes expenses for all special joint applications or treatments. Such items as elastomeric joint material, rubber waterstop, and expansion material are included. Generally, their installation cost is included in the form erection cost. Sandblasting or waterblasting of joints or sealing are included in this item, and their expense should also include separate consideration for the labor and equipment expense involved.

Waterproof or Dampproof

The cost for surface treatments such as waterproofing or dampproofing (when not associated with a significantly large item that is best identified separately) can be included as a Common Concrete Cost item. For example, wall joints are often sealed with a 2-foot-wide waterproofing strip, or only a small portion of a wall received a dampproofing application.

Sandblast

At times, specifications require that surfaces be cleaned or finished by sandblasting. If this expense is not extensive enough to consider as a separate item identified with a particular concrete component, it may be included as an item common to all concrete.

Embedded Items

This expense can be significant. It includes the installation of incidental materials such as anchors, sleeves, conduits, drains, expansion dams, curbing, and flashing.

Additives

Designers of certain concrete mixes may optionally require additives such as retarders or accelerators. There is an add-on cost for such items that can be included as a Common Concrete Cost.

Grout

Specifications often require that construction joints be grouted before placing concrete against them. The added grout cost can be included as a Common Concrete Cost.

Move

This item includes all expenses for equipment and material transportation not included directly with another cost item. It may include the expenses for a service truck and driver to move lumber or for a lowboy to move a crane. Generally, it involves only on-site moving expense. If the estimator chooses to include these moving expenses directly with the various concrete cost items, only that portion of the expenses that was not included elsewhere should be included here.

Repairs

There is always something that needs repairing. It may be ladders, scaffolding, forms, tools, or small equipment. Maintaining these items in good repair requires an expenditure that most often cannot be considered an equipment repair expense and thus cannot be included anywhere except in the Common Concrete Cost.

Engineering

Engineering expense, if not included as an indirect cost item, may become a part of this universal concrete cost. It would then include all field layout and related engineering services necessary to control the concrete work.

Cold Weather

The added expenses involved for heating aggregates, heating water, heating forms, insulating forms, or other measures taken for the protection of concrete from low temperatures are included here.

Power

Power for vibrators, saws, grinders, and other tools is commonly supplied for all concrete work through the use of generators or public supply sources. This item includes all expenses for power installation, supply and/or equipment not included elsewhere.

Ramps and Scaffolding

Ramps, scaffolding, staging, and many other devices are frequently employed for easy, all-purpose access to the work. The expense for the supply, installation, and removal of these devices is included in this Common Concrete Cost item.

Testing

At times, specifications require that the contractor maintain a quality control program for structural concrete. This requires retaining an outside testing agency, or employing an in-house quality control technician. If a technician is used, it also requires the purchase of testing equipment. Testing expense may also be estimated as a contingency safeguard against some anticipated technical problem.

Table 5.1 Placing Concrete

Component	Method	Yield (%)	Preparatory time (hr)	Rate (cy/hr) Actual	Rate (cy/hr) Elapsed
Footing 25–100 cy	Direct	92	$1/2$	35–45	22–23
	Crane		1	30–40	15–26
	Convey		1	35–45	15–28
	Pump		1	30–40	15–26
	Buggy (3)		1	30–40	15–26
Slab on grade 15–40 cy	Direct	92	$1/2$	30–40	16–24
	Crane		1	25–35	10–17
	Convey		1	35–45	11–20
	Pump		1	25–35	10–17
	Buggy (3)		$1^1/4$	30–40	10–17
Abutment, 0–8' or wall, 0–8' 5–15 cy	Direct	96	$3/4$	15–25	5–10
	Crane		$1^1/4$	10–20	3–7
	Convey		1	10–20	3–7
	Pump		1	10–20	3–7
Abutment, 8'+ 10–60 cy	Crane	96	$1^1/2$	15–25	5–13
	Convey		$1^3/4$	15–25	4–13
	Pump		$1^1/4$	15–25	5–14
Wall, 8'+ 20–80 cy	Crane	96	$1^1/2$	15–25	8–15
	Convey		$1^3/4$	15–25	7–14
	Pump		$1^1/4$	15–25	8–15
Column 5–20 cy	Crane	98	$1^1/2$	5–10	2–5
	Convey		$1^3/4$	5–10	2–5
	Pump		$1^1/4$	5–10	2–5
Beam 10–30 cy	Crane	96	$1^1/4$	15–25	6–11
	Convey		$1^1/2$	20–30	5–11
	Pump		1	20–30	7–13
Deck 40–100 cy	Crane	94	$1^3/4$	20–30	12–17
	Convey		2	25–35	12–18
	Pump		$1^1/2$	25–35	14–20
	Buggy (4)		2	35–45	13–22
Slab above grade 20–80 cy	Crane	94	$1^3/4$	20–30	8–16
	Convey		2	30–40	8–19
	Pump		$1^1/2$	25–35	9–19
	Buggy (4)		2	35–45	8–20

			Crew				
Foreman	Carpenter	Finisher	Vibrator	Laborer	Operator	Oiler	Truck driver
1			2	4			1/4
1			2	4	1	1	1/4
1			2	5	1		1/2
1			2	5	1		1/4
1			2	6			1/2
1		2	2	4			1/4
1		2	2	5	1	1	1/4
1		2	2	5	1		1/2
1		2	2	5	1		1/4
1		2	2	6			1/2
1	1	1/2	1	3			1/4
1	1	1/2	1	4	1	1	1/4
1	1	1/2	1	4	1		1/2
1	1	1/2	1	4	1		1/4
1	1	1/2	2	5	1	1	1/2
1	1	1/2	2	5	1		3/4
1	1	1/2	2	5	1		1/2
1	1	1/2	2	5	1	1	1/2
1	1	1/2	2	5	1		3/4
1	1	1/2	2	5	1		1/2
1	1		1	5	1	1	1/2
1	1		1	5	1		3/4
1	1		1	5	1		1/2
1	1	1	2	5	1	1	1/4
1	1	1	2	5	1		1/2
1	1	1	2	5	1		1/4
1	1	3	3	6	1	1	1/2
1	1	3	3	6			3/4
1	1	3	3	6	1		1/2
1	1	4	3	7			1/2
1	1	3	3	6	1	1	1/2
1	1	3	3	6	2		3/4
1	1	3	3	6	1		1/2
	1	3	3	7			1/2

Table 5.2   Concrete Surface Treatment

Treatment	Crew				A & W* 0–8′	A & W* 8′ +
	Fore-man	Fin-isher	La-borer	Truck driver		
Finish:						
Rub	1/4	2	1	1/4	60–75	50–65
Burlap	1/4	2	1	1/4	120–150	100–130
Hammer	1/8	2	1/4	1/8	25–35	20–30
Sandblast	1/4	1	1	1/4	100–140	
Sandblast	1/4	1	1 1/2	1/4		90–130
Grind (float)	1/4	2	1/2	1/4		
Grind (float)	1/4	1	1	1/4		
Rotary Trowel	1/8	1	1/4	1/8		
Application:						
Waterproof 2 ply	1		4	1/2	100–150	
Waterproof 2 ply	1		4	1/2		90–140
Waterproof 3 ply	1		4	1/2	90–140	
Waterproof 3 ply	1		5	1/2		80–130
Dampproof	1		2	1/4	100–150	
(brush − 1 coat)	1		3	1/4		90–140
	1		4	1/4		
Linseed Oil	1/8		1 1/2	1/8	500–750	
(spray − 1 coat)	1/4		2	1/8		400–650
Epoxy Paint	1/8		2	1/4	90–110	
(brush − 1 coat)	1/2		3	1/4		80–100

* A & W = abutment and wall.

Productivity (sf/hr)					
Column	Beam	Fascia-parapet	Deck & slab	Abutment seat	Pier seat
40–55	40–55	55–70			
70–100	70–100	90–120			
10–20	10–20	20–30			
60–100	50–90	70–110			
				15–30	10–25
			200–500		
			200–400		
			150–200		
			140–190		
			200–250		
			500–750		
200–400	200–400	400–600			
60–80	60–80	70–90			

6

ILLUSTRATION OF A COST ESTIMATE

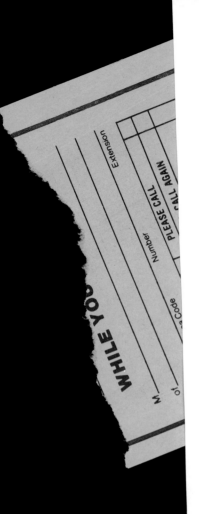

6.1 THE ESTIMATING GOAL

Estimating construction cost, as a fundamental business practice, is one in which many participate—and one on which many rely. Government agencies and private consulting firms often estimate cost as a basis for construction fund appropriations; contractors most frequently estimate cost for competitive bidding purposes. Survival of both government and private sectors depends on their ability to repeatedly produce reasonably accurate cost estimates. With today's broadened markets and ever-expanding technology in construction, there is no doubt that the estimator must constantly strive toward improved understanding of the estimating art. It is in this regard that this author has adopted the goal of improving the estimator's understanding—as well as the evaluation of structural concrete construction.

Thus far, all of the fundamental factors that significantly affect the cost of structural concrete have been explained. Now, an illustration of a method for estimating and assembling cost would be of greatest value to the reader. Therefore, returning to the hypothetical Highway 1 Project introduced in Chapter 2, and using the information and computations provided there, the complete illustration of a structural concrete cost estimate can get underway with very few preliminaries. It is recommended that the estimator first review Chapter 2 and the plans and specifications for Highway 1 to become familiar with the project and take-off material. As the illustration develops, further specific references will be made to various subjects and tables presented throughout the book.

6.2 ORGANIZATION OF A COST ESTIMATE

The estimator usually organizes any cost estimate in a way that provides easy reference for purposes of review or adjustment. Without a well-organized method, the chances for omission and error are multiplied. Estimating structural concrete cost, in particular, demands a systematized assembly of information and computations, and before continuing with the cost estimate for the Highway 1 Project concrete, a procedural outline should be made.

All estimates involve the following significant parts:

1. Plans and specifications
2. Take-off
3. Cost data
4. Cost estimates
5. Summary of cost

Each of these parts contains information absolutely essential to the estimate and, in the order listed, serves as the basis for an outline that describe all features of the estimate. Applying this concept, the following outline for a structural concrete cost estimate has been developed.

OUTLINE FOR A STRUCTURAL CONCRETE COST ESTIMATE

I. Plans and Specifications

II. Take-off
- A. Investigative Material
  1. Plans and Specifications
  2. Project Site Visit
  3. Test Results
- B. Quantity Take-Off
  1. Quantity Computations
  2. Summary of Quantity Take-Off
- C. Preliminary Progress Schedule
- D. Supplier and Subcontractor Contacts

III. Cost Data
- A. Wage Rates
  1. Basic Wage Rates and Fringe Benefits
  2. The Work Week
  3. Effects of Escalation
  4. Effects of Premium and Lost Time
  5. Effects of Insurance and Tax Expense
  6. Bid Wage Rates
- B. Equipment Rates
  1. Ownership
  2. Operating Expense
- C. Materials Prices

1. Additives	13. Epoxy Paint
2. Aggregates	14. Expansion Dams
3. Anchors	15. Expansion Material
4. Backfill	16. Forms
5. Cement	17. Form Liners
6. Concrete Mix	18. Form Lumber
7. Conduits	19. Form Ties
8. Cure Compound	20. Insulation
9. Cure Blankets	21. Joint Seals
10. Curbing	22. Linseed Oil
11. Dampproofing	23. Plywood
12. Drain Pipe	24. Polyethylene

25. Railing
26. Scaffolding
27. Shoring
28. Sleeves

29. Special Tools
30. Reinforcing Steel
31. Waterstop
32. Waterproof

D. Subcontractor Quotations
E. Other Cost Data

IV. Cost Estimates
  A. Form Cost
    1. Form Utilization Plan
    2. Labor and Equipment
    3. Lumber and Hardware
    4. Architectural Form Lining
  B. Shoring
    1. Labor and Equipment
    2. Material
  C. Concrete Placing Cost
    1. Labor and Equipment
    2. Concrete Mix
  D. Concrete Finishing Cost
    1. Labor and Equipment
    2. Material
  E. Special Applications
    1. Labor and Equipment
    2. Materials
  F. Common Concrete Cost

1. Cure
2. Joints
3. Waterproof
4. Dampproof
5. Sandblast
6. Embedded Items
7. Additives
8. Grout

9. Move
10. Repairs
11. Engineering
12. Cold Weather
13. Power
14. Ramps and Scaffolding
15. Testing
16. Other

V. Summary of Cost

Note that this outline will serve as an excellent checklist for all structural concrete cost estimates.

6.3 PROJECT REVIEW AND BUSINESS CONSIDERATIONS

The estimator will recall that Highway 1 is a $1/3$-mile-long highway construction project with an 18-month completion requirement, involving four structures identified as:

Structure 1 Reinforced concrete box culvert
Structure 2 Retaining walls (2)
Structure 3 Three-span simple I-beam bridge
Structure 4 Three-span girder bridge

The concrete for these structures is to be of three classes, each of which represents a bid item for which a cost is to be developed. The classes are as follows:

Class A Concrete Decks, sidewalks, parapets
Class B Concrete Substructures, wall stems, box culvert
Class C Concrete Footings

The take-off for Highway 1, as illustrated in Chapter 2, provided an excellent description of the structural concrete work from an qualitative and quantitative viewpoint. All necessary aspects of the work were identified—including the external conditions that could impact the concrete cost and project progress. Before continuing with the cost estimate, there is one other matter worth mentioning: the *business considerations* that bid preparation involves.

Contractors do not actually always bid every project that they could—or every project for which they prepare an estimate. A contractor with any interest at all will obtain plans and specifications and investigate enough to gain a reasonably clear understanding of the project's needs and how those needs fit into the corporate backlog. This is a business matter in which many estimators find themselves involved, and for which many are held responsible. The completion (or near completion) of a take-off usually signals the best time for this type of consideration.

In actual practice, the decision to submit a bid is not always clear-cut. Often, the reasons are based on business considerations such as the following:

1. How would the project fit into the overall corporate backlog?
2. Does the project offer attractive cash flow prospects?
3. Are the specific resources required to do the job available?
4. What are the risks?

Without further discussion, it is pointed out that the Highway 1 Project involves (1) the volume of work needed and the opportunity to meet planned, moderate growth; (2) cash flow prospects that are not particularly attractive in that early revenue producing items such as clearing and excavation are offset by early investments in bridge materials, steel, and earth support systems; (3) continuous use of resources in labor, supervision, and equipment that are available within the company; and (4) some risk in that the potential for high water in the stream is greatest in planning to build and maintain a temporary roadway and bridge across the stream, along with associated earth cofferdams around the pier excavations of Structure 4. It is decided that a bid should be prepared since the risks are not great and growth and continuity are prevalent factors.

6.4 COST DATA

The data required for estimating the structural concrete cost will consist of wage rates, equipment rates, materials prices, and subcontractor prices. Establishment of this data is of great importance, and considerable care must be taken in its assembly.

Wage Rates

Highway I will be an open-shop project if the bid being prepared is successful. Moderately strong local unions have had an effect on open-shop wage levels in the area to the extent that in many ways the wage rates and benefits for the two are similar. In this case, many of the key personnel for the project would transfer from another of the contractor's projects located in the area, making complete reliance on unknown segments of the open-shop labor market unnecessary.

The basis for all direct labor expense to be used in the estimate will be the *Bid Wage Rates*. Bid Wage Rates reflect the effects of anticipated escalation, premium and lost time, and insurance and tax expense on the basic wages and fringe benefits as they exist at the time of bid. They will now be developed.

Basic Wage Rates and Fringe Benefits

The basic wage rate and fringe benefits represent what will be paid to a worker (or, expended in the worker's behalf) for each straight-time hour worked at the time of bid. In this case, there are disparities between the predetermined wages and fringes provided for in the specifications and those currently being paid to the open-shop employees in the area. The choice of the *basic* rates, therefore, is a matter of deciding which rates must prevail, remembering that the predetermined rates set the minimum that can be paid to any employee on the project. Figure 6.1 is the Wage Rate Determination computation sheet showing the predetermined rates as well as those that are currently prevalent in the open-shop market. Considering the disparities mentioned, the basic wage rates and fringe benefits that will be used for this estimate are circled. It is understood that the contractor provides fringe benefits to all employees at a fixed rate, and any surpluses that result due to higher specification requirements must be paid directly to the employee.

Work Week

It is planned that the structural concrete work will be performed on a 40-hour-per-week basis, with Saturdays being considered available to work at straight-time wage rates if time is lost during the week for inclement weather or a holiday. Recognizing that in practice the average worker gets some overtime (even on a 40 hour per week project), a judgment must be made as to the average number of hours per week that would be representative for each labor classification on this project. Figure 6.1 shows the results of this determination. The hours chosen consider, for instance, that (1) the concrete placing crew will occasionally work overtime in order to complete all work associated with a pour; (2) placing deck concrete involves great potential for overtime; (3) formwork involves very little overtime, except in critical situations; (4) crane operators do maintenance work on their cranes after hours, thereby adding at least 2 hours each week; (5) foremen will work hours similar to those of their crews but without premium pay, since they are salaried; and (6) finishers are frequently the last to leave a pour, resulting in a tendency to work more overtime.

Effects of Escalation

Each July 1 most local construction firms consider the adjustment of employee wages to meet changes in the cost of living and to provide merit recognition to those who have earned it. Consideration of the current inflationary trends indicates that these increases will probably be 8 percent for 1983. Since July 1 is very close to the midpoint of the proposed structural concrete work, the average wage escalation is therefore set at 4 percent. Fringe benefits will also increase in cost at about the same time, because of expected insurance premium adjustments of about 10 percent; this would represent an average increase of 5 percent.

Although realistically founded, the escalation factors do not, in this case, reflect an entirely fair and equitable adjustment for all wages or fringe benefits on July 1. The principal reason is that, initially, many of the employees will receive increases in their pay (due to the higher

Project Highway 1

Location _____

Date 1/1

By Jec

WAGE RATE DETERMINATION

CLASSIFICATION	PREDETERM'D		Hrs/Wk	ACTUAL WAGES					ACTUAL FRINGES				BID RATE
	Wage Rate	Fringes		Basic Rate	Avg. Escal. Time	P+L Time	Ins.+ Toxes	Adjust. Rate	Basic Fringes	Avg. Escal.	P+L Time	Adjust Fringes	
Foreman – labor	(wkly salary)	—	42	10.00	1.09	1.18	1.21	14.85	1.00	1.05	1.18	1.24	16.10
– grade													
– carpenter	(wk'ly salary)	—	41	12.50	1.04	1.21	1.21	19.03	1.00	1.05	1.21	1.27	20.30
– finisher	(wk'ly salary)	—	42	11.25	1.04	1.18	1.21	16.71	1.00	1.05	1.18	1.24	17.95
– ironworker													
Laborer – common	6.00	—	42	5.50	1.00	1.02	1.21	7.41	0.75	1.05	1.00	0.79	8.20
– air/power	6.50	—	42	6.00	1.00	1.02	1.21	8.02	0.75	1.05	1.00	0.79	8.80
Finisher	8.50	0.75	42	9.00	1.04	1.02	1.21	11.55	0.75	1.05	1.00	0.79	12.35
Ironworker – re-bar													
– structural													
Carpenter – journeyman	9.00	1.50	41	9.50	1.00	1.07	1.21	12.30	0.75	—	1.06	1.59	13.90
– helper	7.50	—	41	7.00	1.00	1.01	1.21	9.17	0.75	1.05	1.00	0.79	9.95
Piledriver													
Electrician													
Truck driver	8.00	1.00	42	7.00	1.00	1.02	1.21	9.87	0.75	—	1.00	1.00	10.85
Welder													
Operator – crane	12.00	1.50	43	12.05	1.01	1.09	1.21	16.45	0.75	—	1.06	1.59	18.25
– backhoe													
– loader													
– dozer													
– finisher	8.50	1.50	42	8.50	1.00	1.08	1.21	11.11	0.75	—	1.06	1.59	12.70
– compress.	7.50	1.50	40	7.50	1.00	1.06	1.21	9.62	0.75	—	1.06	1.59	11.20
– coveyor	8.50	1.50	41	8.50	1.00	1.07	1.21	11.00	0.75	—	1.06	1.59	12.60
– pump	8.50	1.50	41	8.50	1.00	1.07	1.21	11.00	0.75	—	1.06	1.59	12.60

Figure 6.1 Wage Rate Determination.

181

than normal requirements set forth in the specifications) because the predetermined minimum rates are higher than those that open-shop employees have normally been getting in the area. The circled basic wage rates and fringe benefits in Figure 6.1 emphasize this point. The estimator must consider each labor classification with particular attention to keeping the employee's average annual earnings at a level similar to those paid on other open-shop projects, so as not to create an imbalance that could affect the area's open-shop wage structure. The *Average Escalation* columns in Figure 6.1 show the results of the estimator's considerations in this regard.

Effects of Premium and Lost Time

In order to adjust wage rates and fringe benefits so that they will reflect the effect of premium and lost time, the estimator must approximate (1) the average number of hours that will be worked each week (as has already been done) and (2) the average number of hours an employee will be paid each year for nonproductive time. With this data, the estimator can assign a time adjustment factor for the wages under each labor classification.

Foremen receive a fixed weekly salary regardless of the hours worked. On the average, foremen work for 10 months each year— March through December. During the winter *layoff*, each foreman receives a Christmas bonus of 2 weeks pay. There are also 5 holidays observed during the working months. The time factor for foremen will be derived through comparison of the time paid and the time worked. The time worked is determined as follows:

Total days per year		365
Not worked:		
Days in January & February	58	
Weekend days—March through December	86	
Holidays	5	
Total not worked		− 149
Work days available (5-day week)		216
Lost days:		
Estimated inclement weather, 14% × 216	30	
Estimated illness, 5% × 216	11	
Estimated Absenteeism, 2.5% × 216	5	
Total lost days		− 46
Actual work days (5-day week)		170
Gained days		
Saturday make-up, 7% × 216	+ 15	
Total gained days		+ 15
Actual days worked		185

The time actually paid is equal to the sum of 44 weeks (10 months), plus 2 weeks of bonus pay or a total of 46 weeks. Based on a 40-hour week, the total hours paid would therefore be 1840. Comparing these hours with the hours actually worked, the time factor for foremen can be computed and entered on the Wage Rate Determination sheet (Figure 6.1).

Labor Foreman   (42 hr/week) $\dfrac{1840}{185 \times 8.4} = 1.18$

Carpenter Foreman   (41 hr/week) $\dfrac{1840}{185 \times 8.2} = 1.21$

Finisher Foreman   (42 hr/week) $\dfrac{1840}{185 \times 8.4} = 1.18$

To determine time factors for hourly paid employees, Table 3.3 is a convenience. Simply estimate the number of lost time hours paid for each year on a year-round basis, and then match those hours to the average number of hours worked each week as established in Figure 6.1.

In this case, the standard among open-shop contractors is to pay carpenters and equipment operators for 6 holidays (48 hours) each year, on the year-round basis, and to pay 2 hours of show-up time for each day that they report to work but do not start work because of inclement weather. Show-up time would occur, it is decided, an average of 20 times each year per qualified employee, paying 40 hours of nonproductive time. The total lost time for holidays plus show-up time would therefore be 88 hours. The time factors for carpenters and equipment operators are found in Table 3.3 and are entered below and in Figure 6.1.

40 hr/week   1.06
41 hr/week   1.07
42 hr/week   1.08
43 hr/week   1.09

The remaining employees will receive no pay for time not worked. Their time factors will therefore be based on the effect of premium time only.

41 hr/week   1.01
42 hr/week   1.02

Fringe benefits for all employees are a function of the hours paid. No overtime factor is involved. Using Table 3.3, it is found that the time factor for those hourly paid employees who annually receive 88 hours of lost time is 1.06. The factor for all others is 1.00. Fringe benefits for foremen are affected in the same way as were foremen's wages.

Effects of Insurance and Tax Expense

The insurance and tax rates that will apply to the gross wages for each employee on the Highway 1 Project are estimated as follows:

Description	Rate (%)	Adjusted %
FICA (Social Security)	6.70	6.70
State unemployment ($6000.00 limit)	5.70	2.85
Federal unemployment	0.70	0.70
Workers' compensation	10.60	10.60
TOTAL		20.85

The insurance and tax factor to be used (Figure 6.1) is 1.21.

Bid Wage Rates

Adjustment of the basic wage rates and fringe benefits (circled) is a simple arithmetic procedure involving multiplication (Figure 6.1). The Bid Wage Rates are finally determined by adding the two adjusted rates, and the sum reflects the total average hourly cost for each hour an employee works. In this illustration, the Bid Wage Rates have been rounded to the nearest 5 cents per hour.

Equipment Rates

Equipment ownership and operating rates have been previously determined, as shown in Figure 6.2. These rates apply to all cost estimates made for the coming year.

Material Prices

During the earlier take-off stages of the estimate (Chapter 2), material suppliers were contacted and advised of the plans to prepare a bid for the Highway 1 Project. They were provided with all necessary infor-

Project ___Highway 1___   EQUIPMENT

Description _Structural Concrete_ Date __1/1__   RATES

Size	Unit	Description	Own. Hourly Cost $	Oper. Hourly Cost $
18	TN	Hydraulic crane, RT	25.00	6.50
40	TN	Truck crane	38.00	9.75
60	TN	Truck crane	45.00	13.00
5	TN	Hydraulic man-lift, telescopic	12.00	4.00
1½	CY	Front end loader, truck type	15.00	7.50
½	TN	Pickup truck	2.00	2.50
3	TN	Flat truck	3.00	3.00
3	M/GL	Water truck	3.00	2.50
40	FT	Deck finisher	12.00	4.50
160	CF	Compressor, trailer mounted, w/hose	2.50	2.90
2.5	kw	Generator, portable, gas oper.	1.10	0.40
1³⁄₈	IN	Vibrator, gas oper	1.25	0.50
2¼	IN	Vibrator, gas oper	1.50	0.55
300	A	Welder, diesel	1.90	2.50
300	A	Welder, electric	1.35	0.60
14	CF	Concrete buggy, gas oper., walk behind	3.15	0.85
1	CY	Concrete bucket	1.15	0.10
1½	CY	Concrete bucket	1.50	0.15
2	CY	Concrete bucket	1.60	0.15
3	CF	Sand blast machine	1.00	0.90
1	EA	Tar kettle	1.10	0.50
1	EA	Scabbler	2.00	1.00
1	EA	Deck grinder	2.00	1.20
1	EA	Hand grinder	1.00	0.60
18	IN	Chain saw	0.90	0.40
10	IN	Bench saw	1.10	0.15
24	IN	Vibratory compactor	2.00	1.00
8	CFM	Spray pump	1.50	0.30
25	KIP	Beam shore support (per day)	2.00	—
30	KIP	Beam shore support (per day)	2.20	—

Figure 6.2 Equipment Rates.

mation regarding quantities and specifications. They have since responded, and all their quotations have been reviewed. Those of greatest advantage have been chosen and are described next.

Lumber and Plywood A local lumber supplier has agreed to supply the entire project needs for lumber and plywood at the following prices, f.o.b. jobsite, exclusive of any state sales tax.

Dimension Lumber	$260 Mbf
3/4-in Plyform, Class I	550 Msf
Rough Boards	220 Mbf
Heavy Structural Timbers	450 Mbf

Form Ties   Form tie prices are based on current supplier price lists, less any usual discounts. Prices exclude local or state sales taxes and include delivery to the jobsite. The list covers all anticipated form tie needs.

Snap Ties, 3M, Spreader Type			Snap Ties, 5M, Spreader Type		
Size (in)	Tie ($)	Working part ($)	Size (in)	Tie ($)	Working part ($)
12	0.50	1.95	12	0.70	2.71
18	0.55	1.95	18	0.79	2.71
30	0.75	1.95	168	3.20	2.71
36	0.85	1.95			
42	0.96	1.95	**Coil Ties, 6M, 15-in Bolts**		
48	1.06	1.95	12	0.54	4.03
72	1.47	1.95	30	0.91	4.03
90	1.77	1.95	48	1.31	4.03
120	2.28	1.95	72	1.85	4.03
180	3.27	1.95			
240	4.32	1.95			
Deck Overhang Bracket, 3M, 54-in Width			**Deck Hanger, 6M, 12-in Flange, 18-in Bolts**		
		65.00	12	1.40	4.36

Concrete Mix   Three commercial concrete suppliers offered to supply the concrete for Highway 1. Their prices are similar and all include the necessary air entrainment, testing, and delivery expense. None offers a discount, and all have established a date for price increases. To compare several quotations of this type, a *Price Comparison Sheet* is convenient. Figure 6.3 shows the comparison of the concrete mix quotations received. AAA Transit Mix offers the best price.

Expansion Dams   Structure 4 requires the installation of two 40-foot-long expansion dams that must be specially fabricated to fit the

PRICE COMPARISON

Project ___Highway 1___

Description ___Concrete Mix___   Date ___1/1___

Detail	Quantity	Unit	Unit Concrete Inc.		Able Supply Co.		AAA Transit Mix Co.			
			Unit	Total	Unit	Total	Unit	Total	Unit	Total
Class A Concrete	602	cy	45.00	27,090.	43.50	26,187.	43.50	26,187.		
Class B Concrete	2160	cy	40.00	86,400.	40.00	86,400.	41.00	88,560.		
Class C Concrete	2001	cy	37.50	75,037.	38.00	76,038.	36.00	72,036		
Class D Concrete	25	cy	35.00	875.	35.00	875.	35.00	875		
Retarder (decks)	431	cy	1.50	646.	1.50	646.	1.00	431		
				190,048.		190,146.		188,089.		
Prices are firm to			12/31	+10%	12/31	+10%	10/1	+7%		
Effect of Escalation	413	cy	N/A	N/A	N/A	N/A	3.05	1,260.		
	296	cy	N/A	N/A	N/A	N/A	0.07	21.		
				190,048.		190,146.		189,370		
Prices include										
Retarder on decks only			yes		yes		yes			
Air entrainment			yes		yes		yes			
Testing			yes		yes		yes			
Discounts			no		no		no			

Figure 6.3 Price Comparison – Materials Prices.

deck cross section as detailed in the plans. Since this type of fabrication is a specialty, only two prices have been received, the best of which is outlined below:

· Material delivered to jobsite (80 lf) $9500.00
· Price is firm for duration of project and includes shop paint.
· Price does not include installation, field paint, joint material, or sales taxes.

Elastomeric Joint Seal 2 1/2 inches by 3 1/2 inches Approximately 90 lineal feet of elastomeric joint seal must be installed in the joints over the piers for Structure 4, as detailed in the plans. The cost for this material, f.o.b. jobsite, is $20.00 per lineal foot; it is a firm price for 1 year. No installation costs or sales taxes are included.

One-Inch Premolded Joint Filler The price for 1-inch joint filler conforming to the specification requirements is $0.85 per square foot, f.o.b. jobsite.

PVC Pipe 30 lineal feet of 4-inch PVC pipe and 100 lineal feet of 6-inch PVC pipe are required for weeps in bridge abutment walls and retaining walls. Prices for the material delivered to the job and exclusive of any sales taxes are:

4-in PVC $1.40 per lf
6-in PVC 2.40 per lf

Six-Inch Perforated PVC Pipe 850 lineal feet of 6-inch drain must be installed behind the Retaining Walls (Structure 2). The best price for this material is $2.60 per lineal foot, including necessary couplings and fittings. The delivery price excludes sales taxes.

Drainage Material A blanket of drainage material 1 1/2 feet thick must be installed against the back of the Retaining Walls as they are backfilled. This material (460 cubic yards), will come from a local gravel supplier, and the price is $8.00 per ton, f.o.b. jobsite, if used within the first year. The price is complete including all sales taxes.

Six-Inch Rubber Waterstop Construction of the box culvert (Structure 1) and the Retaining Walls (Structure 2), requires the use of 6-inch rubber waterstop in construction joints and expansion joints. The best quotation received offers waterstop at $3.00 per lineal foot exclusive of sales tax.

Polyethylene, 6 Mil   The current price for 6-mil polyethylene sheet suitable for curing and protection purposes is $0.04 per square foot delivered and exclusive of sales tax.

Cure Blankets   Burlap cure blankets cost $0.50 per square foot, to which any taxes must be added.

Steel Sectional Scaffolding   The purchase of enough scaffolding to cover 800 to 1000 square feet of wall surface is necessary for various access needs on the project. This material, again, exclusive of taxes, is priced as follows:

5 × 5 Frames	20 each @ $60.00 =	$1200.00
Cross Braces	32 each @ 15.00 =	480.00
Jacks and Plates	10 each @ 20.00 =	200.00
Miscellaneous Hardware		100.00
		$1980.00

Subcontractor Quotations

Within the scope of the structural concrete for Highway 1 there is very little work that can be sublet conveniently without interfering with the effective use of company work forces and equipment that must, in any case, be on the project to conduct the major portion of the work. However, several contractors have expressed interest in subcontracting the responsibility for waterproofing, dampproofing, and linseed oil applications. Subletting these items would not affect the remaining work. Another item of interest to subcontractors is the installation of the 6-inch perforated drainage pipe and the backfill for the retaining walls (Structure 2).

Surface Applications   Four quotations have been received for surface application items. They are compared on a Price Comparison Sheet (Figure 6.4). The ABC Corporation has the most attractive prices for use in this cost estimate.

Drainage, Structure 2   A single quotation has been received from a small contractor who would like to place the 6-inch PVC perforated drain, and all select backfill associated with Structure 2. The prices quoted to furnish and install all material in accordance with the plans and specifications are as follows:

PRICE

COMPARISON

Project _____Highway 1_____

Description _Dampproof, Waterproof, Linseed Oil_   Date __1/1__

Detail	Quantity	Unit	Waterproof Inc.		ABC Corp.		C. Brown Co.		Apply Co.	
			Unit	Total	Unit	Total	Unit	Total	Unit	Total
Dampproof	18,600	sf	1.00	18,600.	1.10	20,460.	1.10	20,460.	-	-
Waterproof	1,000	sf	5.00	5,000.	3.00	3,000.	3.50	3,500.	-	-
Linseed Oil	20,400	sf	0.65	13,260.	0.60	12,240.	-	-	0.60	12,240.
				36,860		35,700		23,960		12,240
Firm for duration of project				Yes		Yes		Yes		Yes

Figure 6.4   Price Comparison – Subcontractor Quotations.

6-in Perforated PVC Drain $ 3.60 per lf

Select Backfill (place measure)   15.00 per cy

Other Cost Data

An accepted practice in the construction estimating profession involves the use of a percentage of the total labor expense as a measure of the funds that will be required to pay for small tools and miscellaneous supplies not directly covered in the cost estimate. The percentage used is influenced by the nature and location of the work being done. For instance, bridge construction crews tend to need more for small tools and supplies than do grading crews. For this estimate, 8 percent of labor expense will cover the small tool and supply requirements for the structural concrete work on Highway 1.

6.5 THE COST ESTIMATE

The cost estimate for structural concrete is a combination of take-off information and cost data with chosen crews, productivity, and material needs. Planning and judgment are the predominating factors in this final consolidation. Beginning with formwork and continuing through every facet of the structural concrete construction for Highway 1, the estimate of cost will now be completely illustrated.

Form Utilization

The structural concrete formwork for Highway 1 will involve many types and sizes of forms. Before form cost can be properly estimated, there must be a conceptual understanding of the overall project form requirements. This understanding is best developed through the use of a Form Utilization Plan.

Form Utilization Plan

A Form Utilization Plan is simply a graphic reorganization of the Preliminary Progress Schedule as it pertains to the formwork involved. Structural components are arranged on the plan in convenient groups that offer the best advantage for tracking forms through their repeated use while, at the same time, avoiding duplicate use projections. Figure 6.5 is the Form Utilization Plan for Highway 1. The formwork for various structural concrete components on this plan are grouped into *Form Sets* which identify specific panel sizes and contact areas. The

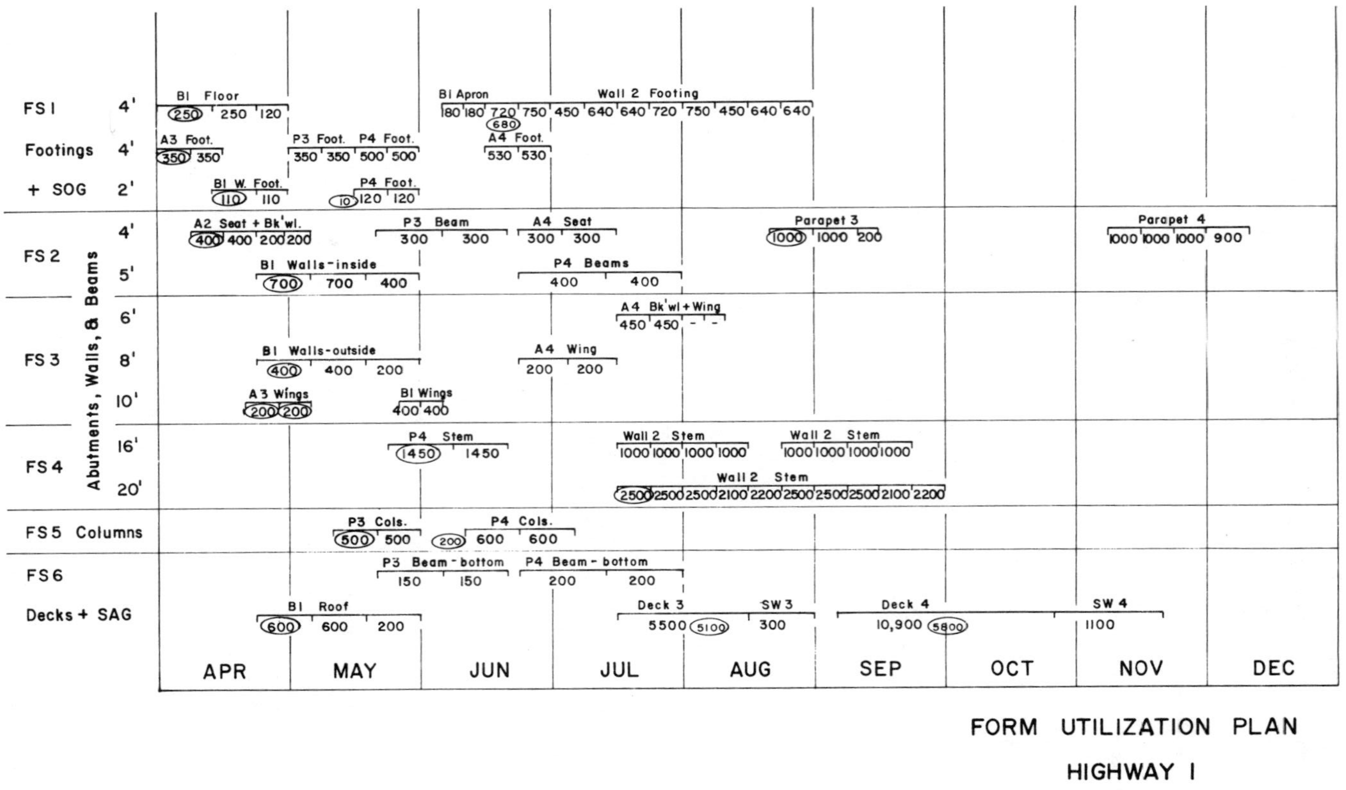

Figure 6.5 Form Utilization Plan.

circled contact areas represent the construction of sufficient forms to serve the area, with the intention of having them become available for further similar applications as work progresses. This plan makes it possible to estimate the form construction cost with considerable reasonableness and accuracy. The only requirement is that the estimator recognize and appreciate the importance of planning at this stage of the estimate.

Form Use Computations

The Form Utilization Plan for Highway 1 (Figure 6.5) categorizes all forms into six sets. The object is to determine the average number of times each new form (circled contact area) will be used in each form set. This can almost be done visually, but computations are best for future reference and planning.

The term *build* is used to designate the contact area for which form materials will be purchased and prefabricated a single time. The forms for the bridge decks and box culvert roof, of course, will require dismantling each time they are stripped, but the material is reused.

Form Set 2 includes parapet walls for which new forms are specifically provided because of their later use and high surface quality requirements. In Form Set 3, note there is a small amount of formwork over 8 feet in height. For practical purposes, all forms in Form Set 3 will be considered to be in the category of 0 to 8 feet high.

FORM USE

Form Set 1 (Footings and slab on grade, 2 and 4 ft high)

	Footing	SOG	Build
2-ft forms			
Box culvert wing		220	110
Pier 4	240		10
4-ft forms			
Box floor slab		620	250
Box apron		360	
Abutment 3	700		350
Pier 3	700		
Abutment 4	1,060		
Pier 4	1,000		
Wall 2A	3,200		720
Wall 2B	3,200		
	10,100	1,200	1,440

$$\text{Form use} = \frac{10{,}100 + 1{,}200}{1{,}440} = 7.8$$

Form Set 2 (Abutments, walls, and beam sides, 4 and 5 ft high)

	Abutment	Wall	Beam	Build
4-ft forms				
Abutment 3	1,200			400
Pier 3			600	
Abutment 4	600			
Parapet 3		2,200		1,000
Parapet 4		3,900		
5-ft forms				
Box—inside		1,800		700
Pier 4			800	
	1,800	7,900	1,400	2,100

$$\text{Form use} = \frac{1,800 + 7,900 + 1,400}{2,100} = 5.3$$

Form Set 3 (Abutments and walls, 6, 8, and 10-ft high)

	Abutment	Wall	Build
6-ft forms			
Abutment 4	900		
8-ft forms			
Box—outside		1,000	400
Abutment 4	400		
10-ft forms			
Abutment 3	400		400
Box wings		800	
	1,700	1,800	800

$$\text{Form use} = \frac{1,700 + 1,800}{800} = 4.4$$

Form Set 4 (Walls, 16 and 20 ft high)

	Wall	Build
16-ft forms		
Pier 4 stem	2,900	1,500
Wall 2A	4,000	
Wall 2B	4,000	
20-ft forms		
Wall 2A	11,800	2,500
Wall 2B	11,800	
	34,500	4,000

$$\text{Form use} = \frac{34,500}{4,000} = 8.6$$

Form Set 5 (Columns)

	Column	Build
Pier 3	1,000	500
Pier 4	1,200	200
	2,200	700

$$\text{Form use} = \frac{2,200}{700} = 3.1$$

Form Set 6 (Decks, slab above grade, and beam deck)

	Deck	SAG	Beam	Build
Pier 3			300	
Pier 4			400	
Box roof		1,400		600
Deck 3	5,500			5,100
Sidewalk 3	300			
Deck 4	10,900			5,800
Sidewalk 3	1,100			
	17,800	1,400	700	10,500

$$\text{Form use} = \frac{17,800 + 1,400 + 700}{10,500} = 1.9$$

FORM USE SUMMARY

Component	Form set	Computation	Average form use
Footing	1	10,100 sf @ 8.1	8.0
Slab on grade	1	1,200 sf @ 8.1	8.0
Abutment, 0–8′	2	1,800 sf @ 5.3	
	3	1,700 sf @ 4.4	
		3,500 sf @ 4.9	5.0
Wall, 0–8′	2	7,900 sf @ 5.3	
	3	1,800 sf @ 4.4	
		9,700 sf @ 5.1	5.0
Wall, 8′+	4	34,500 sf @ 8.6	8.0
Column	5	2,200 sf @ 3.1	3.0
Beam	2	1,400 sf @ 5.3	
	6	700 sf @ 1.9	
		2,100 sf @ 4.2	4.0
Deck	6	17,800 sf @ 1.9	2.0
Slab above grade	6	1,400 sf @ 1.9	2.0

Form Use Summary

With each form set analyzed, it is now relatively easy to arrange the results so that the average number of form uses for each structural component can be projected.

In this case, the preceding Form Use Summary has produced an oddity in that it predicts eight uses for the box culvert floor slab form. Of course this is not possible. It was caused by the inclusion of forms for the box culvert floor slab with footing forms. However, since the planned form application is correct, it is acceptable to use this average figure in computing the cost.

Form Cost

Form cost is a function of the labor, equipment, and material required to complete all formwork. It is influenced by crew productivity and form utilization planning. Highway 1, with its many concrete components and form variations, demonstrates the degree of complexity that can be involved in deriving cost.

Before proceeding with the illustrated form cost computations, it is necessary to define the meanings of certain factors and conditions as they pertain to formwork.

FORMWORK CONDITIONS

1. Installation and material expense for chamfer strip and 2 × 4 keyways is covered by the form crew productivity and material factors used. No added cost need be estimated.
2. Lumber and tie factors cover the cost for miscellaneous hardware such as nails and straps.
3. Stripping crews will oil, repair, and generally maintain forms— including architectural liners. They will also fill concrete tieholes and remove fins when stripping forms, as defined under *Ordinary Finish* in the specifications.

Form Crews and Productivity

Figure 6.6*a* to *f* illustrates the compilation of hourly form crew and equipment expense for building, erecting, and stripping forms for each of the structural concrete components on the Highway 1 Project. The hourly wage rates used are taken from the Highway 1 Wage Rate Determination (Figure 6.1), and the crew sizes and their productivity were determined with the aid of Table 4.12. The crew established for *board finish* represents the add-on expense involved for installing

Project ___Highway 1___

Description ___Build Forms___   Date ___1/1___

CREW HOURLY COST

Labor Classification	Bid Rate	Footings SOG (Ftg 60 / SOG 50)	Abut. 0-8' / Wall 0-8' (Abut 50 / Wall 50)	Wall 8'+ (50)	Columns Beams (Gl 60 / Beam 50)	Board Finish (120)
Foreman Carp.	20.30		½ 10.15	½ 10.15	½ 10.15	
Laborer common	8.20	1 8.20	1 8.20	2 16.40	1 8.20	1 8.20
air/power						
Finisher						
Ironworker						
Carpenter journeyman	13.90	1 13.90	1 13.90	2 27.80	1 13.90	1 13.90
helper	9.95	1 9.95	1 9.95	1 9.95	1 9.95	1 9.95
Truck driver	10.85	¼ 2.71	¼ 2.71	¼ 2.71	¼ 2.71	¼ 2.71
Welder						
Operator crane	18.05	¼ 4.56	¼ 4.56	½ 9.12	¼ 4.56	
conveyor						
pump						
finisher						
compress.						
oiler	11.20			½ 5.60		
Crew Totals		39.32	49.47	81.73	49.47	34.76

Figure 6.6(a) Hourly Crew Cost – Formwork (Build Forms).

Project Highway 1 EQUIPMENT

Description Build Forms Date 1/1 HOURLY COST

	Equipment	Rate	Footings SOG		Abut, 0-8' Wall, 0-8'		Wall, 8'+		Columns Beams		Board Finish					
OWNERSHIP	Pickup	2.00			1/2	1.00	1/2	1.00	1/2	1.00						
	Service truck	3.00	1/4	0.75	1/4	0.75	1/4	0.75	1/4	0.75	1/4	0.75				
	18T Hydr. Crane	25.00	1/4	6.25	1/4	6.25			1/4	6.25						
	40T Trk. Crane	38.00					1/2	19.00								
	2.5 KW Generator	1.10	1	1.10	1	1.10	1	1.10	1	1.10	1	1.10				
	Bench Saw	1.10			1	1.10	1	1.10	1	1.10	1	1.10				
Ownership Totals			8.10		10.20		22.95		10.20		2.95					
EOE	Pickup	2.50			1/2	1.25	1/2	1.25	1/2	1.25						
	Service truck	3.00	1/4	0.75	1/4	0.75	1/4	0.75	1/4	0.75	1/4	0.75				
	18T Hydr Crane	6.50	1/4	1.63	1/4	1.63			1/4	1.63						
	40T Trk Crane	9.75					1/2	4.88								
	2.5 KW Generator	0.40	1	0.40	1	0.40	1	0.40	1	0.40	1	0.40				
	Bench Saw	0.15			1	0.15	1	0.15	1	0.15	1	0.15				
EOE Totals			2.78		4.18		7.43		4.18		1.30					

Figure 6.6(b) Hourly Equipment Cost – Formwork (Build Forms).

Description Erect Forms   Date /1

CREW

HOURLY COST

Labor Classification	Bid Rate	Footings SOG (Foot 70 / SOG 50)		Abut. 0-6' Wall 0-6' (Abut 35 / Wall 50)		Wall 8+ (50)		Columns (35)		Beams (25)		Decks (50)		SAG (40)	
Foreman Carp.	20.30	1	20.30	1	20.30	1	20.30	1	20.30	1	20.30	1	20.30	1	20.30
Laborer common air/power	8.20	2	16.40	2	16.40	2	16.40	2	16.40	2	16.40	3	24.60	2	16.40
Finisher															
Ironworker															
Carpenter journeyman	13.90	2	27.80	2	27.80	3	41.70	2	27.80	2	27.80	4	55.60	3	41.70
helper	9.95	1	9.95	1	9.95	1	9.95	1	9.95	1	9.95	1	9.95	2	19.90
Truck driver	10.85	1/4	2.71	1/2	5.43	1/4	2.71	1/2	5.43	1/2	5.43	3/4	8.14	1/2	5.43
Welder															
Operator crane	18.25	1/2	9.12	1/2	9.12	3/4	13.69	1/2	9.12	3/4	13.69	3/4	13.69	3/4	13.69
conveyor															
pump															
finisher															
compress.															
oiler	11.20					3/4	8.40	1/2	5.60	1/2	5.60	3/4	8.40		
Crew Totals			86.28		89.00		113.15		94.60		99.17		140.48		117.42

Figure 6.6(c) Hourly Crew Cost – Formwork (Erect Forms).

Project ___Highway 1___

Description ___Erect Forms___   Date ___1/1___

EQUIPMENT

HOURLY COST

OWNERSHIP

Equipment	Rate	Footings SOG	Abut. 0-8' Wall. 0-8'	Wall. 8+	Columns	Beams	Decks	SAG
Pickup	2.00	1 2.00	1 2.00	1 2.00	1 2.00	1 2.00	1 2.00	1 2.00
Service truck	3.00	¼ 0.75	½ 1.50	¼ 0.75	½ 1.50	½ 1.50	¾ 2.25	½ 1.50
18 T Hydr. Crane	25.00	½ 12.50	½ 12.50					¾ 18.75
40 T Trk. Crane	38.00			¾ 28.50	½ 19.00	¾ 28.50	¾ 28.50	
60 T Trk Crane	45.00						(¾)(33.75)	
Welder 300 Amp.	1.90		¼ 0.48	¼ 0.48	¼ 0.48	¼ 0.48	½ 0.95	¼ 0.48
2.5 KW Generator	1.10	1 1.10	1 1.10	1 1.10	1 1.10	1 1.10	2 2.20	2 2.20
Bench Saw	1.10		1 1.10	1 1.10	1 1.10	1 1.10	1 1.10	1 1.10
Ownership Totals		16.35	18.48	33.93	25.18	34.68	#3 37.00 (3Du)(42.25)	26.03

EOE

Equipment	Rate	Footings SOG	Abut. 0-8' Wall. 0-8'	Wall. 8+	Columns	Beams	Decks	SAG
Pickup	2.50	1 2.50	1 2.50	1 2.50	1 2.50	1 2.50	1 2.50	1 2.50
Service truck	3.00	¼ 0.75	½ 1.50	¼ 0.75	½ 1.50	½ 1.50	¾ 2.25	½ 1.50
18 T Hydr. Crane	6.50	½ 3.25	½ 3.25					¾ 4.88
40 T Trk. Crane	9.75			¾ 7.31	½ 4.88	¾ 7.31	¾ 7.31	
60 T Trk Crane	13.00						(¾)(9.75)	
Welder 300 Amp	2.50		¼ 0.62	¼ 0.62	¼ 0.62	¼ 0.62	½ 1.25	¼ 0.62
2.5 KW Generator	0.40	1 0.40	1 0.40	1 0.40	1 0.40	1 0.40	2 0.80	2 0.80
Bench Saw	0.15		1 0.15	1 0.15	1 0.15	1 0.15	1 0.15	1 0.15
EOE Totals		6.90	8.42	11.73	10.05	12.48	#3 14.26 (3Du)(16.70)	10.45

Figure 6.6(d) Hourly Equipment Cost—Formwork (Erect Forms).

Project ___Highway 1___

Description ___Strip Forms___   Date ___1/1___

HOURLY COST

Labor Classification	Bid Rate	Footings SOG (Foot 170 / SOG 140)	Abut. 0-8' Wall. 0-8 (Abut 80 / Walls 110)	Wall/8+ (90)	Columns Beams (Col'n 120 / Beam 100)	Decks (#3 150 / #4 130)	SAG (70)
Foreman Carp.	20.30	1/4 5.08	1/4 5.08	1/2 10.15	1/4 5.08	1/2 10.15	1 20.30
Laborer common	8.20	2 16.40	2 16.40	3 24.60	2 16.40	4 32.80	4 32.80
air/power							
Finisher							
Ironworker							
Carpenter journeyman	13.40	1 13.90	1 13.90	1 13.90	1 13.90	1 13.90	1 13.90
helper	9.95	1 9.95	1 9.95	1 9.95	1 9.95	1 9.95	1 9.95
Truck driver	10.85	1/2 5.42	1/2 5.42	1/2 5.42	1/2 5.42	1/2 10.95	1/2 5.42
Welder							
Operator crane	18.25	1/2 9.12	1/2 9.12	3/4 13.49	3/4 13.49	1/2 9.12	1 18.25
conveyor							
pump							
finisher							
compress.	11.20			3/4 8.40	3/4 8.40	1/2 5.60	
oiler							
Crew Totals		59.87	59.87	86.11	72.84	92.37	100.62

Figure 6.6(e) Hourly Crew Cost – Formwork (Strip Forms).

201

Project ___Highway 1___

Description ___Strip Forms___   Date ___1/1___

EQUIPMENT

HOURLY COST

	Equipment	Rate	Footings SOG	Abut. 0-8' Wall 0-8'	Wall 11.8'	Columns Beams	Decks	SAG
OWNERSHIP	Pickup	2.00	1/4 0.50	1/4 0.50	1/2 1.00	1/4 0.50	1/2 1.00	1 2.00
	Service Truck	3.00	1/2 1.50	1/2 1.50	1/2 1.50	1/2 1.50	1 3.00	1/2 1.50
	18 T Hydr Crane	25.00	1/2 12.50	1/2 12.50	3/4 28.50	3/4 28.50	1/2 19.00	1 38.00
	40 T Tk Crane	38.00					(1/2)(22.50)	
	60 T Tk Crane	45.00						
	2.5 KW Generator	1.10	1 1.10	1 1.10	1 1.10	1 1.10	1 1.10	1 1.10
	Ownership Totals		15.60	15.60	32.10	31.60	#3 24.16 (3u)(27.60)	42.60
EOE	Pickup	2.50	1/4 0.62	1/4 0.62	1/2 1.25	1/4 0.62	1/2 1.25	1 2.50
	Service Truck	3.00	1/2 1.50	1/2 1.50	1/2 1.50	1/2 1.50	1 3.00	1/2 1.50
	18 T Hydr Crane	6.50	1/2 3.25	1/2 3.25				
	40 T Tk Crane	9.75			3/4 7.31	3/4 7.31	1/2 4.88	1 9.75
	60 T Tk Crane	13.00					(1/2)(6.50)	
	2.5 KW Generator	0.40	1 0.40	1 0.40	1 0.40	1 0.40	1 0.40	1 0.40
	EOE Totals		5.77	5.77	10.46	9.83	#3 9.53 (3u)(11.15)	14.15

Figure 6.6(f) Hourly Equipment Cost – Formwork (Strip Forms).

rough boards on the forms for Structure 2 needed to meet the architectural finish requirements. The fraction of an hour for a worker or machine signifies that a full time need is not required, since the project has multiple activities and partial time for a single activity is realistic.

The estimator will note that in this case some crews are similar in size and value—and vary in potential productivity—whereas others differ greatly in size and value but produce at similar rates. The experienced estimator can often establish fewer *average* crews and accordingly vary productivity rates—thereby shortening the computation procedure.

Form Labor and Equipment

The form labor and equipment cost will represent the entire direct labor and equipment budget for building, erecting, and stripping the forms for Highway 1. These computations (Figure 6.7a to d) represent the first in which structural concrete component costs are identified in terms of the pay item or class of concrete. They employ information derived from the quantity take-off, the form utilization plan, and the hourly crew and equipment data sheets, and they apply appropriately chosen productivity rates to this information. The capital letters B, E, and S stand for *build, erect,* and *strip*. The object is to find the total number of crew hours required for each building, erecting, or stripping task and to multiply those hours by the hourly crew and equipment rates, thereby finding the total form construction cost for each pay item.

The estimator will note that the cost computations include the architectural rough board add-on cost and that a prediction is made that the boards will not survive more than one-half of the need. The cost, therefore, includes one full replacement of the boards.

Form Lumber and Plywood

The process for finding the total lumber and plywood material expense involves the use of the contact areas found in the take-off, the neat material and loss factors appropriate to the various form applications (as found in Tables 4.6 to 4.11), and the quoted lumber and plywood prices as established with the cost data. Before proceeding with this cost estimate, several added expense items must first be recognized and quantified: rough boards for the Structure 2 face forms, stiffbacks for wall forms over 8 feet high, crosstie and haunch form support systems for the Structure 1 floor slab, and added large sized keyways. The requirements for these items are estimated next.

Project ___Highway 1___

Description ___Class A Concrete___ Date ___1/1___

FORM

COST

Detail		Contact sf	No. Uses	Prod. Rate sf/hr	Total Hours	Labor		Equipment Ownership		Equipment Operation	
						$/hr	Total $	$/hr	Total $	$/hr	Total $
Parapet (Wall,0-8)	B	6100	5.0	50	25	49.50	1,238.	10.20	255.	4.20	105.
	E			50	122	89.00	10,858.	18.70	2,281.	8.40	1,024.
	S			110	55	59.90	3,295.	15.60	858.	5.80	318.
Deck 3	B	5,800	2.0	—	—						
	E			50	116	140.70	16,321.	37.00	4,292.	14.30	1,659.
	S			150	39	92.40	3,604.	24.10	940.	9.50	370.
Deck 4	B	12,000	2.0	—	—						
	E			50	240	140.70	33,768.	40.20	10,128.	16.70	4,008.
	S			130	92	92.40	8,501.	27.60	2,539.	11.20	1,030.
Totals		23,900					77,584.		21,294.		8,516.

Figure 6.7(a) Form Cost Computations – Class A Concrete.

Project _Highway 1_

Description _Class B Concrete_   Date _1/1_

Detail	Contact sf	No. Uses	Prod. Rate sf/hr	Total Hours	Labor		Equipment Ownership		Equipment Operation	
					$/hr	Total $	$/hr	Total $	$/hr	Total $
Box Floor (Sob) B	1,200	8.0	50	3	39.30	118	8.10	24	2.80	8
E			50	24	86.30	2,071	16.30	391	6.90	166
S			140	9	59.90	539	15.60	140	5.80	52
Abutment 3+4 B	3,500	5.0	50	14	49.50	693	10.20	143	4.20	59
(Abut. o-B) E			35	100	89.00	8,900	18.70	1,870	8.40	840
S			90	44	59.90	2,636	15.60	686	5.60	255
Box Wall B	3,600	5.0	50	15	49.50	742	10.20	153	4.20	63
(Wall. o-B) E			50	72	89.00	6,408	18.70	1,346	8.40	605
S			110	33	59.90	1,977	15.60	515	5.86	191
Wall z Stem B	31,600	8.0	50	79	81.70	6,454	23.00	1,817	7.40	585
(Wall. B+) E			50	632	113.20	71,542	33.90	21,425	11.70	7,394
S			90	351	86.10	30,221	32.10	11,227	10.50	3,686
Arch. Fin.	(28,200)	4.0	120	59	34.80	2,053	3.00	177	1.36	77
Pier 4 Stem B	2,900	8.0	50	7	81.70	572	23.00	161	7.40	52
(Wall. B+) E			50	58	113.20	6,566	33.90	1,966	11.70	679
S			90	32	86.10	2,755	32.10	1,207	10.50	336

Figure 6.7(b) Form Cost Computations – Class B Concrete.

Project ___Highway 1___

Description ___Class B Concrete (Cont')___ Date ___1/1___

COST

Detail	Contact sf	No. Uses	Prod. Rate sf/hr	Total Hours	Labor $/hr	Labor Total $	Equipment Ownership $/hr	Equipment Ownership Total $	Equipment Operation $/hr	Equipment Operation Total $
Columns 3+4 B	2,200	3.0	60	12	49.50	594	10.20	122	4.20	50
E			35	63	94.60	5,960	25.20	1,588	10.00	630
S			120	18	72.80	1,310	31.60	569	9.80	176
Beams 3+4 B	2,100	4.0	50	11	49.50	544	10.20	112	4.20	46
E			25	84	99.20	8,333	34.70	2,915	12.50	1,050
S			100	21	72.80	1,529	31.60	664	9.80	206
Box Roof (SAG) B	1,400	2.0	-	-						
E			40	35	117.40	4,109	26.00	910	10.50	368
S			70	20	100.60	2,012	42.60	852	14.10	282
Totals	48,500					168,639		50,241		17,855

Figure 6.7(c) Form Cost Computations – Class B Concrete (cont.).

Project _Highway 1_

Description _Class C Concrete_   Date _1/1_

COST

Detail	Contact sf	No. Uses	Prod. Rate sf/hr	Total Hours	Labor		Equipment Ownership		Equipment Operation	
					$/hr	Total $	$/hr	Total $	$/hr	Total $
Footings B	10,100	8.0	60	21	39.30	825	8.10	170	2.80	59
c			70	144	86.30	12,427	16.30	2,347	6.90	994
s			170	60	59.90	3,594	15.60	936	5.80	348
Totals	10,100					16,846		3,453		1,400

Figure 6.7(d) Form Cost Computations – Class C Concrete.

ADDED LUMBER REQUIRED

Rough Boards, Structure 2 Details for the rough board finish on the face of Structure 2 (plan sheet 1 of 2) show that the following estimated amount of lumber will be required for each square foot of form lining installed.

$$\textit{Form Lining} \qquad \frac{1' \times 1'' \times 12''}{12} = 1.0 \text{ bf/sf}$$

$$\textit{Recess} \qquad \frac{1' \times 1.5'' \times 4''}{12} = 0.5 \text{ bf/sf}$$

$$\text{Total lumber required} \qquad \overline{1.5 \text{ bf/sf}}$$

Stiffbacks, Walls 8'+ 4 × 6 stiffbacks, spaced at 6-foot centers, will be added to the forms used for the Structure 2 wall stems and Structure 4 pier stems. The lumber required per square foot of form is

$$1' \times \frac{4'' \times 6''}{6' \times 12} = 0.33 \text{ bf/sf}$$

Floor Slab and Haunch Form Support, Structure 1 The box culvert floor slab forms can be satisfactorily held in position by employing a system of 2 × 6 crossties from one side form to the other at 8-foot intervals, in addition to the usual braces and blocking used. The haunch forms can be supported by struts nailed to the crossties. The added lumber for this application to the form for a 25-foot floor slab section is as follows:

$$\textit{Crossties} \qquad 4 \text{ each @ } 22' \times \frac{2'' \times 6''}{12} = 88 \text{ bf}$$

$$\textit{Haunch Supports} \qquad 16 \text{ each @ } 3' \times \frac{2'' \times 6''}{12} = 48 \text{ bf}$$

$$\textit{Haunch Supports} \qquad 12 \text{ each @ } 2' \times \frac{2'' \times 6''}{12} = 24 \text{ bf}$$

$$\text{Total lumber required} \qquad \overline{160 \text{ bf}}$$

Keyway The quantities for large keyways are found in the take-off and can be entered directly into the cost computations.

Figure 6-8a to d, shows the entire lumber and plywood cost computations. Note that sales taxes are added to the material expense and that keyway material expense is based on a single use with considerable waste in fabrication.

LUMBER & PLYWOOD COST

Project: Highway 1

Description: Class A Concrete Date: 1/1

Detail	Contact Area sf	No. Uses	Form Area sf	Material Factors		Cost $	
				Neat	Loss	Unit	Total
Parapet (Wall, 0-8') Lumber L	6100	5.0	1,220	2.55	1.36	0.26	1100
Plywood P			1220	1.00	1.36	0.55	913
Deck 3 + 4 L	17,800	2.0	8900	1.30	1.27	0.26	3820
P			8900	1.00	1.27	0.55	6217
	23,900		10,120				12,050
Sales Tax 5%							602
Total Cost							12,652

Figure 6.8(a) Lumber and Plywood Cost Computations – Class A Concrete.

Project ___Highway 1___

Description ___Class B Concrete___ Date ___1/1___

LUMBER & PLYWOOD

COST

Detail		Contact Area sf	No. Uses	Form Area sf	Material Factors		Cost	
					Neat	Loss	Unit	Total
Box Floor (Sog)	L	1,200	8.0	150	2.95	1.34	0.26	154
	P			150	1.00	1.34	0.55	111
Add for haunch		see comps		—	1.60	1.30	0.26	54
Abutment 3+4 (Abut. 0-8)	L	3,500	5.0	700	2.75	1.50	0.26	751
	P			700	1.00	1.50	0.55	578
Box Wall (Wall. 0-8')	L	3,600	5.0	720	2.75	1.36	0.26	700
	P			720	1.00	1.36	0.55	539
Wall 2 Stem (Wall 1.8'+)	L	31,600	8.0	3950	2.70	1.25	0.26	3,466
	P			3950	1.00	1.25	0.55	2,716
stiffbacks				3950	0.35	1.25	0.26	449
rough board	(28,200)		4.0	7050	1.50	1.50	0.22	3,490
Pier 4 Stem (Wall 0.4')	L	2,900	8.0	360	2.70	1.31	0.26	331
	P			360	1.00	1.31	0.55	259
stiffbacks				360	0.35	1.25	0.22	35

Figure 6.8(b) Lumber and Plywood Cost Computations – Class B Concrete.

Project _Highway 1_

Description _Class B Concrete (Con'l)_ Date _1/1_

LUMBER & PLYWOOD

COST

Detail		Contact Area sf	No. Uses	Form Area sf	Material Factors		Cost	
					Neat	Loss	Unit	Total
Column 3×4	L	2200	3.0	730	3.85	1.27	0.26	928
	P			730	1.00	1.27	0.55	510
Beam 3×4	L	2100	4.0	525	2.40	1.41	0.26	462
	P			525	1.00	1.41	0.55	370
Box Roof (SAG)	L	1400	2.0	700	0.80	1.27	0.26	185
	P			700	1.00	1.27	0.55	489
Keyway 3×6		1000 LF		–	1500	1.50	0.26	585
3×8		100 LF		–	200	1.50	0.26	78
		48,500		7835				17,220
Sales tax 5%								861
Total Cost								18,081

Figure 6.8(c) Lumber and Plywood Cost Computations – Class B Concrete (cont.).

Project *Highway 1* — **LUMBER & PLYWOOD COST**

Description *Class C Concrete* Date *1/1*

Detail		Contact Area sf	No. Uses	Form Area sf	Material Factors Neat	Material Factors Loss	Cost $ Unit	Cost $ Total
Footings	L	10,100	8.0	1260	2.55	1.37	0.26	1144
	P			1260	1.00	1.37	0.55	949
Keyway 3×8		1,000 LF		-	1000	1.50	0.26	390
3×12		100 LF		-	100	1.50	0.26	39
6×18		100 LF		-	100	1.50	0.26	39
		10,100		1260				2,561
Sales Tax 5%								128
Total Cost								2,689

Figure 6.8(d) Lumber and Plywood Cost Computations – Class C Concrete.

Form Ties

Essential form tie needs for the project are estimated by multiplying component contact areas by the related tie factors found in Tables 4.6 to 4.10. Material losses for ties are held at 10 percent for all tie parts with the *life* of working parts being limited (in this case) to 15 uses.

To evaluate the form tie needs, it is necessary that the estimator choose the type, size, and length of tie by comparing contact areas to the three-dimensional conditions found in the plans. The result is that the breakdown of contact areas is in greater detail. (See Figure 6.9*a* to *d*.) The estimator may decide, as could be the case with footing forms for example, that long ties can be satisfactorily replaced by added lumber crossties and braces. This is acceptable as long as the added lumber involved is evaluated. In this case, the tie cost as shown will satisfactorily cover essential form support needs.

The deck forms under Class A Concrete will require the use of overhang brackets in addition to the hanger system chosen from Table 4.9. Since the brackets are an add-on material expense, an estimation of the number of brackets required must be made. Assuming the use of brackets with a 3000 pound capacity and with a concentrated load of 1000 pounds on the fascia form created by a mechanical finishing machine with wheels spaced at 7-foot intervals, the number of brackets needed is as follows:

DECK OVERHANG BRACKET REQUIREMENTS

Structure 3 (See plans)

Length of fascia (2 sides)	292 ft
Extent of overhang	3.25 ft

Load per lineal foot of fascia

Concrete	$3.25' \times 0.75' \times 150$ lb/cf =	366 lb
Form	5 sf $\times$ 15 lb/sf =	75 lb
Workers	3.25 sf $\times$ 50 lb/sf =	163 lb
	Total load (excluding finisher)	604 lb

Spacing of brackets
(3000 lb − 1000 lb) ÷ 604 lb/ft = 3.3 ft

Brackets required
292 ft ÷ 3.3 ft each = 89 each

Structure 4 (See plans)

Length of fascia (2 sides)	500 ft
Extent of overhang	2.5 ft

Project ___Highway 1___

Description ___Class A Concrete___   Date ___1/1___

FORM TIE
COST

Detail	Form Ties			Contact Area s.f.	Material Factors		Cost $	
	Length in.	Size M lbs.	Type		Neat	Loss	Unit	Total
Parapet Expendable E	12	3	Strap	6,100	0.08	1.10	0.50	268
(wall, 0-8') what part W					0.08	1.10/15	1.95	70
Deck 3+4 E	12	6	Hanger	17,800	0.03	1.10	1.40	822
W					0.03	1.10/15	4.36	170
Deck Overhang Brackets	54	3	Bracket	(211 uses)@		1.10/20	65.00	754
				23,900				2084
Sales Tax 5%								104
Total Cost								2188

Figure 6.9(a)   Form Tie Cost Computations — Class A Concrete.

FORM TIE

COST

Project ___Highway 1___

Description ___Class B Concrete___   Date ___1/1___

Detail		Form Ties			Contact Area s.f.	Material Factors		Cost $	
		Length in.	Size M lbs.	Type		Neat	Loss	Unit	Total
Box Floor (SOG)	E	240	3	(Use wood ties)	1200	(See lumber cost)			—
	W								—
Abutment 3 (Abut. 0-8')	E	12	3	Snap	1000	0.15	1.10	0.50	83
	W					0.15	1.10/15	1.95	21
	E	36	3	Snap	600	0.08	1.10	0.85	45
	W					0.08	1.10/15	1.95	7
Abutment 4 (Abut. 0-8')	E	18	3	Snap	1200	0.15	1.10	0.55	109
	W					0.15	1.10/15	1.95	26
	E	42	3	Snap	700	0.08	1.10	0.96	59
	W					0.08	1.10/15	1.95	8
Box Walls (Wall 0-8')	E	12	5	Snap	1600	0.11	1.10	0.70	136
	W					0.11	1.10/15	2.71	35
	E	18	5	Snap	2000	0.11	1.10	0.79	191
	W					0.11	1.10/15	2.71	44

Figure 6.9(b) Form Tie Cost Computations – Class B Concrete.

Project _Highway 1_

Description _Class B Concrete (Cont'd)_   Date _1/1_

FORM TIE

COST

Detail		Form Ties			Contact Area	Material Factors		Cost s	
		Length in.	Size M lbs.	Type	s.f.	Neat	Loss	Unit	Total
Wall 2 Stem	E	30	6	Coil	31,600	0.13	1:10	0.91	4,112
(Wall 8'+)	W					0.13	1:10/15	4.03	1,214
Pier 4 Stem	E	72	6	Coil	2,900	0.13	1:10	1.85	767
(Wall 8'+)	W					0.13	1:10/15	4.03	111
Columns 3+4	E	48	6	Coil	2,200	0.25	1:10	1.31	793
	W					0.25	1:10/15	4.03	650
Beams 3+4	E	48	3	Snap	2,100	0.07	1:10	1.06	171
	W					0.07	1:10/15	1.95	21
Box Roof (SAG)		(None required)			1,400	—		—	
					48,500				8,603
Sales tax 5%									430
Total Cost									9,033

Figure 6.9(c) Form Tie Cost Computations – Class B Concrete (cont.).

FORM TIE

COST

Project: Highway 1

Description: Class C Concrete   Date: 1/1

Detail		Form Ties			Contact Area s.f.	Material Factors		Cost $	
		Length in.	Size M lbs.	Type		Neat	Loss	Unit	Total
Abutment 3 Footings	E	72	3	Snap	700	0.08	1.10	1.47	91
	W					0.08	1.10/15	1.95	8
Abutment 4 Footings	E	90	3	Snap	1000	0.08	1.10	1.77	156
	W					0.08	1.10/15	1.95	11
Wall 2 Footings	E	180	3	Snap	6400	0.08	1.10	3.27	1842
	W					0.08	1.10/15	1.95	73
Pier 3 Footings	E	120	3	Snap	700	0.08	1.10	2.22	140
	W					0.08	1.10/15	1.95	8
Pier 4 Footings	E	168	5	Snap	1300	0.11	1.10	3.20	503
	W					0.11	1.10/15	2.71	28
					10,100				2,860
Sales tax 5%									143
Total Cost									3,003

Figure 6.9(d)   Form Tie Cost Computations – Class C Concrete.

Load per lineal foot of fascia

Concrete	2.5′ × 0.8′ × 150 lb/cf	= 300 lb
Form	4 sf × 15 lb/sf	= 60 lb
Workers	2.5 sf × 50 lb/sf	= 125 lb
	Total load (excluding finisher)	485 lb

Spacing of brackets
(3000 lb − 1000 lb) ÷ 485 lb/ft   = 4.1 ft

Brackets required
500 ft ÷ 4.1 ft each   = 122 each

The estimate of cost for deck overhang brackets is based on the total number of planned uses (89 + 122), including losses similar to those for ties (10 percent), and a *life* of 20 cycles. Entering these factors into the computation sheet (Figure 6.9*a*) and applying them to the purchase price for brackets as established with the cost data, a cost is determined. Note that this procedure assumes the continued use of this material on other projects.

Shoring Cost

The external support of forms can be often executed in more than one way. Thus, estimating the cost first requires the conceptual consideration of the support problem and possibly a preliminary design sufficient enough to establish a system capability. The cost can then be estimated as it would be for any work activity.

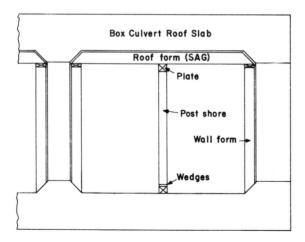

Figure 6.10   Post Shore System — Box Culvert.

Box Culvert Roof Slab Form

The 8-foot-wide box culvert roof form could be constructed with joists of sufficient size, spacing, and strength to avoid the need for any external support, but a relatively simple and inexpensive system of post shores would afford greater overall economy because the self-supporting form would require an additional 1.2 board feet of lumber per square foot—and it would cost much more to build. Referring to Figure 6.10, and using load tables for posts as found in *Formwork for Concrete* (ACI, Special Publication, Number 4)[1] the following is an estimate of the shoring requirements for the box culvert roof slab form:

POST SHORE SYSTEM—BOX CULVERT

Approximate Design

Problem Design for a system of posts located at the center of the roof form span (see Figure 6.10)

Load Per Lineal Foot of Roof Form

Concrete	$4' \times 1.5' \times 150$ lb/cf	=	900 lb
Form	4 sf $\times$ 10 lb/sf	=	40 lb
Workers	4 sf $\times$ 50 lb/sf	=	200 lb
	Total load per lineal foot		1140 lb

Post Design The capacity of a $4'' \times 4'' \times 6'$ post is approximately 11,000 pounds[1]

Spacing of Posts

11,000 lb ÷ 1140 lb/ft = 9.65 ft
Use 8-ft space

Conclusion

The material cost for a post shore system will be adequately represented by $4'' \times 4''$ posts, spaced at 8-foot centers, with 4 × 4 plates at the top and bottom running the length of the form. Material requirements for a 25-foot-long form are:

8 each	$6' \times \dfrac{4'' \times 4''}{12}$ =	64 bf
4 each	$25' \times \dfrac{4'' \times 4''}{12}$ =	133 bf
Wedges and blocks (est.)		25 bf
		222 bf

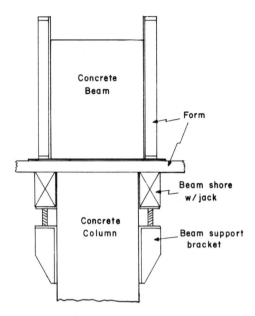

Figure 6.11 Beam Shore System – Pier Beams.

Pier Beam Form

One of the most popular means used for the support of a pier beam form is the beam shore. The reason lies in the simplicity and convenience of beam shores. Figure 6.11 represents the general configuration of the shore system as it would be applied in this case. A simple design is used to approximate material requirements. Referring to the plans and to tables found in *Wood Structural Design Data*[2] published by the National Forest Products Association, the following is an estimate of the beam shore requirements.

BEAM FORM SUPPORT

Approximate Beam Shore Design—Structure 3

Span supported	=	19.5 ft
Total beam length	=	31 ft
Load per lineal foot of beam		
Concrete 4′ × 4′ × 150 lb/cf	=	2,400 lb
Forms 12 sf × 15 lb/sf	=	180 lb
Workers 4 sf × 50 lb/sf	=	200 lb
Shore (approx.) 2 × 50 lb/ft	=	100 lb
Total load per foot (two beam shores)	=	2,880 lb

Load per lineal foot of shore $\qquad$ = 1,440 lb

Approximate shore design load = 1440 lb/ft × 19.5 ft = 28,080 lb

Beam Shore Design

The beam tables show that a 12- by 18-in beam is capable of carrying 29,348 lb over a 20-ft span.

Beam Support Bracket

A single bracket must carry 1440 lb/ft × 15.5 ft, or 22,320 lb. Use a 25,000-lb capacity bracket.

Approximate Beam Shore Design—Structure 4

Span supported	=	17.5 ft
Total beam length	=	19.5 ft

Load per lineal foot of beam

Concrete	4′ × 5′ × 150 lb/cf	=	3,000 lb
Forms	14′ × 15 lb/sf	=	210 lb
Workers	4 sf × 50 lb/sf	=	200 lb
Shore (approx.)	2 × 50 lb/ft	=	100 lb
Total load per foot (two beam shores)			3,510 lb

Load per lineal foot of shore $\qquad$ 1,755 lb

Approximate shore design load = 1775 lb/ft × 17.5 ft. = 30,712 lb

Beam Shore Design

Beam tables show that a 12- by 18-in beam will carry a load of 32,609 lb over a span of 18 ft.

Beam Support Bracket

A single bracket will carry

At center 1755 lb/ft × 17.5 = 30,712 lb
At ends   1755 lb/ft × 10.75 = 18,866 lb

Use 30,000-lb capacity brackets at the center column, and 25,000-lb brackets at the ends.

Conclusions

The materials required to support the pier beam forms are equivalent to the following:

$$2 \text{ each } 40' \times \frac{12'' \times 18''}{12} = 1440 \text{ bf}$$

4 each 25,000-lb brackets (Structures 3 and 4)
2 each 30,000-lb brackets (Structure 4)
6 each 30,000-lb jacks (Structures 3 and 4)

Shoring Crews and Productivity
Figure 6.12a and b shows the crew and equipment necessary for the installation and removal of the shoring systems chosen and the rates at which the crews will produce.

Shoring Labor, Equipment, and Materials
Figure 6.13 displays the shoring labor and equipment cost computations. The material cost is computed as follows:

Post Shore System—Box Culvert
222 bf @ $0.26 bf = $ 58.00

Pier Beam Shore
1440 bf @ $0.45 bf =	648.00
	$706.00
Sales tax 5%	35.00
Total cost	$741.00

Concrete Mix Cost
The prices obtained from AAA Transit Mix Company (Section 6.4, "Cost Data") represented the lowest cost for all concrete mixes. In order to state the cost in terms that reflect material waste, sales tax, escalation, and the use of retarders, the price for each class of concrete must be adjusted as follows:

Class A Concrete—Decks, Sidewalks, and Parapets

Concrete required prior to 10/1
Structure 3–189 cy @ $43.50 cy = $ 8,222.00
Concrete required after 10/1
Structure 4–413 cy @ $46.55 cy = 19,225.00
Retarder required prior to 10/1
Structure 3–135 cy @ $ 1.00 cy = 135.00
Retarder required after 10/1
Structure 4–296 cy @ $ 1.07 cy = 317.00
Subtotal $27,898.00
Sales tax 5% 1,395.00
Subtotal $29,293.00
Average expected yield 95%
Total cost Class A concrete
$29,293.00 ÷ 95% = $30,835.00

Project _____Highway 1_____

Description _Install and Remove Shoring_ Date __1/1__

CREW

HOURLY COST

Labor Classification	Bid Rate	Beam Shores Insh. 25 Rem. 40		Post Shores Insh 75 Rem 150	
Foreman _Carp._	20.30	20.30	1	20.30	1
Laborer common	8.20	16.40	2	16.40	2
air/power					
Finisher					
Ironworker					
Carpenter journeyman	13.90	27.80	2	27.80	2
helper	10.85	2.71	1/4	2.71	1/4
Truck driver					
Welder	18.25	18.25	1		
Operator crane				4.56	1/4
conveyor					
pump					
finisher					
compress.					
oiler					
Crew Totals		85.46		71.77	

Figure 6.12(a) Hourly Crew Cost – Shoring.

223

EQUIPMENT

HOURLY COST

Project __Highway 1__

Description __Install and Remove Shoring__ Date __/ /__

Equipment	Rate	Beam Shores		Post Shores	
OWNERSHIP					
Pickup	2.00	1	2.00	1	2.00
Service truck	3.00	1/4	0.75	1/4	0.75
18 T Hydr. Crane	25.00	1	25.00	1/4	6.25
Chain Saw	0.90	1	0.90	1	0.90
2.5 kW Generator	1.10	1	1.10	1	1.10
300 Amp Welder	1.90	1/2	0.95		
Ownership Totals			30.70		11.00
EOE					
Pickup	2.50	1	2.50	1	2.50
Service Truck	3.00	1/4	0.75	1/4	0.75
18 T Hydr. Crane	6.50	1	6.50	1/4	1.63
Chain Saw	0.40	1	0.40	1	0.40
2.5 kW Generator	0.40	1	0.40	1	0.40
300 Amp Welder	2.50	1/2	1.25		
EOE Totals			11.80		5.68

Figure 6.12(b) Hourly Equipment Cost – Shoring.

224

Project ___Highway 1___

___Class B Concrete___

Description ___Install and Remove Shoring___   Date___/ /___

SHORING

COST

Detail	Support Surface s.f.	Prod. Rate sf/hr	Total Hours	Labor		Equipment Ownership		Equipment Operation	
				$/hr	Total $	$/hr	Total $	$/hr	Total $
Pier Beam Shores									
Install	600	25	24	85.50	2,052	30.70	737	11.80	283
Remove	600	40	15	85.50	1,282	30.70	461	11.80	177
Beam shore support brackets									
25" - 4 @ 70 days				–	–	2.00/d	560.	–	–
30" - 2 @ 40 days				–	–	2.20/d	176.	–	–
Box Culvert Roof Shores									
Install	1200	75	16	71.77	1,148	11.00	176	5.70	91
Remove	1200	150	8	71.77	574	11.00	88	5.70	46
Total Cost					5,056		2,198		597

Figure 6.13 Shoring Cost Computations.

Class B Concrete—Substructure Wall Stems and Box Culvert

All concrete required prior to 10/1
    2160 cy @ $41.00 cy = $88,560.00
Sales tax 5%   4,428.00
Subtotal $92,988.00
Average expected yield 96%
    Total cost Class B concrete
    $92,988 ÷ 96%   = $96,862.00

Class C Concrete—Footings

All concrete required prior to 10/1
    2001 cy @ $36.00 cy = $72,036.00
Sales tax 5%   3,602.00
Subtotal $75,638.00
Average expected yield 92%
    Total cost Class C concrete
    $75,638.00 ÷ 92%   = $82,215.00

Class D Concrete—Overbreak, Nonpay

25 cy @ $35.00 cy   = $ 875.00
Sales tax 5%   44.00
Subtotal $ 919.00
Average expected yield 92%
    Total cost Class D concrete
    $919.00 ÷ 92%   = $ 999.00

Concrete Placing Cost

For the Highway 1 Project a crane will be used to place all structural concrete because there are very few opportunities for direct placement. With good planning, cranes should always be on the project and available for use.

Figure 6.14a and b shows the various hourly rates for placing crews and their equipment and, as chosen with the aid of Table 5.1, their projected rates of productivity.

The concrete placing cost for each class of concrete is computed as shown in Figure 6.15a to c. Once again, these computations utilize the take-off. Note that the cost for placing Class D concrete is subsidiary to the Class C concrete item cost.

Concrete Finishing Cost

Dry finishing is essentially confined to the rubbing of exposed concrete surfaces, grinding of bridge seats to close tolerances, and accomplishing of any necessary correction work on bridge decks. Figure

Project ___Highway 1___

Description ___Place Concrete___ Date ___1/1___

HOURLY COST

Labor Classification	Bid Rate	Foot 22		SOG 14 SAG 10		Abut 0-8' Wall 0-8 A w 4/5		Wall 8+ 14		Column Beams C S 8 8		Deck 3 14 Deck 4 12		Class D Conc. 15	
Foreman Labor	16.10	1	16.10	1	16.10	1	16.10	1	16.10	1	16.10	1	16.10	½	8.05
Laborer common	8.20	4	32.80	5	41.00	4	32.80	5	41.00	5	41.00	6	49.20	3	24.60
air/power	8.80	2	17.60	2	17.60	1	8.80	2	17.60	1½	13.20	3	26.40		
Finisher	12.35			2	24.70	½	6.17	½	6.17	½	6.17	3	37.05		
Ironworker															
Carpenter journeyman	13.90					1	13.90	1	13.90	1	13.90	1	13.90		
helper															
Truck driver	10.85	¼	2.71	¼	2.71	¼	2.71	½	5.42	½	5.42	½	5.42	¼	2.71
Welder															
Operator crane	18.25	1	18.25	1	18.25	1	18.25	1	18.25	1	18.25	1	18.25		
conveyor															
pump															
finisher	12.70											1	12.70		
compress.															
oiler	11.20	1	11.20	1	11.20			1	11.20	1	11.20	1	11.20		
Crew Totals			98.66		131.56		98.73		129.64		125.24		190.22		35.36

Figure 6.14(a) Hourly Crew Cost – Concrete Placing.

EQUIPMENT

HOURLY COST

Project ___Highway 1___

Description ___Place Concrete___   Date ___1/1___

	Equipment	Rate	Footing STDG STRG		Abut.to-8' Wall,o-8'		Wall,8'+		Column Beam		Deck 3		Deck 4		Class D Conc.	
OWNERSHIP	Pickup truck	2.00	1	2.00	1	2.00	1	2.00	1	2.00	1	2.00	1	2.00	1/2	1.00
	Service truck	3.00	1/4	0.75	1/4	0.75	1/2	1.50	1/2	1.50	1/2	1.50	1/2	1.50	1/4	0.75
	18 T Hydr. Crane	25.00			1	25.00										
	40 T Truck Crane	38.00	1	38.00	1	38.00	1	38.00	1	38.00	1	38.00	1	(60T) 45.00		
	1 3/8" Vibrator	1.25			1	2.50	1	1.25	2	2.50	2	2.50	2	2.50		
	2 1/4" Vibrator	1.50	3	4.50	2	2.50	2	3.00	1	1.50	2	3.00	2	3.00		
	1 CY Conc. Bucket	1.15			1	1.15										
	2 CY Conc. Bucket	1.60	2	3.20			2	3.20	1	1.60	2	3.20	2	3.20		
	2.5 KW Generator-Deck Finisher	1.10 / 12.00			1	1.10	1	1.10	1	1.10	1	1.10 / 12.00	1	1.10 / 12.00		
	Ownership Totals			48.45		32.50		50.05		48.20		63.30		70.70		1.75
EOE	Pickup truck	2.50	1	2.50	1	2.50	1	2.50	1	2.50	1	2.50	1	2.50	1/2	1.25
	Service truck	3.00	1/4	0.75	1/4	0.75	1/2	1.50	1/2	1.50	1/2	1.50	1/2	1.50	1/2	0.75
	18 T Hydr. Crane	6.50			1	6.50										
	40 T Truck Crane	9.75	1	9.75			1	9.75	1	9.75	1	9.75	1	(60T) 13.00		
	1 3/8" Vibrator	0.50			2	1.00	1	0.50	2	1.00	2	1.00	2	1.00		
	2 1/4" Vibrator	0.55	3	1.65	2	1.00	2	1.10	1	0.55	2	1.00	2	1.10		
	1 CY Conc. Bucket	0.10			1	0.10										
	2 CY Conc. Bucket	0.15	2	0.30			2	0.30	1	0.15	2	0.30	2	0.30		
	2.5 KW Generator-Deck Finisher	0.40 / 4.50			1	0.40	1	0.40	1	0.40	1	0.40 / 4.50	1	0.40 / 4.50		
	EOE Totals			14.45		11.25		16.05		15.85		21.05		24.30		2.00

Figure 6.14(b) Hourly Equipment Cost – Concrete Placing.

Project _Highway 1_

Description _Class A Concrete_   Date __1/1__

CONCRETE PLACE

COST

Detail	Method	Concrete cy	Prod. Rate cy/hr	Total Hours	Labor $/hr	Labor Total $	Equipment Ownership $/hr	Equipment Ownership Total $	Equipment Operation $/hr	Equipment Operation Total $
Deck 3	Crane	135	14	10	190.20	1,902	63.30	633	21.00	210
Deck 4	"	296	12	25	190.20	4,755	70.30	1758	24.30	608
Sidewalk 3,4 (deck)	"	64	10	6	131.60	790	48.40	290	14.40	86
Parapet (wall, 0-8')	"	107	5	21	98.70	2,073	32.50	682	11.20	235
Totals		602				9519		3363		1139

Figure 6.15(a)   Concrete Placing Cost Computations – Class A Concrete.

Project Highway 1

Description Class B Concrete   Date 1/1

CONCRETE PLACE

COST

Detail	Method	Concrete cy	Prod. Rate cy/hr	Total Hours	Labor $/hr	Labor Total $	Equipment Ownership $/hr	Equipment Ownership Total $	Equipment Operation $/hr	Equipment Operation Total $
Box Floor (SOG)	Crane	128	14	9	131.60	1,184	48.40	436	14.40	130
Abutment 3,4 (Abut. 0-8')	"	103	4	26	98.70	2,566	32.50	845	11.20	291
Box wall (wall, 0-8')	"	71	5	14	98.70	1,382	32.50	455	11.20	157
Wall 2 Stem (wall, 8'+)	"	1,339	14	96	129.60	12,442	50.00	4,800	16.00	1,536
Pier 4 stem (wall, 8'+)	"	274	14	20	129.60	2,592	50.00	1,000	16.00	320
Columns 3,4	"	68	5	14	125.20	1,753	48.20	675	15.80	221
Beams 3,4	"	96	8	12	125.20	1,502	48.20	578	15.80	190
Box Roof (SOG)	"	81	10	8	131.60	1,053	48.40	387	14.40	115
Totals		2,160				24,474		9,176		2,960

Figure 6.15(b) Concrete Placing Cost Computations – Class B Concrete.

Project ___Highway 1___

Description ___Class C Concrete___ Date ___1/1___

CONCRETE PLACE

COST

Detail	Method	Concrete cy	Prod. Rate cy/hr	Total Hours	Labor		Equipment Ownership		Equipment Operation	
					$/hr	Total $	$/hr	Total $	$/hr	Total $
Footings	Crane	2001	22	91	98.70	8,982	418.46	41,404	14.40	1310
Class D Concrete		25	15	2	35.40	71	1.75	3	2.00	4

Figure 6.15(c) Concrete Placing Cost Computations – Class C Concrete.

6.10a and b shows the crew and equipment needs and the expected productivity. Although the crews for the various rubbing tasks are the same, productivity and equipment use varies. Figure 6.17a and b contains the estimate of rub and float labor and equipment cost.

Rubbing concrete surfaces often involves the use of small amounts of mortar composed of cement and sand. This expense should be sufficiently covered by a 3 percent surcharge against labor expense. No added material expense is anticipated for float.

RUBBING MATERIAL COST

Class A Concrete   3% × $6856.00 = $206.00

Class B Concrete   3% × $5333.00 = $160.00

Expansion Dams and Joint Seals

The expansion dams and joint seals as required for the construction of the deck for Structure 4 are itemized and evaluated separately because of their high cost and specifically assigned locations. The expansion dams require particular care in installation so that deck surface grades will be met. They also require field painting. The cost computations for these activities are shown in Figures 6.18a and b and 6.19.

The material expense as taken from the quotations will be as follows:

Expansion Dams

Material	$ 9,500.00
Paint (est.)	75.00
	$ 9,575.00
Sales tax 5%	479.00
Total cost	$10,054.00

Elastomeric Joint Seal Material

90 lf × $20.00 per lf =	$1800.00
Sales tax 5%	90.00
Total cost	$1890.00

Subcontracted Work

It has been decided that some of the work can be subcontracted. The surface applications of waterproofing, dampproofing materials, and linseed oil will be done by the ABC Corporation, and the 6-inch perforated drain system and select backfill materials required for Structure 2 will be installed by the small contractor who had an interest. Their respective prices will therefore be used as they were quoted.

Project ___Highway 1___

Description ___Finishing___   Date ___1/1___

CREW

HOURLY COST

Labor Classification	Bid Rate	Rub Low Walls 70		Rub High Walls 60		Rub Col's & Bms 50		Rub Surface Face 60		Float Bm. Seats A 20 / P 15		Float Deck Grind 350	
Foreman Finisher	17.95	¼	4.49	¼	4.49	¼	4.49	¼	4.49	¼	4.49	¼	4.49
Laborer common air/power	8.20	1	8.20	1	8.20	1	8.20	1	8.20	½	4.10	1	8.20
Finisher	12.35	2	24.70	2	24.70	2	24.70	2	24.70	2	24.70	1	12.35
Ironworker													
Carpenter journeyman helper													
Truck driver	10.85	¼	2.71	¼	2.71	¼	2.71	¼	2.71	⅛	1.35	⅛	1.35
Welder													
Operator crane													
conveyor													
pump													
finisher													
compress.													
oiler													
Crew Totals			40.10		40.10		40.10		40.10		34.64		26.39

Figure 6.16(a) Hourly Crew Cost – Surface Treatment.

Project ___Highway 1___

Description ___Finishing___   Date ___1/1___

EQUIPMENT
HOURLY COST

	Equipment	Rate	Lab Low Walls	Lab High Walls	Lab C.B.& Bms	Lab Parapet Fcns	Float Bm Seats	Float Deck
OWNERSHIP	Pickup truck	2.00	1/4 0.50	1/4 0.50	1/4 0.50	1/4 0.50	1/4 0.50	1/4 0.50
	Service truck	3.00	1/4 0.75	1/4 0.75	1/4 0.75	1/4 0.75	1/8 0.37	1/8 0.37
	Hydraulic lift	12.00		1/8 3.00	1/2 6.00	1/4 3.00		
	HD Grinder	2.00					1 2.00	1 2.00
	Generator	1.10					1 1.10	1 1.10
	Hand grinder	1.00					2 2.00	
	Ownership Totals		1.25	4.25	7.25	4.25	3.97	3.97
EOE	Pickup truck	2.50	1/4 0.62	1/4 0.62	1/4 0.62	1/4 0.62	1/4 0.62	1/4 0.62
	Service truck	3.00	1/4 0.75	1/4 0.75	1/4 0.75	1/4 0.75	1/8 0.37	1/8 0.37
	Hydraulic lift	4.00		1/4 1.00	1/2 2.00	1/4 1.00		
	HD Grinder	1.20					1 1.20	1 1.20
	Generator	0.40					1 0.40	1 0.40
	Hand grinder	0.60					2 1.20	
	EOE Totals		1.37	2.37	3.37	2.37	2.59	2.59

Figure 6.16(b) Hourly Equipment Cost – Surface Treatment.

234

Project *Highway 1* — SURFACE TREATMENT

Description *Class A Concrete* Date *1/1* — COST

Detail	Finish Area s. f.	Prod. Rate sf/hr	Total Hours	Labor		Equipment Ownership		Equipment Operation	
				$ / hr	Total $	$ / hr	Total $	$ / hr	Total $
Rub Parapets and									
Facias	10,100	70	144	40.10	5,774	4.20	605	2.40	346
Float Deck	14,200	350	41	26.40	1,082	4.00	164	2.60	107
Totals					6,856		769		453

Figure 6.17(a) Surface Treatment Cost Computations – Class A Concrete.

Project *Highway 1*

Description *Class B Concrete* Date *1/1*

SURFACE TREATMENT COST

Detail	Finish Area s. f.	Prod. Rate sf/hr	Total Hours	Labor $/hr	Labor Total $	Equipment Ownership $/hr	Equipment Ownership Total $	Equipment Operation $/hr	Equipment Operation Total $
Rub - Abutments	1200	70	17	40.10	682	1.25	21	1.37	23
Box Wall	700	70	10	"	401	1.25	12	1.37	14
Pier 4 stems	1400	60	23	"	922	4.25	98	2.37	55
Columns	2000	50	40	"	1,604	7.25	290	3.37	135
Beams	2000	50	40	"	1,604	7.25	290	3.37	135
Box roof	200	70	3	"	120	1.25	4	1.37	4
Totals	7,500				5,333		715		365
Float - Box floor	1,500	None							
Abutment	400	30	13	34.60	450	4.00	52	2.60	34
Beams	700	25	28	34.60	969	4.00	112	2.60	73
Totals	2,600				1,419		164		107

Figure 6.17(b) Surface Treatment Cost Computations – Class B Concrete.

Project _____ Highway 1 _____

Description _Exp. Dams + Joint Seals_ _____ Date _1/1_ _____

HOURLY COST

Labor Classification	Bid Rate	Exp. Dam 80 Ft. 8 ft/hr 10.15	Paint Exp. Dam cft/hr/cf	Joint Seal 90 ft. 10 ft/hr
Foreman _Carp_	20.30	½ 10.15		
Laborer common air/power	8.20	1	8.20	1	8.20	2	16.40
Finisher				
Ironworker				
Carpenter journeyman	13.90	2	27.80		
helper				
Truck driver	10.85	¼	2.71		¼	2.71
Welder				
Operator crane	18.25	½	9.12		
conveyor				
pump				
finisher				
compress.				
oiler				
Crew Totals		57.78	8.20	19.11

Figure 6.18(a) Hourly Crew Cost – Joint Treatment.

237

Project __Highway 1__

Description __Exp Dams + Joint Seals__   Date __1/1__

EQUIPMENT HOURLY COST

Equipment	Rate	Exp.Dam 80 Ft.	Paint Exp-Dam	JointSeal 90 Ft.
OWNERSHIP				
Pickup truck	2.00	1/2 1.00		
Service truck	3.00	1/4 0.75		1/4 0.75
18 T Hyd Crane	25.00	1/2 12.50		
300 A Welder	1.90	1 1.90		
160 Compressor	2.50			1 2.50
Ownership Totals		16.15	None	3.25
EOE				
Pickup truck	2.50	1/2 1.25		
Service truck	3.00	1/4 0.75		1/4 0.75
18 T Hyd Crane	6.50	1/2 3.25		
300 A Welder	2.50	1 2.50		
160 Compressor	2.90			1 2.90
EOE Totals		7.75	None	3.65

Figure 6.18(b) Hourly Equipment Cost—Joint Treatment.

Project ___Highway 1___

Description ___Class A Concrete___   Date ___1/1___

JOINT TREATMENT
COST

Detail	Length l.f.	Prod. Rate lf/hr	Total Hours	Labor		Equipment Ownership		Equipment Operation	
				$/hr	Total $	$/hr	Total $	$/hr	Total $
Expansion dams	80								
Install	80	8	10	57.98	580	16.15	162	7.75	78
Paint	80	6	27	8.20	221	-	-	-	-
Totals					801		162		78
Elastomeric joint seals	90	10	9	19.11	172	3.25	29	3.65	33

Figure 6.19 Joint Treatment Cost Computations – Class A Concrete.

239

Common Concrete Cost

The balance of the structural concrete cost items for Highway 1 is such that the costs are not conveniently identified with any single specific class of concrete. Therefore, they are costs common to all concrete work.

Cure

Includes all expense for labor, equipment, and materials required for the maintenance of the concrete cure. Initial placement of curing protection is included with the cost for placing concrete—or with the cost for stripping forms. Specifications require a 7-day cure of all concrete. The procedure for curing is as follows:

1. For footings, slabs on grade, abutments, walls, and beams, cover with wet blankets until form is stripped; then cover with polyethylene.
2. For columns and parapets, cover with wet blankets for entire cure period.
3. For decks and slabs above grade, cover with polyethylene for entire cure period.

The Preliminary Progress Schedule indicates curing concrete will be a constant requirement throughout the 6-month period April through September. It is estimated that the following materials must be purchased:

	Area (sf)	Polyethylene (sf)	Blankets (sf)
Footings	18,000	15,000	2,000
SOG	2,700	2,000	
Abutments	3,500	4,000	1,000
Walls	33,500	15,000	2,000
Beams	2,100	1,000	1,000
Decks	16,400	12,000	
Sidewalks	2,100	1,000	
Parapets	6,100		2,000
Columns	2,200		500
SAG	2,900	3,000	
Totals		53,000	9,000

The entire cost for curing is estimated as follows:

ESTIMATE OF CURE COST

Cure Crew Time

April–September	116 days @ 3 hr/day	= 348 hr
October–November	36 days @ 2 hr/day	= 72 hr
December	5 days @ 1 hr/day	= 5 hr
Total crew hours		425 hr

Labor Cost

Foreman	1/4 hr @ $16.10	= $ 4.03 hr
Laborer	1 hr @ 8.20	= 8.20 hr
Truck driver	1 1/4 hr @ 10.85	= 13.56 hr
Total labor cost		$25.76 hr × 425 hr
		= $10,948.00

Equipment Ownership

Pickup truck	1/4 hr	@	$2.00 = $0.50 hr
Service truck	1/4 hr	@	3.00 = 0.75 hr
Water truck	1 hr	@	3.00 = 3.00 hr
Total equipment ownership costs			$4.25 hr × 425 hr
			= $1806.00

EOE

Pickup truck	1/4 hr	@	$2.50 = $0.62 hr
Service truck	1/4 hr	@	3.00 = 0.75 hr
Water truck	1 hr	@	2.50 = 2.50 hr
Total equipment operating expenses			$3.87 hr × 425 hr
			= $1645.00

Material

Curing blankets	9,000 sf	@	$0.50 = $4500.00
Polyethylene (6 mil)	53,000 sf	@	0.04 = 2120.00
Subtotal			$6620.00
Sales tax 5%			631.00
Total material costs			= $6951.00

Supplies

$10,948.00 × 8%	= $ 876.00

Joints

This expense is for various expansion and sealing materials used in construction and expansion joints throughout the work. They are as follows:

6" Waterstop for box and walls	900 lf
Other joint material	Various
Expansion dams	See Class A concrete
Joint seal	See Class A concrete
Large keyways	See lumber cost

Referring to the materials price data obtained, the material cost for joints is as follows:

JOINT MATERIAL COST

6" waterstop	900 lf @ $3.00 = $2700.00
1" joint material	700 sf @ 0.85 = 595.00
Miscellaneous joint materials (est.)	= 205.00
	$3500.00
Sales tax 5%	175.00
Total material cost	$3675.00

Embedded Items

This expense is for all embedded items not specifically identified elsewhere. Installation is included with the formwork.

EMBEDDED MATERIAL COST

4" PVC weeps	30 lf @ $1.40 = $ 42.00
6" PVC weeps	100 lf @ 2.40 = 240.00
Screens	10 ea @ 1.00 = 10.00
	$292.00
Sales tax 5%	15.00
Total material cost	$307.00

Move

Move cost covers all of the expenses for the continuous on-site movement of materials and equipment. Included are (1) service truck time not already covered under other direct costs, (2) labor for loading and unloading materials not otherwise covered in the cost, (3) labor and equipment necessary for cleanup details, and (4) outside trucking services for moving heavy equipment from one location to another. The cost is computed as follows:

Service Crew Time

April–September	116 days @ 4 hr/day = 464 hr
October–November	36 days @ 2 hr/day = 72 hr
December	5 days @ 2 hr/day = 10 hr
Total crew time	546 hr

Labor Cost

Foreman	1/4 hr @ $16.10 =	$ 4.03 hr
Laborer	1 hr @ 8.20 =	8.20 hr
Truck driver	1 hr @ 10.85 =	10.85 hr
Total labor cost		$23.08 hr × 546 hr
		= $12,602.00

Equipment Ownership

Pickup truck	1/4 hr @ $2.00 =	$0.50 hr
Service truck	1 hr @ 3.00 =	3.00 hr
Total ownership cost		$3.50 hr × 546 hr
		= $1911.00

EOE

Pickup truck	1/4 hr @ $2.50 =	$0.62 hr
Service truck	1 hr @ 3.00 =	3.00 hr
Total EOE cost		$3.62 hr × 546 hr
		= $1977.00

Supplies

8% × $12,602.00 = $1008.00

Subcontract

Trailer services (est.) 10 moves @ $250.00 = $2500.00

Repairs

For this project it is estimated that there will be one full-time worker to maintain all warehoused materials and small equipment and to keep everything in good, usable order; the cost for this person will be as follows:

REPAIR COST

April–October	134 days × 8 hr =	1072 hr
Laborer 1072 hours @ $8.80 per hr		= $9434.00
Materials (est)		= $1500.00
Supplies 8% × $9434.00		= $ 755.00

Power

The project must utilize portable power services since no commercial service is available. Maintain two spare 2.5-kilowatt generators on a standby basis for the entire period April through November. The cost will be as follows:

POWER

Equipment standby

152 days @ 8 hr/day   =   1216 hr

Standby expense

2 @ $1.10 per hr × 1216 hr   = $2675.00

Ramps and Scaffolding

Safe access to and along the concrete work must be continuously maintained for the personnel that do the formwork and place, finish, and cure the concrete. This requires the installation of ramps and scaffolding, the expense for which is common to all concrete cost. The estimate of cost to meet these needs is as follows:

RAMP AND SCAFFOLD COST

Wood Wall Scaffolds (Figure 4.16)

Total requirements	
Walls	180 lf
Beams	80 lf
Columns	80 lf
Total length	340 lf
Crew productivity	16 lf/hr
Total crew time	21 hr

Wood Walkways

Total requirements	
Decks	500 lf
Crew productivity	30 lf/hr
Total crew time	17 hr

Wood Scaffold and Walkway Cost

Labor Cost

Foreman	½ hr @ $20.00/30.00 =	$10.15 per hr
Carpenter	1 hr @ 13.90 =	13.90 per hr
Carpenter helper	1 hr @ 9.95 =	9.85 per hr
Laborer	1 hr @ 8.20 =	8.20 per hr
Total labor cost		$42.20 per hr × 38 hr
		= $1604.00

Equipment Ownership

Pickup	½ hr @	2.00 =	1.00 per hr
Service truck	¼ hr @	3.00 =	0.75 per hr
Generator	1 hr @	1.10 =	1.10 per hr
Total ownership cost			$2.85 per hr × 38 hr
			= $108.00

EOE

Pickup	½ hr @ $2.50 =	$1.25 per hr
Service truck	¼ hr @ 3.00 =	0.75 per hr
Generator	1 hr @ 0.40 =	0.40 per hr
Total EOE cost		$2.40 per hr × 38 hr
		= $91.00

Material

Lumber	340 lf @ 8 bf/lf × $0.26 bf =	$ 707.00
	500 lf @ 6 bf/lf × 0.26 bf =	780.00
Miscellaneous material (est.)	=	250.00
Total material cost		$1737.00

Supplies and Small Tools

8% × $1604.00	= $ 128.00

Sectional Scaffolding

Enough sectional steel scaffolding is to be purchased to cover 800 to 1000 square feet of wall surface. As obtained earlier, the price for the scaffold material is $1980.00. It is estimated that this scaffolding will be used an equivalent of 10 times. Assuming that three laborers can erect or dismantle scaffolding at the rate of five frames per hour, the following is the cost.

Sectional Scaffolding Cost

Erect 20 frames 10 times	=	200
Dismantle 20 frames 10 times	=	200
Total frames		400

Crew time required 400 ÷ 5 =	= 80 hr

Labor 3 hr @ $8.20	= $ 24.60
Total labor $24.60 per hr × 80 hr	= $1968.00

Material

Scaffold (quoted)	$1980.00
Planks, ladders	500.00
	$2480.00
Sales tax 5%	124.00
Total material cost	$2604.00

Supplies
8% × $1968.00   = $ 157.00

Ramps and Scaffolding Summary

	Labor	Equipment ownership	EOE	Material	Supplies
Wood scaffold	$1604.00	$108.00	$91.00	$1737.00	$128.00
Steel scaffold	1968.00			2604.00	157.00
	$3572.00	$108.00	$91.00	$4341.00	$285.00

Common Concrete Cost Summary
The cost for each of the Common Concrete Cost items must now be summarized and allotted to the appropriate bid items. Figure 6.20 lists each of the CCC items, including many for which there was no cost estimated. The reason for this is to show that the unused cost categories were considered and found to require no further consideration.

6.6 SUMMARIZING THE COST

The summarization of cost for the Highway 1 structural concrete, Classes A, B, and C, can now be completed. Each summary will identify cost by activity, and the component costs will have been completely transformed into pay item terms. Figure 6.21a to c displays the results.

The estimator should note that (1) various take-off quantities are shown for reasons of information and have no other purpose in the summarization; (2) the unit prices shown are a function of cost based on the quantity of concrete calculated in the take-off, and the bid cost must therefore be adjusted to suit the quantity difference; (3) Common Concrete Cost is not generally detailed on the summary sheets; and (4) the unit cost for every cost item is not necessarily completed. This exercise is left to the discretion of the estimator.

6.7 COST ADJUSTMENTS

The total cost approach as it applies to structural concrete has now been fully explained. Throughout the process, the value of many of the activities were based on productivity judgments (with little comparison of the elapsed time required) as compared with the activity

COST

SUMMARY

Project Highway 1

Description Common Concrete Cost.   Date 1/1

Detail	Quantity	Unit	Labor		Equipment Ownership		Equipment Operation		Material		Supplies		Subcontracts		Total Cost	
			Unit	Total	Unit	Total	Unit	Total	Unit	Total	Unit	Total	Unit	Total	Unit	Total
Core	4,763	cy		10,948		1,806		1,645		6,951		876			4.67	22,226
Joints			See Class B Concrete cost summary - subcontracted							3,675					0.77	3,675
Waterproof			" " " " "													
Dampproof			" " " "		"		"		"							
Sandblast			None anticipated													
Embedded items										307					0.06	307
Rubbing			See Class A Concrete mix													
Grout			None anticipated													
MORC				12,602		1,911		1,977		1,500		1,008		2,500	4.20	19,998
Repairs				9,434		–						755			2.45	11,689
Engineering			Indirect item													
Cold Weather			None anticipated													
Power				3,572		2,675		91		4,341		285			0.56	2,675
Pumps & Scaffold			Included in mix price			108									1.76	8,397
Testing			Included in mix price													
Totals CCC	4,763	cy		36,556		6,500		3,713		16,774		2,924		2,500		28,967
Class A Concrete	602	cy		4,620		821		465		2,120		370		316		8,717
Class B Concrete	2,160	cy		12,578		2,948		1,684		7,607		1,326		1,134		31,276
Class C Concrete	2,001	cy		15,358		2,731		1,560		7,047		1,228		1,050		28,974
	4,763	cy														

Figure 6.20 Common Concrete Cost Summary.

COST

SUMMARY

Project _Highway 1_

Description _Class A Concrete – 610 cy_ Date _1/1_

Detail	Quantity	Unit	Labor Unit	Labor Total	Equipment Ownership Unit	Equipment Ownership Total	Equipment Operation Unit	Equipment Operation Total	Material Unit	Material Total	Supplies 8% Unit	Supplies 8% Total	Subcontracts Unit	Subcontracts Total	Total Cost Unit	Total Cost Total
Form labor + equipt	23,900	sf		77,584		21,294		8,516				6,207			188.71	113,601
" lumber	10,120	sf								12,652					21.02	12,652
" ties	23,900	sf								2,188					3.63	2,188
Concrete mix	602	cy								30,835					51.22	30,835
place	602	cy		9,519		3,363		1,139				762			24.56	14,783
finish-rub	10,100	sf		5,774		605		346		206		462			12.28	7,393
- float	14,200	sf		1,082		164		107				87			2.39	1,440
linseed oil	20,400	sf												12,240	20.33	12,240
Expansion dam	80	lf		802		162		78		10,054		63			18.84	11,159
Joint seal	90	lf		172		29		33		1,890		14			3.55	2,138
Common Conc. (Bgt)	602	cy		4,620		821		469		2,120		370		316	14.48	8,716
Totals	602	cy	165.37	99,553	43.92	26,438	17.50	10,688	99.58	59,945	13.23	7,965	20.86	12,556	360.71	217,145
Adjust to Contract Quantity	610	cy		100,876		26,789		10,830		60,742		8,071		12,723		220,031

Figure 6.21(a) Cost Summary – Class A Concrete.

COST

SUMMARY

Project ___Highway 1___ Date __1/1__

Description __Class B Concrete - 2,125 cy.__

Detail	Quantity	Unit	Labor Unit	Labor Total	Equipment Ownership Unit	Equipment Ownership Total	Equipment Operation Unit	Equipment Operation Total	Material Unit	Material Total	Supplies Unit	Supplies Total	Subcontracts Unit	Subcontracts Total	Total Cost Unit	Total Cost Total
Form labor + equip.	48,500	sf		68,639		50,841		17,855				13,491			116.12	250,826
" lumber	7,835	sf								18,081					8.37	18,081
" ties	40,500	sf								9,033					4.18	9,033
Shoring	1,800	sf		5,056		2,198		597		741		404			4.16	8,996
Concrete mix	2,160	cy								96,862					44.84	96,862
place	2,160	cy		24,474		9,176		2,960				1,958			17.86	38,568
finish - R	7,500	sf		5,333		715		365		160		427			3.24	7,000
" F	363	sf		1,419		164		107				114			0.84	1,804
Dampproof	18,500	sf												20,460	9.47	20,460
Waterproof	1,000	sf												3,000	1.39	3,000
6" PVC drain	850	lf												3,060	1.42	3,060
Drainage backfill	460	cy												6,900	3.19	6,900
Common Conc. Cost	2,160	cy		16,578		29,948		1,684		7,607		1,326		1,134	14.48	31,276
Totals	2,160	cy	102.55	221,499	30.58	66,042	10.91	23,568	61.34	132,484	8.20	17,720	16.00	34,554	229.57	495,866
Adjust to Contract Quantity	2,125	cy		217,910		64,972		23,186		130,337		17,433		33,994		487,831

Figure 6.21(b) Cost Summary – Class B Concrete.

Project __Highway 1__

Description __Class C Concrete - 2,020 cy__   Date __1/1__

Detail	Quantity	Unit	Labor Unit	Labor Total	Equipment Ownership Unit	Equipment Ownership Total	Equipment Operation Unit	Equipment Operation Total	Material Unit	Material Total	Supplies Unit	Supplies Total	Subcontracts Unit	Subcontracts Total	Total Cost Unit	Total Cost Total
Form labor & equip.	10,100	sf		16,846		3453		1400				1548			1.52	23,047
lumber	1,260	sf								2689					1.34	2689
ties	10,100	sf								3003					.30	3003
Concrete mix	2,001	cy								82,215					41.05	82,215
place	2,001	cy		8982		4404		1310				219			.70	15,415
Class D concrete	25	cy		71		3		4		999		6			0.54	1083
Common Conc. Cost	2,001	cy		15,358		2731		1560		7047		228	1050		14.48	28,974
Totals	2001	cy	20.66	41,257	5.29	10,591	2.14	4,274	47.95	95,953	165	3301	1050	78.17	156,426
Adjust to Contract Quantity	2,020	cy		41,649		10,692		4,314		96,864		3332	1,060			157,911

Figure 6.21(c) Cost Summary — Class C Concrete.

durations shown on the Preliminary Progress Schedule. Without a Preliminary Progress Schedule of much greater detail, this type of comparison would not be possible, and at this stage greater scheduling detail is not practical. So long as the estimator has used a well-founded approach to all steps taken in the estimating process, no further check is needed.

It should be noted that worker's hours and the number of workers on the project are always somewhat flexible—depending on scheduled needs. Equipment, however, is constantly on the project, and ownership cost is continuous and without much flexibility. A check on the total equipment ownership cost can be made by projecting the overall period of time that each item of equipment will be on the project and multiplying the total time by the equipment depreciation rate.

For Highway 1, the average annual equipment depreciation is based on use of the equipment for 1600 hours. The monthly use would therefore be 133 hours. Using the Preliminary Progress Schedule to judge the elapsed time (in months), the overall equipment ownership expense is independently estimated as follows:

TOTAL EQUIPMENT OWNERSHIP COST

Item	Number of items	@ Time (months)	Total hours	@ Total ownership rate	= Total ownership cost
18-tn Hydraulic crane	1	$8^1/2$	1130	$25.00	$ 28,250.00
40-tn Truck crane	1	6	798	38.00	30,324.00
60-tn Truck crane	1	$1/2$	66	45.00	2,970.00
5-tn Hydraulic lift	1	1	133	12.00	1,596.00
$1/2$-tn Pickup truck	1–3	17	2261	2.00	4,522.00
3-tn Flat truck	1	$8^1/2$	1130	3.00	3,390.00
3 M gal Water truck	1	6	798	3.00	2,394.00
40-ft Deck finisher	1	1	133	12.00	1,596.00
160-cf Compressor	1	8	1064	2.50	2,660.00

TOTAL EQUIPMENT OWNERSHIP COST (Continued)

Item	Number of items	@ Time (months)	Total hours	@ Total ownership rate	= Total ownership cost
2.5-kW Generator	3–5	24	3192	1.10	3,511.00
1³/₈-in Vibrator (gas)	3	24	3192	$ 1.25	3,990.00
2¹/₄-in Vibrator (gas)	3	24	3192	1.50	4,788.00
300-A Welder (diesel)	1	6	798	1.80	1,516.00
1 cy Concrete bucket	1	6	798	1.15	917.00
1¹/₂-cy Concrete bucket	2	12	1596	1.50	2,394.00
2-cy Concrete bucket	2	12	1596	1.60	2,554.00
1 Deck grinder	1	¹/₂	66	2.00	132.00
1 Hand grinder	3	3	399	1.00	399.00
18-in Chain saw	2	12	1596	0.90	1,436.00
10-in Bench saw	1	8	1064	1.10	1,170.00
8-cfm Spray pump	1	¹/₂	66	1.50	99.00
25-kip Beam shore support	4–6	5	665	2.00	1,330.00
Total ownership cost					$101,940.00

For comparison, the sum of the equipment ownership columns in the estimated cost for Classes A, B, and C concrete is $102,651.00. A large difference may prompt the estimator to review the estimate and possibly make some adjustment.

6.8 CONCLUSION

Estimators everywhere vary their approach to the determination of cost and, as a result, get various answers. The answers in the illustrations presented in this book hold far less importance than do the concepts explained in their assembly. It must be remembered that the object has been to use an estimating procedure that best serves as a vehicle for explaining the many facets of structural concrete construction and its cost. With understanding and practice an estimator should find ways to shortcut the procedures presented here and to develop individual techniques while still maintaining the good organization and the necessary checks and balances that serve to yield the quality cost estimate.

REFERENCES

[1] *Formwork for Concrete*, SP4, 4th ed., American Concrete Institute, Detroit, Mich., 1979.

[2] *Wood Structural Design Data*, National Forest Products Association, Washington, D.C., 1978.

A

STRUCTURAL PLANS–
HIGHWAY 1

The plans contained here are complete to the extent that they fulfill
the needs of illustrating a structural concrete take-off and cost estimate. They are not reflective of any structural design and are not intended to be used for any purpose other than illustration in this book.
(See Figures A.1 to A.5.)

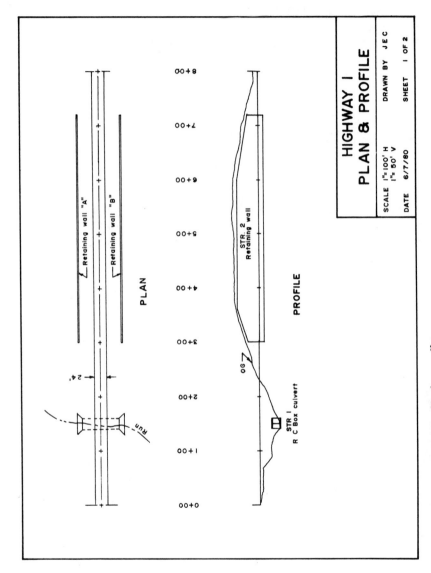

Figure A.1(a)   Plan and Profile (page 1).

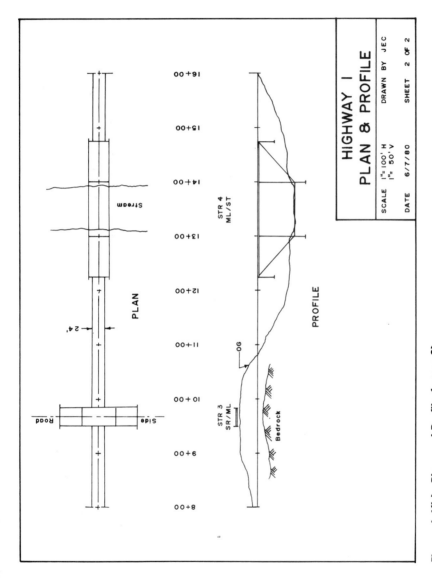

Figure A.1(b)   Plan and Profile (page 2).

257

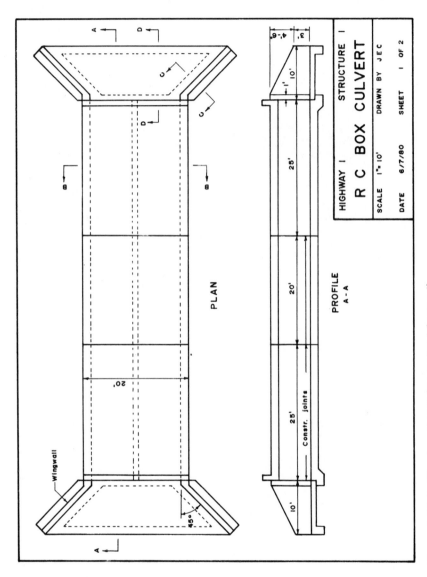

Figure A.2(a) Structure 1, R C Box Culvert (page 1).

258

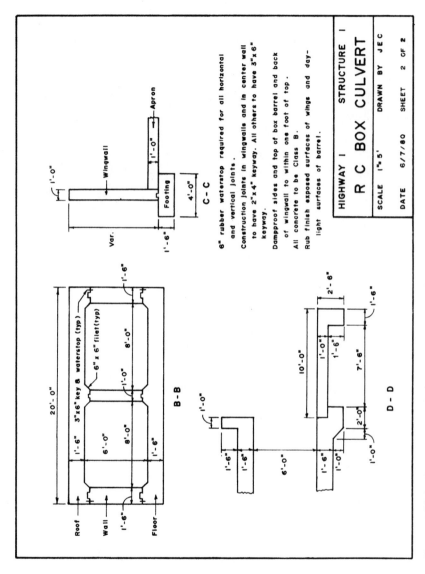

Figure A.2(b) Structure 1, R C Box Culvert (page 2).

The following notes appear on the drawing:

6" rubber waterstop required for all horizontal and vertical joints.

Construction joints in wingwalls and in center wall to have 2"x4" keyway. All others to have 3"x6" keyway.

Dampproof sides and top of box barrel and back of wingwall to within one foot of top.

All concrete to be Class B.

Rub finish exposed surfaces of wings and daylight surfaces of barrel.

HIGHWAY I   STRUCTURE I

R C BOX CULVERT

SCALE I"= 5'   DRAWN BY JEC

DATE 6/7/80   SHEET 2 OF 2

C - C

Apron

Wingwall

Footing

I'- 0"

4'- 0"

I'- 6"

Var.

B - B

20'- 0"

3"x6" key & waterstop (typ.)

6" x 6" fillet (typ.)

Roof

Wall

Floor

I'- 6"   6'- 0"   8'- 0"   I'- 6"

8'- 0"

I'- 0"

I'- 0"

I'- 6"

D - D

10'- 0"

2'- 6"

I'- 6"

7'- 6"

I'- 0"

I'- 6"

2'- 0"

I'- 0"

6'- 0"

I'- 6"

I'- 6"

I'- 6"

I'- 0"

I'- 0"

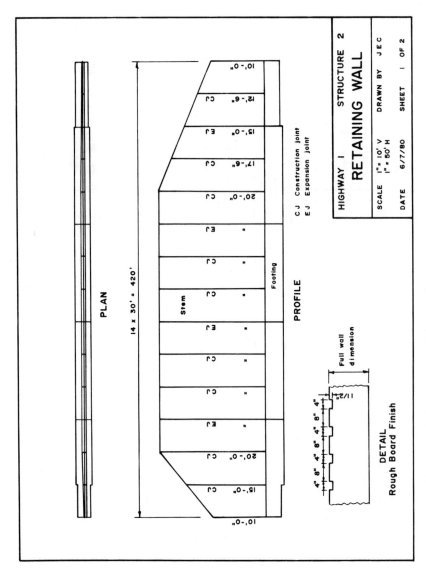

Figure A.3(a) Structure 2, Retaining Wall (page 1).

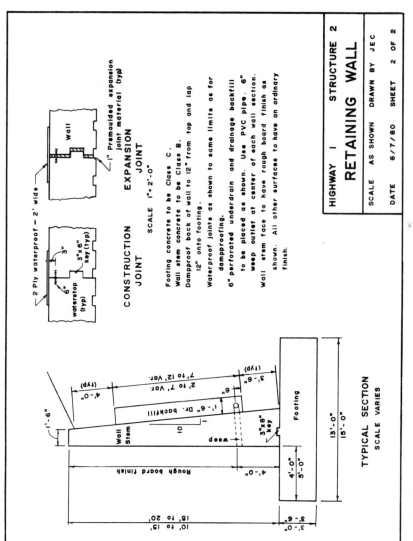

CONSTRUCTION JOINT
SCALE I" = 2'-0"

EXPANSION JOINT
SCALE I" = 2'-0"

Footing concrete to be Class C.
Wall stem concrete to be Class B.
Dampproof back of wall to 12" from top and lap
12" onto footing.
Waterproof joints as shown to same limits as for
dampproofing.
6" perforated underdrain and drainage backfill
to be placed as shown. Use PVC pipe. 6"
weep outlet at center of each wall section.
Wall stem face to have rough board finish as
shown. All other surfaces to have an ordinary
finish.

TYPICAL SECTION
SCALE VARIES

HIGHWAY I	STRUCTURE 2
RETAINING WALL	
SCALE AS SHOWN	DRAWN BY JEC
DATE 6/7/80	SHEET 2 OF 2

Figure A.3(b) Structure 2, Retaining Wall (page 2).

261

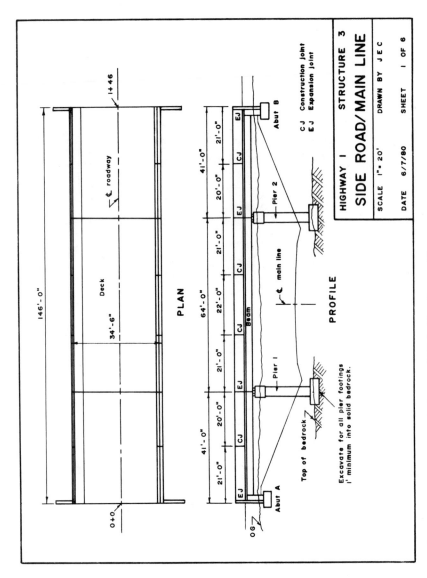

Figure A.4(a)   Structure 3, Side Road/Main Line (page 1).

262

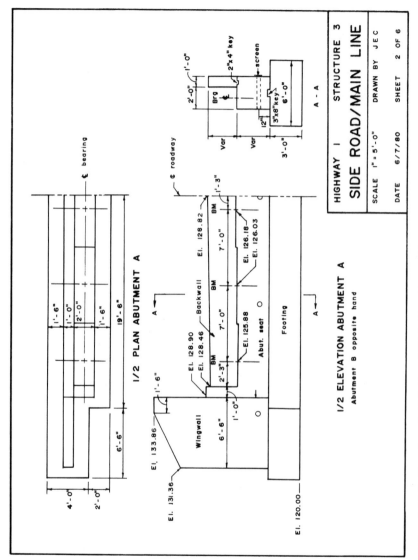

Figure A.4(b) Structure 3, Side Road/Main Line (page 2).

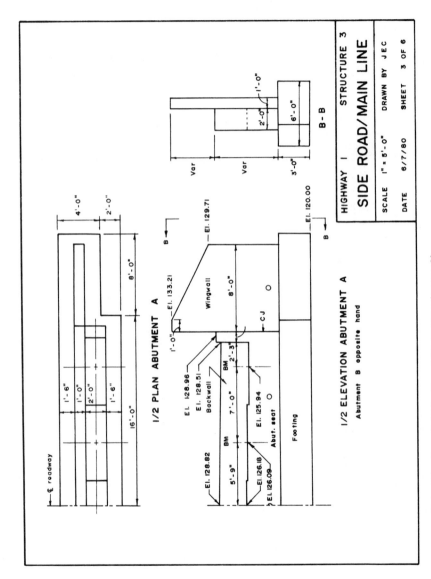

Figure A.4(c) Structure 3, Side Road/Main Line (page 3).

264

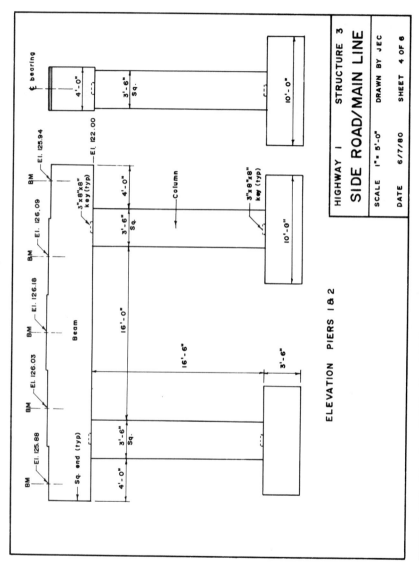

Figure A.4(d) Structure 3, Side Road/Main Line (page 4).

265

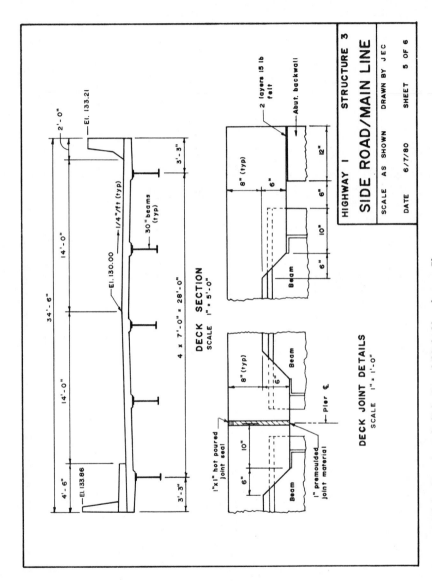

Figure A.4(e) Structure 3, Side Road/Main Line (page 5).

266

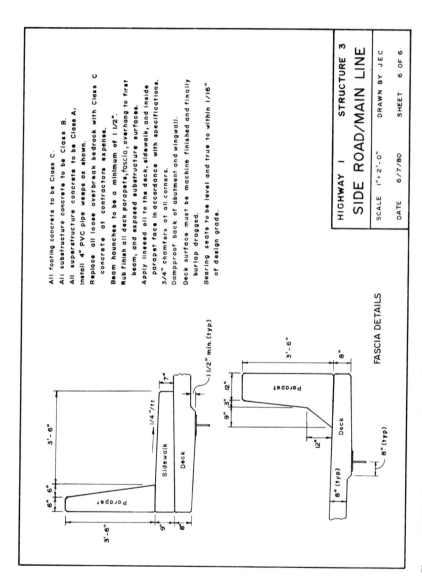

All footing concrete to be Class C.

All substructure concrete to be Class B.

All superstructure concrete to be Class A.

Install 4" PVC pipe weeps as shown.

Replace all loose overbreak bedrock with Class C concrete at contractors expense.

Beam haunches to be a minimum of 1 1/2".

Rub finish all deck parapets, fascia, overhang to first beam, and exposed substructure surfaces.

Apply linseed oil to the deck, sidewalk, and inside parapet face in accordance with specifications.

3/4" chamfers at all corners.

Dampproof back of abutment and wingwall.

Deck surface must be machine finished and finally burlap dragged.

Bearing seats to be level and true to within 1/16" of design grade.

FASCIA DETAILS

HIGHWAY 1	STRUCTURE 3
SIDE ROAD/MAIN LINE	
SCALE 1"=2'-0"	DRAWN BY JEC
DATE 6/7/80	SHEET 6 OF 6

Figure A.4(f) Structure 3, Side Road/Main Line (page 6).

267

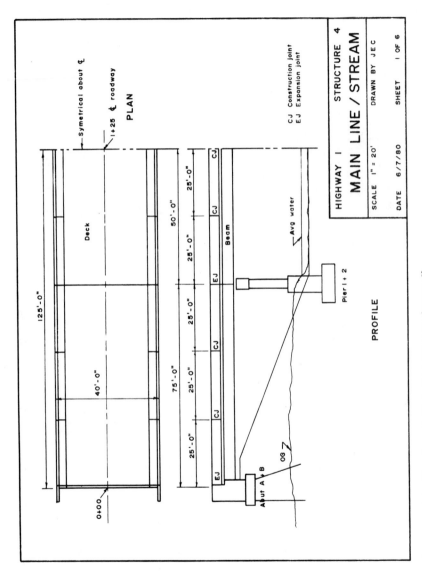

Figure A.5(a) Structure 4, Main Line/Stream (page 1).

268

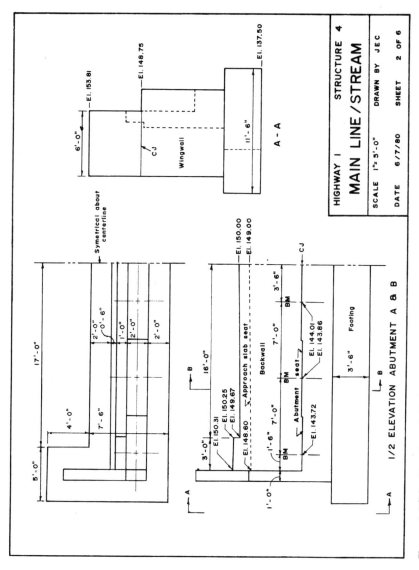

Figure A.5(b)   Structure 4, Main Line/Stream (page 2).

269

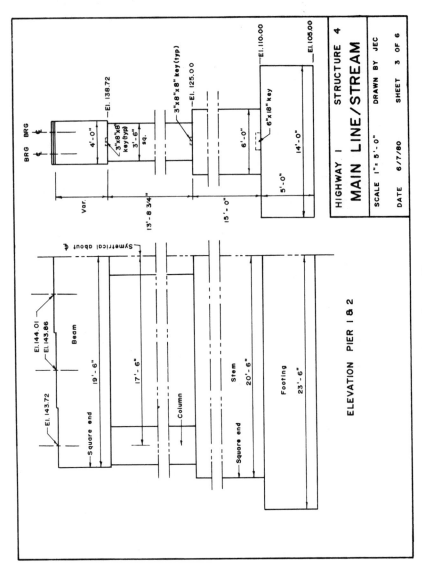

Figure A.5(c)   Structure 4, Main Line/Stream (page 3).

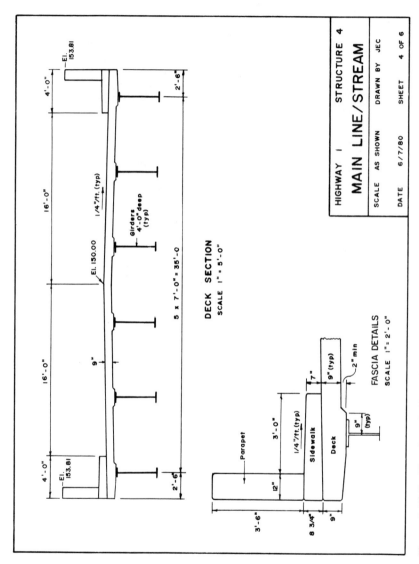

Figure A.5(d) Structure 4, Main Line/Stream (page 4).

DECK SECTION
SCALE 1" = 5'-0"

FASCIA DETAILS
SCALE 1" = 2'-0"

El. 153.81

4'-0"   16'-0"   16'-0"   4'-0"

El. 150.00

1/4"/ft. (typ)

Girders 4'-0" deep (typ)

9"

5 x 7'-0" = 35'-0

2'-6"

Parapet

12"

3'-0"

1/4"/ft. (typ)

Sidewalk

Deck

3'-6"

8 3/4"

9"

7"

9" (typ)

2" min

9" (typ)

HIGHWAY 1   STRUCTURE 4
MAIN LINE/STREAM

| SCALE AS SHOWN | DRAWN BY JEC |
| DATE 6/7/80 | SHEET 4 OF 6 |

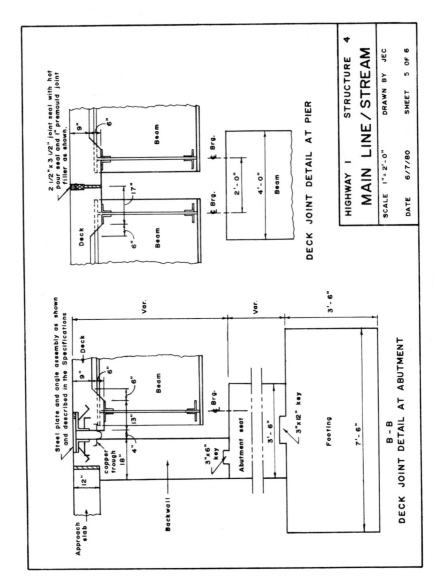

Figure A.5(e) Structure 4, Main Line/Stream (page 5).

Pier footings and stems are to be placed in the dry.

Access to site is entirely subsidiary to the work.

Dampproofing shall be applied to all unexposed surfaces of abutment walls and of wingwalls to within 1' of exposed surfaces.

All beam haunches shall be a minimum of 2" deep by 18" wide as shown.

All exposed surfaces shall be rub finished.

Approach slabs are not included in this work.

Beam bearing seats shall be finished level to within 1/16" of design grade.

A seal of Class D concrete, 6" thick, shall be placed below the pier footings. Cost shall be subsidiary to the footing concrete.

All footing concrete shall be Class C.

All substructure concrete shall be Class B.

All superstructure concrete shall be Class A.

Apply linseed oil to deck, sidewalk, and inside of parapet.

All protruding corners and edges shall be chamfered 3/4".

Surface of deck must be machine finished and burlap dragged.

Use a 2 x 4 keyway between wall and footing for wingwalls.

HIGHWAY 1	STRUCTURE 4
MAIN LINE / STREAM	
SCALE AS SHOWN	DRAWN BY JEC
DATE 6/7/80	SHEET 6 OF 6

Figure A.5(f) Structure 4, Main Line/Stream (page 6).

B SPECIFICATIONS FOR STRUCTURAL CONCRETE- HIGHWAY 1

These specifications are based on the *Standard Specifications for Highway Bridges* (12 ed., 1977) as adopted by The American Association of State Highway and Transportation Officials. They are used, with the permission of AASHTO, to illustrate the examples of structural concrete cost estimating found in this book.

1 DESCRIPTION

This work shall consist of furnishing and placing portland cement concrete for structures as required in accordance with these specifications and in reasonably close conformity with the dimensions, lines, and grades as shown on the plans.

2 CLASSIFICATION AND PROPORTIONING

The following classes of concrete are included in these specifications and shall be used where required by the plans.

Concrete class	Compressive strength (lb/in²)	Cement content (bags/cy)	Proportion by weight (approximate)	Air entrainment (%)	Water per bag (gal)
A	3500	6.5	1–2–3	5.5–7.5	6.0
B	3000	6.0	1–2–3.5	5.0–7.0	5.5
C	2500	5.5	1–2–3.5	4.5–6.5	5.0
D	1500	4.5	1–3–4.5	4.0–6.0	5.0

Bridge deck concrete shall include the use of a retarding chemical admixture. Entrained air may be obtained by the use of air entraining portland cement, an approved additive, or a combination of both.

3 BATCHING

All measuring and batching of materials shall be done at an approved commercial batching plant. The plant shall be subjected to periodic inspection by an authorized representative of the Owner.

The proportion of ingredients per batch shall be that approved by the Owner.

Proper facilities shall be provided, at the batch plant, for the Owner's representative to inspect and test the ingredients and the processes used in batching.

4 MIXING AND DELIVERY

Mixing of concrete ingredients may be done at the batching plant or in truck mixers. Delivery shall be made in truck mixers approved by the Owner. Discharge of the concrete shall be complete within 1 1/2 hours after the introduction of the mixing water to the cement and aggregates.

5 TESTING

The Contractor shall provide all labor, equipment, materials, and facilities necessary to assure the quality of the concrete. This requirement shall include all field sampling, curing, and testing necessary to assure that all delivered materials meet the requirements for quality and strength as set forth in the specifications. Test facilities shall be properly equipped and capable of the following:

· Slump testing
· Air content determination
· Cylinder compressive strength testing
· Curing under conditions identical to the concrete represented
· Determination of the weight per cubic foot of concrete

6 COLD WEATHER

The Contractor shall be responsible for the quality of the concrete placed. When it is necessary to place concrete at or below 40° Fahrenheit, the Contractor must employ an approved method of protection to ensure that no freezing occurs. One or more of the following methods may be used as approved by the Owner.

a. Heating of mix water
b. Heating of aggregates
c. Heating of forms
d. Insulation of forms
e. Use of insulating blankets

No cold weather deck concrete shall be placed.

7 FORMS

The choice of form materials used shall be at the option of the Contractor. Forms shall be mortar tight and sufficiently rigid to prevent distortion due to the pressure of the concrete and other loads incident to the construction operations including vibration.

Form Face Lumber

All form lumber for exposed surfaces shall be of concrete form exterior plywood, not less than 5 ply and not less than $3/4$ inches in thickness. The foregoing may be modified for certain curved surfaces as approved by the Owner.

Form lumber for unexposed surfaces may be dressed tongue and groove, or square edge sized 4 sides of uniform width and thickness. The minimum thickness, after finishing, shall be $3/4$ inches.

Forms shall be filleted at all sharp corners.

Studs

Studs shall have a minimum nominal size of 2×6 inches. They shall not be spaced, center to center, more than 16 inches. All studs shall be capped at the top with a plate of not less than 2×6 inches nominal size.

Wales

All wales shall be at least 4×6 inches minimum section or equivalent. Spacing of wales shall be no greater than 36 inches. A row of wales shall be placed within 6 inches of the bottom of each pour unless studding extends below the bottom of the pour and can be secured by wales fastened to ties in the previous pour.

Form Ties

Metal form ties and anchors to hold forms in alignment and location shall be so constructed as to permit their removal to a depth of at least 2 inches from the concrete surface without injury to the concrete. All cavities resulting from the removal of the metal ties shall be filled with cement mortar of the same proportions used in the body of the work and the surface finished smooth and even.

Surface Treatment

All forms shall be treated with an approved oil prior to placing reinforcing steel. No materials shall adhere to the forms that will discolor or disfigure the surface of the concrete.

Metal Ties

Metal forms, in design and use, shall meet all the criteria and requirements of wood forms. The thickness of the form skin shall be such that the forms will remain true to shape. All bolt and rivet heads shall be countersunk. Clamps, pins, and other connecting devices shall hold the forms rigidly together and allow removal without injury to the concrete.

Removal

Unless otherwise permitted, load bearing forms may not be removed until concrete test cylinders have attained 80 percent of the minimum compressive strength of the class of concrete required by the plans or these specifications. If removal is not controlled by cylinder tests, the following periods may be used as a guide:

Floor Slabs, Beam Bottoms, Arches, and Shored Surfaces	14 days
Columns	7 days
Walls, Stems, Beam Sides, and Others	3 days
Footings	2 days

Metal Deck Forms

The Contractor may elect to use corrugated metal bridge deck forms. The forms must be at least 20 gauge with a unit working stress in all metal parts of not more than 75 percent of the minimum yield strength. In no case shall unit working stress exceed 36,000 pounds per square inch. Design criteria shall take into consideration weight of materials, weight of plastic concrete, and live load of 50 pounds per square foot. Deflection of the forms shall not exceed $1/2$ inch.

The metal bridge deck forms shall meet the requirements of American Iron and Steel Institute Specifications for cold formed steel. All material shall be galvanized.

Corrugated metal forms shall be placed in accordance with approved erection plans. All installation shall be such that the minimum specified cover on all reinforcing bars is obtained and such that the specified concrete deck thickness is maintained above the crest of the corrugations.

8 SHORING

All shoring methods used shall be approved by the Owner. When required, shoring shall be adequate for the type of construction involved. Suitable provision shall be made to secure the permanent camber required in the structure, and means of adjustment shall be provided so as to correct any possible settlement or deflection during construction. The Owner may require the Contractor to employ screw jacks, or hardwood wedges, to take up any slight settlement of the forms.

9 CONSTRUCTION JOINTS

Construction joints shall be formed only at the locations shown on the plans, unless otherwise approved by the Owner. When the placing of concrete is to be interrupted and a construction joint formed, provision shall be made for interlocking with the succeeding layer by roughening the surface and providing keyways, dowels, or other construction as shown on the plans or as ordered by the Owner.

In joining fresh concrete to concrete that has already set, the surface shall be roughened in a manner that will not leave loosened particles or damaged concrete on the surface. The surface shall be thoroughly cleaned and washed of all loose and foreign material and it shall be kept wet until the fresh concrete is placed.

Construction joints exposed to view or any other joints where seepage of water is objectionable may require use of an approved waterstop of rubber, synthetic material, or copper in accordance with details on the plans. Waterstop shall be placed not less than 3 inches from the face of the concrete and shall extend into each section of the concrete a distance of not less than 2 inches.

Construction joints for bridge decks shall be located where and as called for on the plans. A $1\frac{1}{2} \times 2$ inch shear key shall be formed in all deck construction joints.

10 EXPANSION JOINTS

Expansion joints shall be constructed in accordance with the details shown on the plans.

Metal joints shall have their sliding surface planed true and smooth, the marks of the plane paralleling the movement of the joint. All sliding surfaces should be thoroughly coated with graphite or grease prior to being placed in position. Special care shall be taken to avoid placing concrete in such a manner as to interfere with their free action. Details shall be in accordance with the plans.

Open joints shall be placed at locations designated on the plans and shall be formed by the insertion of and subsequent removal of a wood strip, metal plate, or other approved material. Care shall be taken to accomplish removal without damage to the concrete.

Filled compression and expansion joints shall be made with a pre-molded, self-expanding material as shown on the plans. Joint filler shall be cut to fit exactly as shown on the plans. If pour grade or caulking filler is called for, that portion of the joint shall be formed with a separate material.

Elastomeric joint seals shall be as detailed on the plans.

11 PLACING CONCRETE

The Contractor shall have sufficient skilled labor and adequate equipment at all times during the placing operation to properly place, consolidate, and finish the concrete as required.

All concrete shall be placed during daylight hours in forms cleaned and approved. No concrete shall be placed that fails to meet the delivery time requirements of Section 4. The method of placing shall be such as to avoid the possibility of segregation of the constituents and to avoid displacement of reinforcing bars or void forms.

Concrete shall not be deposited in running water.

Concrete shall not be deposited in the forms more than 6 feet from its final position. Dropping of unconfined concrete more than 5 feet will not be permitted. Use of long chutes for conveying concrete will not be permitted without consent of the Owner. When chutes are used, they shall be made of metal or have a metal lining.

Bridge decks shall be finished by an approved mechanical finisher. Screed rails shall not be placed within the roadway area unless permitted by the plans or specifications.

Concrete shall be deposited in continuous horizontal layers of a thickness not to exceed 12 inches; however, slabs shall be placed in a single layer.

Concrete shall be consolidated with mechanical vibrators of approved type. When required, vibrating shall be supplemented by hand spading. Vibrators shall be internal to the concrete. A sufficient number of vibrators shall be used to properly consolidate each batch immediately after it is placed in the forms. They shall be manipulated so as to work the concrete thoroughly around reinforcement and embedded fixtures and into corners and angles of the forms. Vibrators shall be capable of transmitting vibration to the concrete at frequencies of not less than 4500 impulses per minute under load.

In certain cases, a foundation leveling course and seal of Class D concrete is called for beneath a footing. When required, the concrete shall be struck-off to grade with a screed and not otherwise vibrated.

12 FINISHING

All concrete shall be finished in accordance with the following described methods:

a. *Ordinary Finish*   The external surface of all concrete shall be thoroughly worked during placing by means of approved tools. The working shall be such as to force all coarse aggregate from the surface and thoroughly work the mortar against the forms to produce a smooth finish free from water and air pockets, segregated materials, or honeycomb. The surface of the hardened concrete shall be finished immediately after the removal of the forms. All voids and honeycomb on the surface shall be filled and finished to conform to the surrounding concrete surface. All fins and irregular projections shall be removed from all surfaces except from those which are not to be exposed.

b. *Float Finish*   This finish, for horizontal surfaces, shall be achieved by placing an excess of material in the forms and removing or striking- off the excess with a template, forcing the coarse aggregate below the mortar surface. After the concrete has been struck-off, the surface shall be made uniform by longitudinal or transverse floating. When the concrete has hardened sufficiently, the surface shall be given a broom finish or a burlap drag finish or left smooth as required.

c. *Rub Finish*   After removal of forms, rubbing of the exposed surfaces shall start as soon as conditions will allow. The concrete shall be kept saturated with water for at least 3 hours prior to starting. Surfaces to be finished shall be rubbed with a medium coarse carborundum stone using a small amount of mortar on its face. The mortar shall be composed of cement and fine aggregate mixed in porportions used in the concrete being finished. Rubbing shall be continued until all form marks, projections, and irregularities have been removed, all voids filled, and a uniform surface obtained.

   The paste produced by this rubbing shall be left in place.

   The final rubbing shall be done with a fine carborundum stone and water. This rubbing shall continue until the entire surface has a smooth texture and uniform color. After the final rubbing is complete and the surface is dried, it shall be rubbed with burlap to remove loose face powder.

d. *Architectural Finish* Where called for in the plans, an architectural finish of a pattern shown shall be formed using form lining material attached to the inside of the form surface. After the forms are removed, the surface of the concrete shall be treated as required for an ordinary finish.

e. *Deck Finish* Bridge decks shall be finished with an approved transverse mechanical screed of the power actuated oscillating type. The screed shall be sufficiently rigid and easy to control in order to provide substantially uniform treatment over the entire deck surface. No rails will be permitted within the roadway area without approval of the Owner. After the concrete has been consolidated and brought to proper elevation by the screed, it shall be further smoothed by use of a longitudinal float of suitable and approved design. The float shall be worked from a bridge with a dragging motion while in position parallel to the roadway centerline and passed gradually from one side of the deck to the other. The deck shall be given a final burlap drag finish.

13 CURING

All concrete shall be cured for a period of not less than 7 days after placing. When the ambient temperature is expected to fall below 40° Fahrenheit, the Contractor shall provide suitable measures to maintain the concrete surface temperature between 40 and 90° Fahrenheit for the duration of the curing period. Regardless of the curing medium selected, the entire surface of the newly placed concrete shall be kept damp by applying water with an atomizing nozzle until the exposed surface is sufficiently hard to be covered by the selected curing medium.

All exposed surfaces of newly placed concrete shall be cured by any one of the following methods.

a. *Water Curing* Continuously sprinkling or flooding of all exposed surfaces for the entire cure period.

b. *Burlap Curing* The entire exposed surface of the concrete shall be covered with two layers of approved burlap. The burlap shall be soaked with water and kept wet for the entire curing period.

c. *Polyethylene Sheeting* White polyethylene sheeting, covering the entire exposed surface of the concrete and fastened to provide a near airtight condition in contact with the surface where possible.

d. *Membrane Curing Compound* Liquid membrane curing compound shall be applied to all exposed concrete surfaces at a minimum rate of 1 gallon per 200 square feet. Application should be even and continuous.

14 LINSEED OIL TREATMENT

Decks, sidewalks, and the inside surface of concrete parapets shall be treated with an application of linseed oil.

Material Linseed oil treatment material shall consist of a mixture of equal volumes of boiled linseed oil and mineral spirits.

· Preblended mixtures shall be furnished unless otherwise authorized.
· Boiled linseed oil shall conform to ASTM D 260, Type 1.
· Mineral spirits shall conform to ASTM D 235. Mixture shall be $^{50}/_{50}$ by volume.

Application After 30 days curing time and when the concrete surface is dry and clean, the first application shall be made at a rate of 1 gallon per 400 square feet. The second application shall be made at a rate of 1 gallon per 600 square feet after the first coat has been fully absorbed and the concrete has regained its dry appearance. Application shall be made through the use of a sprayer.

15 DAMPPROOFING

This work consists of furnishing and applying dampproofing to surfaces in accordance with the plans.

Materials used for dampproofing shall be asphalt conforming to AASHTO-M115, Type B, with a primer conforming to AASHTO-M116.

The surface to which dampproofing is to be applied shall be cleaned of all loose foreign material and dirt and shall be dry. When necessary, the Owner may require the surface to be scrubbed with water and a stiff brush, after which it shall be allowed to dry prior to application of the primer.

Application shall be brush painted at the rate of not less than two coats of primer using a minimum of $^1/_8$ gallon per square yard per coat, followed by one application of asphalt seal coat applied at a rate of $^1/_{10}$ gallon per square yard.

16 WATERPROOFING

Waterproofing consists of furnishing and applying a membrane system to the surface of concrete at locations shown on the plans.

Materials used for waterproofing shall conform to the following requirements:

Primer	AASHTO-M116
Seal Asphalt	ASTM D 449, Type C
Woven Glass Fabric	Fed. Spec. HH-C-00466

The surfaces which are to be waterproofed shall be smooth and free from projections or holes which might puncture the membrane fabric. The surface shall be thoroughly cleaned of loose or foreign substances.

No priming or waterproofing shall be done in wet weather or when the air temperature is below 35° Fahrenheit.

Application of the primer shall be at a rate of $1/10$ gallon per square yard. Primer shall cure for 24 hours before the waterproofing membrane is applied.

Waterproofing fabric and seal coats shall be applied as follows:

a. Mop hot asphalt, at about 300° Fahrenheit, over the surface.

b. Press fabric into place, eliminating any air bubbles.

c. Mop another coat of hot asphalt over the first layer.

d. Press a second layer of fabric into place as before.

e. Apply a final coat of asphalt at a rate heavy enough to cover and conceal the fabric.

The total application of asphalt shall not be less than 1.3 gallons per square yard.

17 MEASUREMENT

The quantity to be measured for payment will be the number of cubic yards of the class of concrete specified. The volume will be computed to the nearest 0.1 cubic yard by the prismoidal method using dimensions shown on the plans. No deductions will be made for the volume of concrete displaced by reinforcing bars, structural steel, expansion joint material, scuppers, weeps, conduits, pile tops, chamfers, or any pipe smaller than 12 inches in diameter.

Class D concrete used as a leveling course will not be measured for payment.

No measurement will be made of concrete used to displace over-excavated foundations in earth or rock. However, in blasted rock foundation excavation, all loose rock must be removed and replaced with the same class concrete as called for in the foundation.

18 PAYMENT

Accepted quantities of structural concrete will be paid for at the contract unit price per cubic yard for the particular class of concrete specified. This price shall be full compensation for performing the work specified and for furnishing all labor, equipment, materials, and tools necessary to complete the work. Included in and incidental to the price for concrete are all waterstops, joint filler, joint seals, expansion dams, scuppers, drainage pipe, dampproofing, waterproofing, embedded conduit, admixtures, finishes, shoring, curing, forming, concrete mix inserts, and select backfill material.

INDEX

ABOUT THE AUTHOR

JOHN E. CLARK, P.E., has thirty years of diverse experience in the construction industry as a contractor and consulting engineer, spanning the design and construction of highways, bridges, dams, power and treatment plants, tunnels, subways, and mining facilities.

This broad expertise has produced several authoritative papers on the subjects of construction claims and cost estimating and has made him an active lecturer before both domestic and international conferences.